Viaje al Español

Self-access Spanish Course

Book 1

santillana

Viaje al Español 1 includes the following materials:

Coursebook,
2 audio cassettes,
1 video cassette, Units 1 - 7,
1 video cassette, Units 8 - 13.

Viaje al Español is a joint production of the Spanish radio and television corporation (RTVE) and the University of Salamanca.

Team of linguists University of Salamanca:
Prof. Dr. Julio Borrego Nieto,
Prof. Dr. Juan Felipe García Santos,
Prof. Dr. José Gómez Asencio,
Prof. Dr. Emilio Prieto de los Mozos
with the collaboration of Prof. John Hyde.

Translation of the English version:
John Hyde

Script writers:
Joaquín Oristrell, Yolanda García Serrano, Juan Luis Iborra.

Producer TVE:
José Manuel Escudero

Audio cassettes:
Radio Nacional de España under the direction of Gonzalo Corella

Layout:
Jaime Agulló (TVE)

Design:
Experimenta, S. L.

Graphic design:
Cuaderna, S. C.
Cover photograph: TURESPAÑA
Photographs: Departamento de Imagen Fija de los Servicios Informativos de TVE; TURESPAÑA y Cuaderna, S. C.
Drawings: Kiko Feria, Laura Lombardi, José Luis García Morán

Executive producer:
Iñigo Yrízar (TVE)

General Coordinator:
Prof. Dr. Víctor García de la Concha (University of Salamanca)

© 1991 by RTVE, Madrid y Universidad de Salamanca
© 1991 by Santillana, Madrid
PRINTED IN SPAIN
Impreso en España
Talleres Gráficos Mateu Cromo, S. A.
Ctra. de Pinto a Fuenlabrada s/n. Pinto (Madrid)
ISBN: 84-294-3419-4
Depósito Legal: M-29318-1991

Contents

Contents

Contents

Introduction

VIAJE AL ESPAÑOL is the result of the joint participation of various institutions of the Spanish State: the Ministry of Foreign Affairs and the Ministry of Culture, Radio-Television Española and the University of Salamanca. The course has been developed under the auspices of the Council of Europe, as part of its Modern Languages Project.

1. AIMS AND COMPONENTS OF THE COURSE

VIAJE AL ESPAÑOL aims to present the authentic use of Spanish in real communication situations, based on the kinds of language activities which its potential users will need to engage in. Sequencing has therefore been carried out primarily on the basis of communication needs rather than the difficulty of grammar structures. Vocabulary has also been selected on the same basis. The level which students are expected to reach by the end of the Course is that which is defined by the Council of Europe as the Threshold Level. This level of competence allows the learner to satisfy his most general communication needs in the target language.

Emphasis is therefore placed on learning how to do things by using Spanish. The variety chosen as the model for active learning is Spanish as spoken by educated people throughout the Spanish-speaking world, that variety which is neutral with respect to age group, social class, region or country. However the fact that the Course has been designed in Spain, and specifically at the University of Salamanca, has led to the adoption of educated Castillian as the model for the pronunciation of the actual examples which appear in the Course.

The core components of VIAJE AL ESPAÑOL include the following elements: 65 video-tape units broadcast on television, 5 coursebooks, and the corresponding audio cassette tapes. Supplementary components also include radio programmes and practice audio-tapes, workbooks and complementary texts, an interactive videodisc and computer programmes. It is not absolutely necessary to use all the component elements of the Course in order to reach the expected level; the user can combine different components according to his own needs and possibilities. However, all combinations should include the coursebooks, since these form the backbone of the Course.

VIAJE AL ESPAÑOL is divided into five stages, each one containing 13 units. Each of these five stages has its own corresponding coursebook, audio-tape and video-tape.

Each of the 65 video units is divided into various fixed sections: **Presentations** of language items which form the learning objectives for the unit, **Illustrations** of those items in authentic communication situations, a **TV Comedy** in which the items which have been learnt appear repeatedly, a **Review Section** which draws attention to some especially interesting grammar and vocabulary points, and a final **Summary**. The different sections of each unit are structured as follows:

Presentation 1	A short narrative sequence in which the Presenter introduces new language items.
Illustrations	Illustraton of each of those items in real- life situations.
TV Comedy 1	The corresponding episode from the TV Comedy ("Viaje para dos"), in which the new language items appear together with other items which, for the most part, are already familiar to the learner.
Presentation 2	The presentatiom of a second series of new language items.
Illustrations	Illustration of each of those items.
TV Comedy 2	Continuation and conclusion of the corresponding episode from "Viaje para dos".
Review section	This section is called "Tome nota" (Take note) and reinforces some particularly important aspects of the unit.
Summary	This section is called "En resumen" and includes a short summary of what has been learnt in the unit.

2. THE COUSEBOOK ORGANISATION AND USE

What is the coursebook?

The coursebooks are designed primarily for self-learning; for that reason, they include explanations and exercises in preference to pair or group activities. Nevertheless, their possible use in groups or in class has also been provided for. You may in fact find that you make more satisfactory progress if you can arrange to follow the Course together with at least one other person (friend, colleague, and so on).

The coursebooks are parallel to the television programmes. However, with the help of the corresponding audio-tapes, they can also be used independently. A later section of this Introduction considers how to get the maximum benefit from the coursebooks and the other component elements of the Course.

How is the coursebook organised?

Open the book to the first unidad - unit. You will see that the unit is divided into different modules, each module covering an activity which you will carry out using Spanish (give your name, greet someone, call someone's attention, introduce someone, and so on). Look at the first module. The aim of this module is for you to learn how to give your name and identify yourself. You are given the linguistic expression for this (Soy Luis Cánovas) together with a short explanation of the structure and use of this expression. You are provided with the necessary vocabulary to enable you to carry out the required language activities. You may also receive some simple grammatical information. Finally, you are encouraged to complete a series of exercises and activities. You will see that the remaining modules in Unit 1 and the following units are organised in exactly the same way.

Exercises

Each exercise is numbered and labelled with one of a series of symbols which indicate the following:

 Listen to the tape.

 Answer orally.

 Answer in writing.

 Read (at least once, aloud).

 Pair or group work; here you will need to carry out various activities with at least one other person.

Some of these symbols may appear together. For example:

 Listen to the tape and then answer orally.

 Listen to the tape and then answer in writing.

Although many exercises include revision material, those headed Y por fin - (And finally) are especially designed for this purpose. This final exercise also serves to combine different items which have already been learnt and practised separately.

Introduction XI

Audio-tape exercises

The audio-tape exercises are numbered exactly the same as in the coursebook, with the number given in Spanish (for example, Ejercicio uno - Exercise one). After that, also in Spanish, you will hear one of the following instructions (depending on the kind of exercise in question): repita - repeat, conteste - answer (orally), pregunte - ask, escriba - write, escuche - listen, or marque - tick, underline, put a cross, etc. You will hear a bell ring which indicates exactly when you should speak. This ring may be either <u>single</u> or <u>double</u>:

• A single ring is followed by a pause so that you can answer without stopping the tape.
• A double ring is followed by a similar pause, but not long enough for you to give your answer. For these exercises, you will have to stop and start the tape.
• The end of each exercise is indicated by a short sequence of musical notes. Do not hesitate to stop the tape or to rewind and listen again as often as necessary.

Vocabulary

The vocabulary is introduced gradually, as communication needs require. The vocabulary items are highlighted and appear together with the translation in English: The abbreviations which appear to the right of some words indicate the following:

(m.)	masculino - masculine
(f.)	femenino - feminine
(m. y f.)	the same word is used for both the masculine and the feminine forms
(pl.)	plural - the word is only used in the plural
(v.i.)	verbo irregular - irregular verb. The forms used to conjugate these irregular verbs are outlined in sections ☞ 16 and ☞ 17 of the RINCÓN DE LA GRAMÁTICA. In the absence of any such indication, a verb will be a regular verb.
niño, -a	the word has one form for the masculine (niño) and a different form for the feminine (niña).

Grammar

Throughout each unit you will be given the essential grammar explanations to enable you to carry out the required language activities. These grammar explanations are given in schematic form and are highlighted against a grey background. If you wish to have further complementary information on a particular grammar point, you will find it useful to consult the RINCÓN DE LA GRAMÁTICA at the back of the book. You will be referred to this grammar section frequently by means of the symbol ☞ and the number of the paragraph or paragraphs in question.

Besides various modules of this kind, each unit includes a further series of fixed sections which are indicated in the following way: **Transcription of the TV dialogues**

This is a transcription of the verbal component of the **Presentaciones** (Presentations) and the **Telecomedia** (TV Comedy), i.e., those sections of the television units which carry the story-line. The transcription is followed by an appendix, called **Cajón de sastre** (Odds and ends), in which you are given varied information on different aspects of the transcribed text. Much of this information is of a sociocultural or sociolinguistic nature.

Usted ya puede...- You now know how to...

This is a list of the linguistic functions and the corresponding expressions and structures which you have learnt throughout the unit. The list follows the order of appearance of the language items in the unit.

Appendixes

At the end of the book you will find the following appendixes:

• **Vocabulary List**, an alphabetical list containing all the vocabulary that has been introduced throughout the book;
• **Grammar Summary** (EL RINCÓN DE LA GRAMÁTICA), already explained in other parts of this Introduction;
• **Answer Key**, with answers to all the exercises.

3. HOW CAN YOU GET THE MOST OUT OF THE COURSE?

As mentioned earlier, the different component elements of the Course permit various possible combinations. The following suggestions indicate the standard combination of components: the coursebooks, audio-tapes and television programmes.

The coursebook

1. First of all, study and practise the guidelines on PRONUNCIATION AND SPELLING which appear immediately after this Introduction.
2. Read carefully the presentation of the material and the explanations which are given in each module. Pay careful attention to the photographs and illustrations; they play an important role in helping you to understand better how the language expressions are used in communication situations.
3. Look at the grammar explanations and consult the RINCÓN DE LA GRAMÁTICA when instructed to do so. Use the grammar information to do the exercises, but do not worry if you are not at first correct in every grammatical detail. The correct use of linguistic forms is important, but it should not be allowed to hinder the learning process or ability to communicate meaning successfully.
4. Study the new vocabulary in the unit; you cannot use a language if you do not learn the basic vocabulary. Pay attention to the abbreviations which appear alongside many words in the vocabulary lists: **(m.)**, **(f.)**, etc. This information will provide valuable help. When you see **(v.i.)** (irregular verb) alongside a word, go to the RINCÓN DE LA GRAMÁTICA, to find its conjugation and the ways in which it differs from regular verbs.
5. Go through the exercises in the order in which they appear. Do not worry if you cannot finish any particular exercise; your use of the coursebook should be flexible. Move on to the next exercise and try returning to the problem later.

Once you have done all the above you will be ready to get the maximum benefit from the television programmes. As we have seen, the essential content of each television unit is the same as the corresponding unit in the coursebook. But remember that, although the coursebook is closely linked to the television programmes, it can be used independently and is structured in a slightly different way.

The television programmes

If you have a video recorder and can view the television programmes repeatedly, try to avoid the temptation of reading the translation of the **Transcriptions of the TV Dialogues** in the book; first watch the TV programme and try to understand as much as possible of what is said and done. If you do not fully understand, refer to the Spanish transcription at the same time as you view the video-tape again. If there is no other alternative, then look at the translation as a last resort. View the video-tapes as many times as you can.

If you do not have a video recorder, read the dialogues in Spanish before watching the television broadcast. If you find that at some point during the Course you can do without reading the transcription beforehand, then do so. Do not resort to the translation unnecessarily. Note further that you may occasionally come across expressions and structures which you do not know, especially in the TV Comedy. These are included for two reasons: first, to give you some experience of the kind of difficulties you will come across when you speak and listen to Spanish in real communication situations, and second to exploit the capacity which all human beings have to deduce meaning from the context of what is seen, or from what is already known. Do not worry if you do not fully understand some parts; this is to be expected and is true even in your native language.

What should you do after that?

After watching the television programme, return to the coursebook. Go over the explanations, the grammar, and the vocabulary. Do the exercises again and check your answers. Use the indexes to find the information which may help you.

4. HOW LONG SHOULD YOU SPEND STUDYING?

As long as you possibly can. We do not wish to set a minimum number of hours per week. But remember that the ability to communicate in a language is above all a question of application and perseverance. You will probably make more satisfactory progress by studying half an hour every day than by crammimg five or six hours into the weekend.

¡Buen viaje! - Have a good journey!

Pronunciation and spelling

1 The spelling of words in Spanish corresponds quite closely to pronunciation. Listen to the beginning of tape number 1. You will hear a man's voice say the word vocales - vowels. After that a woman's voice will give you the name of the letters for each vowel, and a male voice will pronounce the words which contain that vowel in the list below. After that you will hear consonantes - consonants and the process will be repeated. The list will take you through the tape step by step. When you have finished the list of consonants, stop the tape and read the OBSERVATIONS which follow.

After that, read the section on el acento - word stress. Start the tape again and listen to the words which appear in that paragraph.

Listen to the tape several times until you are easily able to reproduce what you hear and can read the written words aloud without the help of the tape.

2 **Vowels:**

Letter	Name of the letter	Pronunciation
a	a	a, da, papá
e	e	e, te, Pepe
i	i	i, ti, Pili
o	o	o, lo, moto
u	u	u, su, sube

3 **Consonants:**

Letter	Name of the letter	Pronunciation
b	be	bebe, subir, blanco
c	ce	c + a, o, u: casa, cosa, cura, octavo
		c + e, i: cena, cine, ciudad
ch	che	chico, mucho, coche
d	de	dedo, ciudad, dónde
f	efe	feo, café, fruta
g	ge	g + a, o, u: gato, amigo, agua
		g + e, i: gente, página
		gu + e, i: pagues, guitarra
h	hache	**this letter is not pronounced:** hay, ahora, hola
j	jota	jamón, jefe, cajón
k	ka	kilo, kilómetro
l	ele	lunes, limón, alto
ll	elle	llover, calle, allí
m	eme	mamá, camisa, comprar

Letter	Name of the letter	Pronunciation
n	ene	bueno, alemán, noche
ñ	eñe	año, niño, baño
p	pe	papá, pasaporte, plato
q	cu	**qu only occurs with** e and i: queso, aquí
r	erre	**non-initial:** hora, Carlos, comprar; **initial:** rubia, rosa, rojo
rr	erre doble	arriba, perro, corre
s	ese	solo, casa, mismo, dos
t	te	aceite, tomate, rato
v	uve	vaso, avión, invitar
x	equis	taxi, extra
y	y griega	playa, yo, vaya **word-final:** y, estoy, hay
z	zeta	azúcar, cerveza, izquierda

OBSERVATIONS:

1. The names of letters are feminine: "la a", "la uve".

2. Note that occasionally the same sound may be represented by more than one letter:

   • **b** and **v** sound the same.
   • **c** before **a**, **o** and **u** sounds the same as **qu** before **e** or **i**. It also sounds the same as **k**.
   • **c** before **e** or **i** sounds the same as **z**.
   • **g** before **e** or **i** sounds the same as **j**.
   • **gu** before **e** or **i** sounds the same as **g** before **a, o, u**. The **u** is pronounced in groups formed by **güe** and **güi** (note the diaeresis on the **u**): **cigüeña, pingüino**.
   • The **r** at the beginning of a word is pronounced the same as the **rr** which appears between vowels.

3. Note that **y** has two very different pronunciations: when it appears at the end of the word and in the word "y" it sounds the same as the vowel **i**.

4. In many varieties of Spanish (but not in the variety chosen as the model in this Course), the pronunciation of **c** before **e, i** and the pronunciation of **z** sound the same as **s**. This is called "seseo". It occurs in the speech of educated people as well, and is not incorrect.

4 In Spanish, one of the last three syllables of each word is pronounced with greater force, because the stress falls on that syllable. Listen to the following words on the tape and note the contrast between the stressed syllable and the unstressed syllables:

co<u>mer</u>	pa<u>pel</u>	ciu<u>dad</u>	ale<u>mán</u>
<u>co</u>che	<u>mar</u>tes	<u>Car</u>men	<u>ár</u>bol
<u>mé</u>dico	<u>sá</u>bado	bo<u>lí</u>grafos	<u>cá</u>mara

It is very important to pronounce each word with the stress in the right place. Follow these guidelines:

1. If the word has an accent in the written form, stress that syllable: ale<u>mán</u>, <u>ár</u>bol, <u>cá</u>mara.

2. If the word has no accent in the written form:
   and ends in "-n", "-s" or a vowel, stress the penultimate syllable: <u>co</u>che, <u>mar</u>tes, <u>Car</u>men.
   if it does not end in "-n", "-s" or a vowel, stress the last syllable: co<u>mer</u>, pa<u>pel</u>, ciu<u>dad</u>.

1 Soy Juan Serrano

In this unit you will learn how to establish first contact with other people in Spanish: say who you are, greet people, say goodbye, call someone's attention and introduce other people.

(I) **Soy Luis Cánovas.**   I am Luis Cánovas.

This is how to say who you are.

1. Soy Juan Serrano

 1. Listen and repeat when you hear the signal.

FORENAMES AND SURNAMES IN SPANISH:

ser = to be

To say who you are use the verb ser, with the form soy in the singular or with the form somos for more than one person.

☞ 16.3   ☞ 20

Spanish people have two surnames. To identify oneself the forename and the first surname are normally used (more formal), or only the forename (less formal).

Andrés Cueto
José Gómez Asencio
Marta Rosales
Rafael
Elena
Javier Conde
Manolo
Carlos Pérez López
María
Julio García

 2. Listen and repeat the above names when you hear the signal.

 3. Listen and point to the respective names as you hear them.

 4. Fill in the blanks in the pictures.

Marta Rosales

Javier Conde y Julio García

Elena

Rafael y María

Julio García

 5. You and your partners all say your names in order to identify yourselves.

Hola.	Hello.	Adiós.	Goodbye.
¿Qué tal?	How are you?	Hasta luego.	Goodbye, See you later.

These expressions are used for greeting people.

These expressions are used for saying goodbye.

6. Listen and repeat when you hear the signal.

Adiós and hasta luego are generally interchangeable. But it is preferable to use adiós if there is going to be a long separation.

Adiós and hasta luego may be used together:

    — Adiós.

    — Adiós, hasta luego.

OTHER FORMS OF GREETING:

Hola and ¿qué tal? are informal greetings which you can use at any time.

Other forms of greeting, however, depend on the time of day:

Buenos días Good morning (until lunch is over)	Buenas tardes Good afternoon / Good evening (until night falls)	Buenas noches Good evening (until dawn)

Hola can be combined with other greetings:

    Hola, ¿qué tal?

    Hola, buenos días.

7. Listen and repeat when you hear the signal.

8. Fill the blanks with suitable expressions either for greeting people or for saying goodbye.

To greet someone in passing (for example, when two people pass in the street) you can use any of the expressions which you have learned already, whether it is an expression for greeting someone or an expression for saying goodbye.

9. Listen to the tape and tick off on the list below the expressions for greeting people and for saying goodbye as you hear them.

Hola.

¿Qué tal?

Adiós.

Hasta luego.

Buenos días.

Buenas tardes.

Buenas noches.

10. Fill each blank with one of the expressions from the list in the previous exercise.

• •

Oiga, por favor.　　　　　Excuse me, please.
This is how to call someone's attention.
Sí, dígame.　　　　　　Yes. Can I help you? [i.e. "Yes, tell me"]
And this is how to reply.

11. Listen and repeat when you hear the signal.

> Perdón, por favor and oiga are expressions for calling someone's attention. They can be used either alone or together: oiga, por favor; perdón, por favor,… Expressions for replying to this are ¿sí? and dígame; these can also be used together:¿sí? dígame and sí, dígame.

12. One person in the group calls another's attention by using one of the expressions which you have just learned, or a combination of expressions. The other person replies.

IV — **Luis Cánovas.**

This is how to introduce someone.

— Encantada.   How do you do./I'm very pleased to meet you.

And this is how to reply.

hermano (m) = brother
hermana (f) = sister
mujer (f) = wife
marido (m) = husband
padre (m) = father
madre (f) = mother
padres (m. pl.) = parents
hijo (m) = son
hija (f) = daughter
hijos (m. pl.) = children
amigo (m) = (male) friend
amiga (f) = (female) friend
novio (m) = boyfriend
novia (f) = girlfriend

To introduce someone it is sufficient to point to the person as you say his/her name or an expression which indicates that person's relationship to you:

— Luis Cánovas.

— Mi hermana.

The expression ésta es... (and variants) is not necessary, but it appears from time to time, especially when the relationship is mentioned:

— Ésta es mi hermana.

— Éste es mi novio.

The reply encantado (used by a man) or encantada (used by a woman) is more formal than the reply ¿qué tal? (used by either men or women).

13. Listen and repeat when you hear the signal.

14. Listen and repeat the words which appear in the written form in the vocabulary list above.

15. On the tape you will hear five dialogues. Put a cross beside those which involve introducing someone.

1
2
3
4
5

éste	es	mi	herma**no**	
ésta	es	mi	herma**na**	
éstos	son	mis	herma**nos**	
éstas	son	mis	herma**nas**	☞ 1, 2, 3

mi	herma**no**	
	herma**na**	
mis	herma**nos**	
	herma**nas**	☞ 1, 2, 3

éste		
ésta	es	
ésto**s**		
ésta**s**	son	
	The verb SER	☞ 14, 15

The expression which is used to give one's name in order to identify oneself (soy Luis Cánovas) is also used to introduce oneself. In this case the reply will be the same as we have seen already: encantado, encantada or ¿qué tal?.

16. Look at the family photo below. Imagine that you and some of your partners are the members of this family. Introduce yourselves to your other partners. They reply.

FAMILIA PÉREZ-LÓPEZ

1. Soy Juan Serrano

● TRANSCRIPTION OF THE TV DIALOGUES
"SOY JUAN SERRANO"

Presentación. Primera parte

MEGAFONÍA: Tren situado en vía cinco, *Viaje al Español*.
PRESENTADOR: Por favor... ¡Oiga, por favor! Hola. Soy Luis Cánovas. Bienvenidos a *Viaje al Español*.
AZAFATA: Perdón... Oiga... Oiga, por favor.
PRESENTADOR: ¿Sí? Dígame.
AZAFATA: Buenos días. Por favor, ¿*Viaje al Español*?
PRESENTADOR: Sí, sí, buenos días. Hola. Soy Luis Cánovas.
AZAFATA: Encantada. Yo soy Marta Rosales. ➡ ①
PRESENTADOR: ¿Qué tal? Por aquí, por aquí.

Telecomedia. Primera parte

EMPLEADO: Buenos días. Buenos días. Buenos días.
JUAN: Buenos días... ¡Días!
EMPLEADO: Buenos días... Buenos días.
JUAN: ¡Por favor!
EMPLEADO: ¿Sí? Sí, dígame.
JUAN: Oiga, por favor... Perdón... Perdón... ➡ ② Perdón, yo... Yo soy Juan Serrano. Encantado. Por favor... Oiga, por favor... Señorita, por favor... la puerta. ➡ ③
ANCIANITA 1: Buenos días.
JUAN: Hola.
ANCIANITA 2: Hola.
JUAN: Hola, buenos días. ➡ ④ Perdón.
ANCIANITA 1: Hasta luego.
ANCIANITA 2: Hasta luego.
JUAN: Adiós.
ANCIANITAS 1 Y 2: ¡Ohhh!

Presentación. Segunda parte

MARTA: Luis, Luis, por favor.
PRESENTADOR: ¿Sí?
MARTA: Éste es mi novio.
NOVIO: Hola, ¿qué tal? ➡ ⑤
PRESENTADOR: Encantado.
MARTA: Bueno, hasta luego.
NOVIO: Adiós.
PRESENTADOR: Adiós, hasta luego. Hasta luego.

Telecomedia. Segunda parte

JUAN: Hola, buenos días. Perdón... Yo soy Juan Serrano. Encantado.
CARMEN: ¿Qué tal?. Yo soy Carmen Alonso.
CARMEN Y JUAN: Por favor.
CARMEN: ¡Oiga!, por favor.
JAVIER: ¡Hola, Carmen!
CARMEN: ¡Javier!
JAVIER: Ésta es Mercedes, mi mujer.
CARMEN: Yo soy Carmen, encantada. ➡ ⑥ Éste es...
JUAN: Yo soy Juan Serrano. Encantado.
CARMEN: Javier Sandoval.
JAVIER: ¿Qué tal?
JUAN: Encantado.
JAVIER: Perdón.
MERCEDES: ¡Oiga!
JUAN: ¿Dígame?
CARMEN: ¿Qué tal?

Presentation. Part One

ANNOUNCEMENT: The train standing on track five, *Viaje al Español*.
PRESENTER: Please... Excuse me, please! Hello. I'm Luis Cánovas. Welcome to *Viaje al Español*.
STEWARDESS: Excuse me. Excuse me. Excuse me, please.
PRESENTER: Yes? Can I help you?
STEWARDESS: Good morning. Please, *Viaje al Español*?
PRESENTER: Yes, yes. Good morning. Hello. I'm Luis Cánovas.
STEWARDESS: How do you do. I'm Marta Rosales. ➡ ①
PRESENTER: Hello. This way. This way.

TV Comedy. Part One

STEWARD: Good morning. Good morning. Good morning.
JUAN: Good morning... Morning?
STEWARD: Good morning. Good morning.
JUAN: Please!
STEWARD: Yes? Yes. Can I help you?
JUAN: Excuse me, please. I'm sorry. I'm sorry. ➡ ② Excuse me, I... I'm Juan Serrano. How do you do. Please! Excuse me, please... Miss, please... The door. ➡ ③
1ST OLD LADY: Good morning.
JUAN: Hello.
2ND OLD LADY: Hello.
JUAN: Hello. Good morning. ➡ ④ I'm sorry.
1ST OLD LADY: Goodbye.
2ND OLD LADY: Goodbye.
JUAN: Goodbye.
OLD LADIES: Ohhh!

Presentation. Part Two

MARTA: Luis! Luis, please!
PRESENTER: Yes?
MARTA: This is my boyfriend.
BOYFRIEND: Hello. How are you? ➡ ⑤
PRESENTER: How do you do.
MARTA: Well, goodbye.
BOYFRIEND: Goodbye.
PRESENTER: Goodbye. Goodbye. Goodbye.

TV Comedy. Part Two

JUAN: Hello. Good morning. Excuse me, please. I'm Juan Serrano. How do you do.
CARMEN: How do you do. I'm Carmen Alonso.
CARMEN AND JUAN: Excuse me, please.
CARMEN: Excuse me, please!
JAVIER: Hello, Carmen!
CARMEN: Javier!
JAVIER: This is Mercedes, my wife.
CARMEN: I'm Carmen. How do you do. ➡ ⑥ This is...
JUAN: I'm Juan Serrano. How do you do.
CARMEN: Javier Sandoval.
JAVIER: How do you do.
JUAN: How do you do.
JAVIER: Excuse me.
MERCEDES: Excuse me!
JUAN: Yes. Can I help you?
CARMEN: How do you do.

1. Soy Juan Serrano

MERCEDES: ¡Por favor!
JUAN: ¡Perdón!
JAVIER: ¿Qué tal?
JUAN: Adiós. Hasta luego. Por favor...
PRESENTADOR: Hasta luego.

MERCEDES: Please!
JUAN: Excuse me!
JAVIER: How are you?
JUAN: Goodbye. Goodbye. Please!
PRESENTER: Goodbye.

● **CAJÓN DE SASTRE**

(1) Yo is a personal pronoun which expresses the subject of the verb. Verbs in Spanish do not normally need the presence of the pronoun to indicate the subject, but they may sometimes appear, as in this sentence. Do not worry about this point for the moment. ☞ 10

(2) As you can see here, the word perdón has other uses besides calling someone's attention. The same is true of por favor. You will meet these further uses in future units.

(3) The words señorita and señora are forms of address. They are frequently used in order to call a woman's attention (¡señora, por favor!).

(4) Remember that buenos días and buenas tardes are not used to say goodbye. However, buenas noches is sometimes used in this way.

(5) The expression ¿Qué tal? is used to greet people but, as you have already seen, it is also used as an informal reply when being introduced to someone. The same is true of hola.

(6) When men are introduced to each other they shake hands. If a woman is involved (i.e. man to woman, or woman to woman) the normal procedure is to exchange a kiss on both cheeks. However, shaking hands and exchanging kisses are not used in everyday greetings between people who already know each other (unless some considerable time has elapsed or it is a special occasion, and so on).

● **USTED YA PUEDE...**

say who you are;	(Yo) soy Luis Cánovas.
greet people;	Hola. ¿Qué tal? Buenos días. Buenas tardes. Buenas noches.
say goodbye;	Adiós. Hasta luego.
call someone's attention;	Oiga. Perdón. Por favor.
reply when someone calls your attention;	¿Sí? Dígame.
introduce yourself;	Soy Luis Cánovas.

1. Soy Juan Serrano

| introduce other people; | Luis Cánovas, mi hermana. Ésta es mi hermana. |
| reply when someone is introduced to you. | Encantado, -a. ¿Qué tal? |

2 Calle de Goya, 7

In this unit you will learn how to give your name and address. You will also learn further ways of establishing contact with other people.

I Me llamo Luis Cánovas.   My name is Luis Cánovas. [i.e. "I call myself"]
This is how to give your name.

¿Cómo se llama usted? What is your name? [i.e. "How do you call yourself?"]
This is how to ask someone their name.
Luis Cánovas.
And this is how to reply.

2. Calle de Goya, 7

1. Listen and repeat when you hear the signal.

| **llamarse** = to be called |
| **niño (m)** = boy |
| **niña (f)** = girl |

El niño se llama José, y la niña, Ana.

To give your name, use the verb llamarse. For the moment you should learn the following forms of this verb:

(yo)	me llamo	my name is
(usted)	se llama	your name is
(el niño)	se llama	the boy's name is

☞ 16.1, 16.2

In Spanish there are two different forms used for addressing other people: usted and tú. We will first introduce usted, which is more formal. In Unit 6, the two different forms of address will be compared and contrasted.

2. Fill the blanks in the dialogue below.

A) —Buenos días.

B) —Hola. Buenos días.

A) —Soy Alfonso Pérez. Y éste es mi hijo.

B) —¿   se llama?

A) —¿Yo? Me   Alfonso Pérez Muñoz.

B) —No, usted no. ¿Cómo   llama el niño?

A) —Ah, el niño. Se   Emilio.

| el niño |
| la niña |
| los niños |
| las niñas |

☞ 4

3. Fill the blanks with what you hear on the tape.

1. MAN: WOMAN: Carmen Morán.

2. MAN: Oscar.

3. WOMAN: llama Julio.

4. Each person in the group writes his name (real or invented) on a slip of paper, which he then places somewhere for all to see. Ask a partner his name or the name of another partner. Your partner should reply.

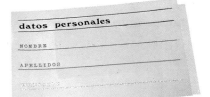

datos personales

NOMBRE

APELLIDOS

To fill in forms and official documents you will be asked to give your name in the following way: ¿nombre?   ¿apellidos?

5. Join each forename to the corresponding surnames:

NOMBRES	APELLIDOS
Carmen	Muñoz López
Juan	Pérez Martín
Oscar	Alonso Casaseca
Marta	Serrano Ribera

nombre (m) = forename
apellido (m) = surname

● ●

(II)

Vivo en Madrid.
I live in Madrid.
This is how to say where you live.
¿Dónde vive?
Where do you live?
And this is how to ask for the same information.

¿Dónde vive?

En Madrid. En la calle de Alcalá, 8.

6. Listen and repeat when you hear the signal.

calle (f) = street
vivir = to live
número (m) = number
plaza (f) = square
derecha (f) = right-hand side
izquierda (f) = left-hand side
piso (m) = floor, storey

To ask where someone lives, use the interrogative form dónde together with the different forms of the verb vivir. The reply begins with the word en, and may be more general (en Madrid) or more specific:

street	en la calle de Alcalá
number	8
floor	tercero
door	derecha

0	cero = zero				
1	uno, -a = one	1.°	primero, -a = first		
2	dos = two	2.°	segundo, -a = second		
3	tres = three	3.°	tercero, -a = third		
4	cuatro = four	4.°	cuarto, -a = fourth		
5	cinco = five	5.°	quinto, -a = fifth		

6	seis = six	6.°	sexto, -a = sixth
7	siete = seven	7.°	séptimo, -a = seventh
8	ocho = eight	8.°	octavo, -a = eighth
9	nueve = nine	9.°	noveno, -a = ninth
10	diez = ten	10.°	décimo, -a = tenth

☞ 9

2. Calle de Goya, 7

7. Listen and repeat.

8. Join the names of the people who speak to their respective addresses.

Elena	Plaza Mayor, 5, 1º
Emilio Prieto	Calle de Málaga, número 8
Alfonso Muñoz	C/ Goya, 9, 4º derecha
Marta Pérez López	Pl. de América, 7, 7º izquierda

9. Look at the cards and fill in the blanks below.

1
José Gómez Asencio
Aribau, 4, 5.° izda.
08001 Barcelona

2
Juan F. García Santos
Libreros, 6, 2.° dcha.
28028 Madrid

3
Julia Nieto López
Ruiseñor, 5
Santa Marta
37191 Salamanca

4.
Elena Serrano Díaz
Plaza de Santo Tomás, 5, 4.° izda.
51002 Zamora

1. José Gómez _____ en Barcelona. _____ la _____ Aribau.
2. Juan F. García Santos vive _____ la calle Libreros, _____ 6.
3. Julia Nieto _____ en _____ calle Ruiseñor, 5.
4. Elena Serrano vive _____ Zamora. _____ la _____ de Santo Tomás, 5, cuarto piso, _____

PRONOUNS
yo = I
usted - tú = you
él, ella = he, she
nosotros, nosotras = we
ellos, ellas = they
☞ 10

The words on the left are personal pronouns. You should begin to familiarise yourself with them, but do not worry for the moment about their exact uses.

The verb VIVIR: present tense			
	(yo) vivo	=	I live
	(tú) vives	=	you live
	(usted) (él, ella) ⎤ vive	=	you live / he, she lives
	(nosotros,-as) vivimos	=	we live
	(vosotros,-as) vivís	=	you live
	(ustedes) (ellos, ellas) ⎤ viven	=	you live / they live

You will already have noticed that Spanish verbs have a variety of different forms. In the table on the previous page you can see the forms for the present tense of a regular verb of the -ir class (or conjugation).

☞ 14

 10. Listen and repeat when you hear the signal.

 11. Ask your partners where they live.

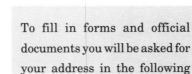 To fill in forms and official documents you will be asked for your address in the following way: ¿Dirección?

dirección (f) = address

 12. Fill in the above form with your personal details.

 13. On the tape an official will ask you some questions. When you hear the signal, reply with your personal details.

 14. Look at the cards in Exercise 9. Choose one of them and imagine that you are the person on the card you have chosen. On the tape an official will ask you some questions. Reply with the details from the card which you have chosen.

2. Calle de Goya, 7

 TOME UN TAXI.   TAKE A TAXI.

 15. Follow the text in the pictures below as you listen to the tape.

Are you free?

This is how to take a taxi.

Yes.

This is how to give an affirmative answer to a question.

—Where to?
—To 8 Alcalá Street.

This is how a taxi driver asks where you want to go and how to reply.

Notice how to take a taxi and say where you want to go. Learn these expressions by heart, but do not worry for the moment about the different elements which make up each expression.

Notice that an affirmative reply is expressed by sí. A negative reply is expressed by no.

To say where you want to go, use the word a before the address:

A la calle de Alcalá, 8

a + el = al

☞ 4

16. Listen and repeat when you hear the signal.

Careful! Watch the boy!

This is how to warn someone of some danger.

By using the word ¡cuidado! you warn someone of some danger. By using con you can also express what that danger consists of:

¡Cuidado con el perro!

 17. Listen and repeat when you hear the signal.

 18. Listen and repeat when you hear the signal.

Thank you. Thank you very much.

This is how to thank someone.

Perdón (or perdone) and lo siento are expressions for apologising for causing some kind of bother. They can be used either alone or in combination: perdón (or perdone); lo siento; perdón, lo siento. Expressions for replying to this are nada, nada and no se preocupe, which can also be used in combination.

19. Listen and repeat when you hear the signal.

Not at all./Don't mention it.

And this is how to reply.

 20. Listen and repeat when you hear the signal.

See you tomorrow.
Bye. See you tomorrow.

This is another way of saying goodbye.

To say goodbye to someone and at the same time express when you expect to see that person again, use an expression with hasta:

Hasta mañana.

Hasta el lunes.

Hasta el día 4.

LOS DIAS DE LA SEMANA

THE DAYS OF THE WEEK

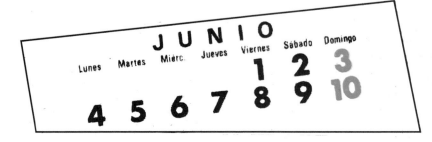

lunes (m) = Monday

martes (m) = Tuesday

miércoles (m) = Wednesday

jueves (m) = Thursday

viernes (m) = Friday

sábado (m) = Saturday

domingo (m) = Sunday

21. On the calendar below write the numbers which you hear on the day of the week to which they correspond.

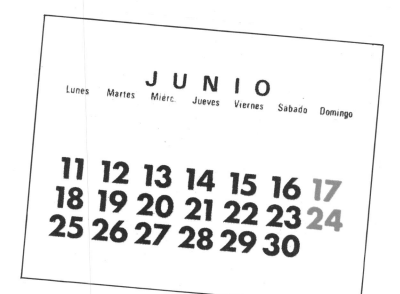

día (m) = day
semana (f) = week
mañana = tomorrow

 22. Today is domingo, tres. On the tape various people say goodbye to you. What day do they expect to see you again? Indicate this by putting a cross on the calendar above.

 23. Look at the places on the map. Listen to the tape and write the name of each place in the space provided below.

sí = yes
no = no
aeropuerto (m) = airport
estación (f) = station
hotel (m) = hotel
hospital (m) = hospital
taxi (m) = taxi

número 1:
número 2:
número 3:
número 4:

 24. Imagine that you go from point 1 on the map to point 4, stopping en route at points 2 and 3. At each point you take a taxi. Listen to the tape and reply to the taxi driver.

25. What would you say in the following situations?

1. On the bus, you tread on someone's foot.

2. Your friend unknowingly approaches a dangerous dog.

3. A friend gives you a book as a present.

4. You want to take a taxi, but you do not know if it is free or not.

5. Someone asks you if you have any children.

perro, -a = dog; bitch

26. Reply to what the voices say to you on the tape.

TRANSCRIPTION OF THE TV DIALOGUES
"¡TAXI!"

Presentación. Primera parte
PRESENTADOR: Hola, buenos días…
SEÑORA: ¡Eh, cuidado!
PRESENTADOR: Lo siento, señora.
MOZO: Perdón, lo siento, señor.
PRESENTADOR: No se preocupe.
SEÑORA: ¿Está libre?
TAXISTA: Sí, sí.
SEÑORA: Uno, dos, tres, cuatro, cinco, seis… ¡Cuidado! ¡Cuidado!
PRESENTADOR: ¡Taxi!
SEÑORA: ¡Taxi! ¡Taxi! Oiga, por favor…
TAXISTA: ¿A dónde vamos?
SEÑORA: Al hotel Imperial.
PRESENTADOR: ¡Taxi!

Presentation. Part One
PRESENTER: Hello. Good morning.
WOMAN: Hey! Careful!
PRESENTER: I'm sorry, madam.
PORTER: Excuse me. I'm sorry, sir.
PRESENTER: Don't worry.
WOMAN: Are you free?
TAXI DRIVER: Yes, yes.
WOMAN: One, two, three, four, five, six … Careful! Careful!
PRESENTER: Taxi!
WOMAN: Taxi! Taxi! Excuse me, please.
TAXI DRIVER: Where to? [i.e. "Where are we going to?"]
WOMAN: To the Imperial Hotel.
PRESENTER: Taxi!

Telecomedia. Primera parte
CARMEN: ¡Óscar!
ÓSCAR: ¿Quién es?
CARMEN: ¡Ah! Éste es Juan Serrano.
ÓSCAR: Encantado. Yo soy Óscar.
JUAN: ¿Qué tal?
CARMEN: Muchas gracias.
JUAN: De nada. Adiós.
ÓSCAR: Adiós.
JUAN: Oiga. Oiga.
EMPLEADO: ¡Cuidado!
JUAN: ¿Está libre?
TAXISTA: Sí. ¿A dónde vamos? ¡Oh, no! Uno, dos, tres, cuatro, cinco, seis.
JUAN: Lo siento.
TAXISTA: No se preocupe.

TV Comedy. Part One
CARMEN: Óscar!
ÓSCAR: Who is that?
CARMEN: Ah! This is Juan Serrano.
ÓSCAR: How do you do. I'm Óscar.
JUAN: How do you do.
CARMEN: Thank you very much.
JUAN: Not at all. Goodbye.
ÓSCAR: Goodbye.
JUAN: Excuse me! Excuse me!
EMPLOYEE: Careful!
JUAN: Are you free?
TAXI DRIVER: Yes. Where to? Oh, no! One, two, three, four, five, six.
JUAN: I'm sorry.
TAXI DRIVER: Don't worry.

Presentación. Segunda parte
DEPENDIENTE: ¿Cómo se llama usted?
PRESENTADOR: Luis Cánovas.
DEPENDIENTE: ¿Dónde vive?
PRESENTADOR: En Madrid. Y usted, ¿cómo se llama? ¿y dónde vive?
DEPENDIENTE: ¿Dirección?

Presentation. Part Two
SHOP ASSISTANT: What's your name?
PRESENTER: Luis Cánovas.
SHOP ASSISTANT: Where do you live?
PRESENTER: In Madrid. And you? What's your name? And where do you live?
SHOP ASSISTANT: Address?

PRESENTADOR: Calle Alcalá ➡ ① , 8, segundo izquierda ➡ ②

DEPENDIENTE: Gracias.
PRESENTADOR: De nada. Bueno, hasta el lunes.
DEPENDIENTE: Sí, sí, hasta el lunes.
PRESENTADOR: Uno, dos, tres, cuatro, cinco, seis, siete, ocho, nueve, diez…

Telecomedia. Segunda parte

CARMEN: ¡Cuidado!
GUARDIA: Buenos días.
ÓSCAR: Perdón, lo siento.
GUARDIA: Documentación. ¿Nombre?
ÓSCAR: ¿Perdón? ➡ ③
GUARDIA: ¿Cómo se llama usted?
ÓSCAR: Óscar Muñoz López.
GUARDIA: ¿Dirección?
ÓSCAR: Calle ➡ ④ Alfonso X, 7, primero derecha.
JUAN: ¡Oiga, por favor!
CARMEN: ¿Sí?
JUAN: Perdón… mi maletín.
ÓSCAR: ¿Es éste?
JUAN: Sí, sí. Es éste.
ÓSCAR: Perdón, yo no…
CARMEN: Ay, lo siento.
JUAN: Nada, nada, no se preocupen. Adiós.
ÓSCAR: Adiós.
CARMEN: Hasta mañana.
ÓSCAR: Hasta mañana.
TAXISTA: ¿A dónde vamos ahora?
JUAN: A la calle Goya.
TAXISTA: Ésta es la calle Goya.
JUAN: Vamos al número 7.
TAXISTA: Éste es el número 7.
JUAN: ¡Ah!
PRESENTADOR: ¡Adiós!

PRESENTER: Alcalá Street ➡ ① , number eight, second floor, left-hand flat ➡ ②.
SHOP ASSISTANT: Thank you.
PRESENTER: Don't mention it. Well, see you on Monday.
SHOP ASSISTANT: Yes, yes. See you on Monday.
PRESENTER: One, two, three, four, five, six, seven, eight, nine, ten.

TV Comedy. Part Two

CARMEN: Careful!
POLICEMAN: Good morning.
ÓSCAR: Excuse me. I'm sorry.
POLICEMAN: Papers, please. Name?
ÓSCAR: I'm sorry? ➡ ③
POLICEMAN: What's your name?
ÓSCAR: Óscar Muñoz López.
POLICEMAN: Address?
ÓSCAR: Alfonso X Street ➡ ④, number seven, first floor, right-hand flat.
JUAN: Excuse me, please!
CARMEN: Yes?
JUAN: I'm sorry. My briefcase.
ÓSCAR: Is this it?
JUAN: Yes, yes. This is it.
ÓSCAR: I'm sorry. I didn't ...
CARMEN: Oh, I'm sorry.
JUAN: No problem. [i.e. "Nothing."] No problem. Don't worry. Goodbye.
ÓSCAR: Goodbye.
CARMEN: See you tomorrow.
ÓSCAR: See you tomorrow.
TAXI DRIVER: Where to now?
JUAN: To Goya Street.
TAXI DRIVER: This is Goya Street.
JUAN: To number 7.
TAXI DRIVER: This is number 7.
JUAN: Oh!
PRESENTER: Goodbye.

● CAJON DE SASTRE

① Although strict academic norms say that de should be used in addresses (calle de Goya, plaza de España), people frequently omit this word: calle Goya.

② The majority of Spanish people live in urban areas. Single-family houses are rare in cities, most people living in blocks of flats. Each floor is numbered (1.°, 2.°, 3.°, etc.) and the various pisos flats on each floor are identified by the letters of the alphabet (2.°A, 3.°C, etc.). If there are only two flats on each floor, they are identified according to whether they are on the right or on the left coming up the stairs (2.° izquierda, 3.° derecha). For the names of the letters of the alphabet, see the section on "Pronunciation and Spelling" (p. XV).

③ Here you have another use of perdón: a polite way of asking someone to repeat when you have not fully understood.

④ Apart from calle and plaza, you will also come across the following: avenida avenue and paseo drive. The respective abbreviations for these four words are as follows: C/, Pl., Avda., and P°.

● **USTED YA PUEDE...**

give your name;	Me llamo Luis Cánovas.
ask someone their name;	¿Cómo se llama usted?
say where you live and give your address;	Vivo en Madrid. Vivo en la calle de Alcalá, 8, 3.° derecha.
ask where someone lives;	¿Dónde vive usted?
reply to questions with your full name and address when filling in official forms;	¿Nombre? ¿Apellidos? ¿Dirección?
take a taxi;	¿Está libre?
reply to a taxi driver when he asks you where you want to go;	—(¿A dónde vamos?) —Al aeropuerto.
reply affirmatively or negatively to a question;	Sí. No.
warn someone of some danger;	¡Cuidado! ¡Cuidado con el perro!
apologise and accept an apology;	—Perdón… Lo siento. —Nada, nada. No se preocupe.
thank someone and reply;	—Gracias. —De nada.
say goodbye to someone, expressing when you expect to see that person again;	Hasta mañana. Hasta el lunes.
count up to 10.	Uno, dos, tres…

3 ¿Dónde está?

In this unit you will learn how to say where people and things are, and to ask if someone is available. You will also learn further expressions for establishing contact with other people.

I **¿Dónde están mis gafas?**   Where are my glasses?

This is how to ask where someone or something is.

Ahí, en la mesa.   There, on the table.

And this is a possible reply.

3. ¿Dónde está?

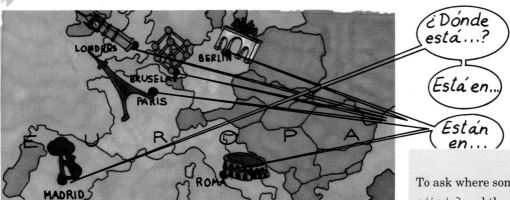

1. Listen and repeat when you hear the signal.

estar (v. i.) = to be in a certain place

gafas (f. pl.) = glasses

bolígrafo (m) = ballpoint pen

mesa (f) = table

foto (f) = photo

sobre (m) = envelope

cajón (m) = drawer

oficina (f) = office

baño (m) = bathroom, toilet

España (f) = Spain

Europa (f) = Europe

To ask where something is, use ¿dónde? and the corresponding form of the verb estar:

> ¿Dónde está Berlín?
> ¿Dónde están las fotos?

To say where something is, use a form of the verb estar together with the word en:

> El bolígrafo está en el cajón.
> Madrid y Roma están en Europa.

2. Look at the picture above and those on the previous page. Listen and indicate whether what you hear is true (T) or false (F).

1. T F   2. T F   3. T F   4. T F   5. T F   6. T F

3. Fill the blanks with one word only in each case.

1.—¿_____ están mis gafas?
—Ahí, _____ la mesa.

2.—¿_____ está Juan?
— _____ la calle.

3.—El bolígrafo está _____ el cajón.

4.—¿Dónde _____ Madrid?
— _____ en España.

5.—Roma y Berlín _____ en Europa.

6.—¿Dónde _____ Londres y Bruselas?
— _____ Europa.

The word en expresses the same meaning as both 'in' and 'on' in English:

> Está en la mesa.   It is on the table.
> Está en el cajón.   It is in the drawer.

But en is not used with the words aquí, ahí and allí, which are also frequently used to express location.

aquí   ahí   allí

 4. Listen and repeat when you hear the signal.

Spanish divides space into three separate planes: the area which is relatively close to the speaker, aquí; an intermediate area, or the area which is relatively close to the hearer, ahí; and the area which is relatively distant from the speaker, allí.

 5. Point to different partners and objects and say where they are by using aquí, ahí, allí.

EXAMPLE:

> Juan está allí.
> El sobre está ahí.

SER	ESTAR
soy	estoy
eres	estás
es	está
somos	estamos
sois	estáis
son	están

☞ 13, 16

Spanish uses two verbs, ser and estar, where English uses only one, 'to be'. This is one of the most notable characteristics of Spanish and it causes problems for foreign speakers. You will find various references to this in successive units in the Course.

So far you have seen the following:

to identify or introduce yourself and others – ser:

> Soy Luis Cánovas.
> Ésta es mi hermana.

to say where something is – estar:

> Luis está en la calle. ☞ 20

6. The people in the pictures here introduce or identify themselves and others. They also say where they are. Fill in the blanks in what they say.

Juan y Carmen

en Madrid

Luis Cánovas. en la oficina

Marta Rosales. en Roma.

Rafael y María. en París.

● ●

(II) ¿Está el señor Escudero?   Is Mr Escudero in/here/there?

This is how to ask if someone is available when you want to see them.

¿Está el señor Escudero?

Y la señorita Barrio, ¿está?

No, no está

Sí. Un momento por favor.

7. Listen and repeat when you hear the signal.

MÁS NOMBRES Y APELLIDOS:

Antonio Prado
Diego Ibarra
Ricardo
Julio Nieto
Roberto Mauri

8. Listen and repeat when you hear the signal.

To ask if someone is available, use the verb estar (está or están).

In informal situations:
¿Está Julio Nieto?
¿Están Ricardo y Carmen?

In more formal situations:
¿Está el señor Ibarra?
¿Está la señora Mauri?
¿Está la señorita Barrio?
¿Está don Julio?
¿Está don Julio Nieto?
¿Está doña Ana?
¿Está el director?

director, -a	= manager
secretario, -a	= secretary
jefe (m. y f.)	= boss
señor (m)	= Mr.
señora (f)	= Mrs.
señorita (f)	= Miss

FORMS OF ADDRESS:

<u>señor</u> Ibarra

<u>señora</u> Mauri

<u>señorita</u> Barrio

<u>don</u> Julio

<u>doña</u> Ana

señor, señora,

señorita + apellido

don, doña + nombre

9. The people in the picture are in a meeting. Imagine that there is a janitor at the door. You go up to him and ask for the people on the list below.

señor Ibarra

señorita García

don Julio Nieto

señora Alonso

don Roberto Mauri

doña María Prado

Questions such as ¿Está el Sr. Escudero? may be answered as follows: **Affirmative:** Sí, sí está.

Negative: No, no está.

In this situation you may frequently be asked to wait:

Un momento, por favor.

10. Look again at the picture in Exercise 9. What replies would the janitor give to the questions you asked him there?

11. Dramatise Exercises 9 and 10 with your partners.

You will already have noticed that questions in Spanish, as in other languages, require a special intonation pattern. They may also frequently involve a change of word order:

<u>Juan</u> está en la oficina.

¿Está <u>Juan</u> en la oficina?   ¿Dónde está <u>Juan</u>?

Question marks are written both at the beginning (in inverted position) and at the end of the question: ¿...?

12. Listen to the following sentences on the tape and put question marks round those which are questions.

Carmen está en la oficina   Juan está aquí

Dónde está el baño   Está Carmen en la oficina

Está aquí Juan   El baño está allí

To negate the verb, place no before it:

Juan está aquí. — Juan <u>no</u> está aquí.

13. Some of the following sentences are false. Rewrite those sentences by using no in order to make them true.

París está en España.

Carmen es un niño.

El señor Cánovas se llama Luis.

El segundo día de la semana es el domingo.

Londres está en Europa.

● ●

¿Es usted el Sr. García?   Are you Mr García?

This is how to ask someone if he/she is the person you are looking for.

 14. Read the following dialogues aloud.

 15. Now cover the dialogues in the previous exercise. Try to repeat what each person says. If possible, dramatise the dialogues with your partners.

Questions such as ¿Es usted el Sr. García? may be answered as follows:

Afirmative: Sí, soy yo.

Negative: No, no.

No, no soy yo.

No, soy Luis Cánovas.

Note the following distinction –

to ask if someone is available, we use the verb estar:

¿Está la señorita Barrio?

to ask someone if he/she is the person we are looking for, we use the verb ser:

¿Es usted la señorita Barrio?

16. Read the following text and fill the blanks with one word only in each case.

1. A young woman enters an office block looking for el señor Prado. She speaks to a janitor.

YOUNG WOMAN: Por favor, ¿ _____ el señor Prado?

JANITOR: Sí, sí _____.

2. The janitor points to a group of people thinking that el señor Prado is among them. The young woman approaches the group and asks one man if he is the person she is looking for.

YOUNG WOMAN: ¿ _____ usted el señor Prado?

MAN: No, no _____ yo. El señor Prado _____ allí.

YOUNG WOMAN: Gracias.

3. The young woman, who seems to be in quite a hurry, speaks to the person who has been pointed out to her.

YOUNG WOMAN: Perdón, ¿ _____ usted el señor Prado?

SR. PRADO: Sí, sí, _____ yo. Dígame.

4. She then asks him a question.

YOUNG WOMAN: ¿ _____ aquí su mujer?

SR. PRADO: No, mi mujer no _____ aquí. _____ en la oficina.

5. As soon as she hears the answer she runs rapidly towards the exit. El Sr. Prado is very surprised. Finally he manages to shout:

SR. PRADO: ¡Oiga, oiga! ¿ _____ se llama usted?

But the young woman has already disappeared.

3. ¿Dónde está?

17. Follow the text in the pictures below as you listen to the tape.

May I (come in)?

1

This is how to request permission to enter.

Come in! Come in!

2

And this is how to reply.

Can I help you? [i. e. "What do you want?"]

3

This is how to ask someone what they want (in a shop or other service encounter).

[Wait] one moment, please.

4

This is how to ask someone to wait.

5

6

11	12	13	14
once	doce	trece	catorce
15	16	17	
quince	dieciséis	diecisiete	
18	19	20	
dieciocho	diecinueve	veinte	
1000	2000	11000	
mil	dos mil	once mil	

Learn the following expressions —
to ask if you may come in, say:

¿Se puede?

to which the reply is:

¡Pase!

¡Adelante!

¡Pase, adelante!

The expressions espere un momento, or simply un momento, are used to ask someone to wait.

18. Dramatise situations in which the following might be used: ¿Se puede? - ¡Pase!/¡Adelante! - ¿Qué desea? - Espere un momento, por favor.

19. As you hear the numbers on the tape, cross them off on the card.

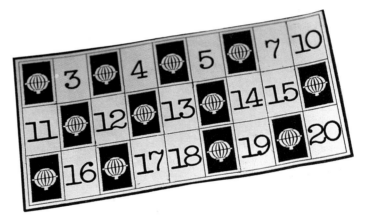

20. On the tape you will hear sequences of three numbers. Write each sequence down when you hear the signal.

1.
2.
3.
4.
5.

3. ¿Dónde está?

● **TRANSCRIPTION OF THE TV DIALOGUES**
"¿DÓNDE ESTÁ?"

Presentación. Primera parte

PRESENTADOR: Hola, buenos días. Un momento, por favor. Hasta luego.

SEÑORA: ¡Huy! ¿Qué desea?

PRESENTADOR: ¿Está el Sr. Escudero?

SEÑORA: ¿Qué?

PRESENTADOR: ¡El Sr. Escudero!

SEÑORA: Huy, perdón. ¿Qué desea?

PRESENTADOR: ¿El Sr. Escudero, por favor?

SEÑORA: Huy, no, no está.

PRESENTADOR: ¿Y la señorita Barrio?

SEÑORA: ¿La señorita Barrio? Espere un momento. ¿Es usted el Sr. García?

PRESENTADOR: No, soy Luis Cánovas.

SEÑORA: ¡Huy!, ¿Luis Cánovas? Pues no, no, no… la señorita Barrio no está aquí.

PRESENTADOR: Gracias. ¡Cuidado!

SEÑORA: Perdone, lo siento.

PRESENTADOR: Nada, nada. No se preocupe.

SEÑORA: Adiós, hasta luego.

Telecomedia. Primera parte

TÉCNICO SONIDO: Buenos días, Carmen.

CARMEN: Hola, buenos días.

TÉCNICO SONIDO: Roberto Mauri. Carmen Alonso. ¡Carmen Alonso!

AYUDANTE: Ah… encantado.

CARMEN: Encantada.

TÉCNICO SONIDO: Adiós. Hasta luego.

CARMEN: Hasta luego.

JOVEN: Buenos días. ¿Qué desea?

JUAN: Buenos días. ¿Está el Sr. Ibarra?

JOVEN: Un momento, por favor. ¿Diego Ibarra?

JUAN: Sí, sí.

JOVEN: Espere un momento. Por favor, ¿está Diego Ibarra? Un momento. ¿Es usted Juan Serrano?

JUAN: Sí, soy yo.

JOVEN: Sí, sí. De acuerdo. Tercer piso.

JUAN: Muchas gracias.

DIEGO: ¿Está Ricardo? Un momento. No, no está. Soy Diego. Sí, un momento, por favor. Sí, sí…

CARMEN: Buenos días.

SECRETARIA: Hola, ¿qué tal?

DIEGO: Sí, sí, sí…

Presentación. Segunda parte

PRESENTADOR: ¿Se puede?

SECRETARIA: Pase, ¡adelante! ¡adelante! ¡adelante!

PRESENTADOR: Buenos días.

SECRETARIA: ¿Dónde están mis gafas?

PRESENTADOR: ¿Dónde están sus gafas?

SECRETARIA: Sí, mis gafas.

PRESENTADOR: En…

SECRETARIA: ¡Ah! ¿Aquí? Gracias. Ah, es usted Luis Cánovas. Un momento, por favor. ¿Dónde está el sobre?… ¿Dónde está el sobre?… Ah, sí, está allí. 16, 4, 18, 20. Mil, dos mil, tres mil, cuatro mil, cinco mil. Diez mil y quince mil. ➡ ①

Presentation. Part One

PRESENTER: Hello. Good morning. One moment please. See you later.

WOMAN: Oh! Can I help you?

PRESENTER: Is Mr Escudero here?

WOMAN: What?

PRESENTER: Mr Escudero!

WOMAN: Oh! I'm sorry. Can I help you?

PRESENTER: Mr Escudero, please?

WOMAN: Oh, no. He's not here.

PRESENTER: And Miss Barrio?

WOMAN: Miss Barrio? [Wait] one moment. Are you Mr García?

PRESENTER: No. I'm Luis Cánovas.

WOMAN: Oh! Luis Cánovas? Well, no, no,… Miss Barrio is not here.

PRESENTER: Thank you. Careful!

WOMAN: Excuse me. I'm sorry.

PRESENTER: No problem. Don't worry.

WOMAN: Goodbye. Goodbye.

TV Comedy. Part One

SOUND TECHNICIAN: Good morning, Carmen.

CARMEN: Hello. Good morning.

SOUND TECHNICIAN: Roberto Mauri. Carmen Alonso. Carmen Alonso!

ASSISTANT: Ah … Pleased to meet you.

CARMEN: How do you do.

SOUND TECHNICIAN: See you. Goodbye.

CARMEN: Goodbye.

YOUNG WOMAN: Good morning. Can I help you?

JUAN: Good morning. Is Mr Ibarra here?

YOUNG WOMAN: One moment, please. Diego Ibarra?

JUAN: Yes. Yes.

YOUNG WOMAN: Just a moment. Is Diego Ibarra there, please? One moment. Are you Juan Serrano?

JUAN: Yes, I am.

YOUNG WOMAN: Yes. Yes. OK. Third floor.

JUAN: Thank you very much.

DIEGO: Is Ricardo there? One moment. No, he's not here. It's [i.e. "I am"] Diego. Yes, one moment, please. Yes. Yes.

CARMEN: Good morning.

SECRETARY: Hello. How are you?

DIEGO: Yes. Yes.

Presentation. Part Two

PRESENTER: May I come in?

SECRETARY: Yes. Come in! Come in!

PRESENTER: Good morning.

SECRETARY: Where are my glasses?

PRESENTER: Where are her glasses?

SECRETARY: Yes, my glasses.

PRESENTER: On …

SECRETARY: Ah! Here? Thank you. Ah, you are Luis Cánovas. One moment, please. Where is the envelope? Where is the envelope? Ah, yes. It's over there. 16, 4, 18, 20. One thousand, two thousand, three thousand, four thousand, five thousand, ten thousand [and] fifteen thousand. ➡ ①

PRESENTADOR: Gracias.

SECRETARIA: De nada.

PRESENTADOR: Doce mil, trece mil, catorce mil, quince mil. Hasta luego.

Telecomedia. Segunda parte

DIEGO: Adiós. Hasta el lunes. Hasta luego.

JUAN: ¿Se puede?

DIEGO: Adelante. ¿Qué desea?

JUAN: Soy Juan Serrano.

DIEGO: ¡Ah! ¿El profesor Serrano? ➡ ②

JUAN: Sí.

DIEGO: Pase, profesor. Yo soy Diego Ibarra. ¿Dónde está el sobre del profesor?

SECRETARIA: Aquí.

DIEGO: ¿Y las fotos? ➡ ③

SECRETARIA: Están allí.

DIEGO: ¿Dónde está Carmen?

SECRETARIA: Allí.

DIEGO: Espere un momento, por favor.

SECRETARIA: Diez, once, doce, trece, catorce, quince...

JUAN: ¡Por favor!

SECRETARIA: Sí, dígame, profesor.

JUAN: ¿Dónde está el baño?

SECRETARIA: Allí.

JUAN: Gracias.

DIEGO: ¿Y el profesor?

SECRETARIA: Está en el... Aquí está el profesor.

DIEGO: Ésta es...

JUAN: Carmen Alonso.

DIEGO: Y éste es...

CARMEN: ¡Juan Serrano!

SEÑORA: Lo siento.

PRESENTADOR: No se preocupe. Hasta luego.

PRESENTER: Thank you.

SECRETARY: Don't mention it.

PRESENTER: Twelve thousand, thirteen thousand, fourteen thousand, fifteen thousand. Goodbye.

TV Comedy. Part Two

DIEGO: Goodbye. See you on Monday. Goodbye.

JUAN: May I come in?

DIEGO: Come in. Can I help you?

JUAN: I'm Juan Serrano.

DIEGO: Ah, Juan Serrano the teacher? [i. e. "Teacher Juan Serrano?"] ➡ ②

JUAN: Yes.

DIEGO: Come in, sir [i. e. "teacher"]! I'm Diego Ibarra. Where is the teacher's envelope?

SECRETARY: Here.

DIEGO: And the photos? ➡ ③

SECRETARY: They are over there.

DIEGO: Where is Carmen?

SECRETARY: In there.

DIEGO: Just one moment, please.

SECRETARY: 10, 11, 12, 13, 14, 15 ...

JUAN: Excuse me, please!

SECRETARY: Yes? What is it, sir?

JUAN: Where is the toilet?

SECRETARY: There.

JUAN: Thank you.

DIEGO: But [i. e. "And"] (Where is) the teacher?

SECRETARY: He's in the ... Ah, here he [i. e. "the teacher"] is.

DIEGO: This is ...

JUAN: Carmen Alonso!

DIEGO: And this is ...

CARMEN: Juan Serrano!

WOMAN: I'm sorry.

PRESENTER: Don't worry. Goodbye.

● **CAJÓN DE SASTRE**

① The unit of Spanish currency is the peseta. At this moment in time the following monedas coins and billetes notes are in circulation:

Monedas: 1 - 5 - 10 - 25 - 50 - 100 - 200 - 500 pesetas

Billetes: 1000 - 2000 - 5000 - 10000 pesetas

② You already know the most usual forms of address such as señor, -a, don, doña, etc. There are also other words, such as profesor, -a teacher, doctor, -a doctor, etc. which are used in the same way.

As you have already seen, señorita miss is the form of address used for a single woman or for a young woman. But be careful not to use the corresponding masculine form, señorito, as a form of address. Use señor to address a man.

③ Foto is the shortened form of fotografía. Many everyday words are shortened in this way; for example, televisión ➡ tele, motocicleta ➡ moto, etc.

3. ¿Dónde está?

USTED YA PUEDE...

ask where someone or something is;	¿Dónde están mis gafas?
and reply;	En la mesa. / Están aquí.
say where someone or something is;	Madrid está en España.
ask if someone is available;	¿Está la señorita Barrio?
and reply;	Sí, sí está. / No, no está.
ask someone if he/she is the person you are looking for;	¿Es usted el Sr. García?
and reply;	Sí, soy yo. / No, no soy yo.
request permission to enter;	¿Se puede?
and reply;	¡Pase! ¡Adelante!
ask someone what he/she wants (in a shop or other service encounter);	¿Qué desea?
ask someone to wait;	Espere un momento.
use numbers from 11 to 20 and thousands.	Once, doce, trece, catorce, quince, dieciséis, diecisiete, dieciocho, diecinueve, veinte; mil, dos mil, once mil,…

4 ¿De quién es?

In this unit you will learn how to say who something belongs to; how to ask for a word to be spelled; and how to ask for various things in different places and situations.

I **Esa maleta es mía.** That suitcase is mine.

This is how to say who something belongs to.

¿De quién es esta maleta? Whose is this suitcase?

This is how to ask for the same information.

Es mía. It is mine.

Es del señor Cánovas. It is Mr Cánovas's.

And this is how to reply.

billete (m) = ticket

casa (f) = house

chaqueta (f) = jacket, coat

coche (m) = car

libro (m) = book

maleta (f) = suitcase

abrigo (m) = overcoat

1. Listen and repeat when you hear the signal.

a + el = al de + el = del ☞ 4

To ask who something belongs to, use de quién and the corresponding form of the verb ser: ¿De quién es esa maleta? ¿De quién son estos libros?

Possession may also be expressed by using ser and the word de: Esa maleta es de Luis Cánovas. or by using words such as mi, su, mío, nuestro, suyo, suyos, and so on:

Ésta es mi maleta.

Es su casa.

Ese libro es mío.

Los billetes son suyos. ☞ 6

2. Look at the pictures above. Listen to the tape and indicate whether what is said is true or false.

1. T F   2. T F   3. T F   4. T F

3. Look at the pictures below and answer the questions as shown in the following example:

—¿De quién es la chaqueta?

—Es de Julio.

| Julio | Rafael | Elena | Marta |

Those words which are referred to in grammar books as 'possessives' (mi, su, mío, etc.) have a complex variety of different forms, as you have already seen in the grammar appendix. ☞ 6 Try to practise them with the two exercises which follow. Do not worry if you do not manage to get them all perfectly correct.

4. Do the same as shown in the following examples.

| yo - libros | —————— | mis libros |
| ustedes - hotel | —————— | su hotel |

nosotros - casas		ellos - coches	
usted - gafas		ustedes - bolígrafo	
él - chaqueta		ellas - maletas	
yo - billetes		usted - libro	

5. Write sentences as shown in the following examples.

| yo - libros | —————— | Los libros son míos. |
| ustedes - hotel | —————— | El hotel es suyo. |

usted - gafas

ella - libros

yo - coche

nosotras - billetes

ellas - bolígrafo

él - chaqueta

ustedes - casa

yo - abrigo

6. Fill in the blanks in what the people say in the pictures below.

¿Son estas maletas?

Sí, mías

¿Es este coche?

Sí,

<u>este</u> coche   <u>ese</u> coche   <u>aquel</u> coche

☞ 5

Este coche

Ese coche

Aquel coche

The words este, ese, aquel are used to indicate things or people. Remember that Spanish divides space into three different planes:

—relatively near the speaker: este - aquí.

—relatively distant from the speaker: aquel - allí.

—an intermediate plane, or near the hearer: ese - ahí.

7. Look at the picture below. Imagine you are the person who appears in the picture. Refer to the objects which you can see there by using este, ese, aquel in the appropriate form.

The words este, ese, aquel may appear accompanied by an immediately following noun (esas gafas son de la secretaria) or they may appear without a noun. In this case they are pronounced the same but appear with an accent in the written form:

—¿Esas gafas?   —Sí, ésas.

8. Look at the pictures below as you listen to the tape. Then answer the questions which appear at the foot of each picture.

Who is Mr López?
Put a cross against him.

Which glasses does the customer want?
Put a cross against them.

9. Identify your partners by using este, ese or aquel. For example:

Éste es ▓▓▓▓▓▓▓▓▓▓▓▓▓.

Ésa es ▓▓▓▓▓▓▓▓▓▓▓▓.

Aquéllos son ▓▓▓▓▓▓▓▓ y ▓▓▓▓▓▓▓▓▓▓▓.

10. Imagine you are a lazy, demanding boss. Indicate what objects you want your partners to hand you. For example:

¡Ese bolígrafo!

"Cánovas" se escribe con "v".   "Cánovas" is spelled with a "v".
This is how to say how a word is spelled.
¿Cómo se escribe "Cánovas"?   How do you spell "Cánovas"?
And this is how to ask for the same information.

escribir (v. i.) = to write
así = like this, in this way

It is rarely necessary to spell words in Spanish. The normal question when confronted with a strange word is ¿Cómo se escribe?. In answering the question people normally write the word down and then show the written form as they say: así.

11. Answer the questions you are asked on the tape.

However, a few letters of the alphabet do cause spelling problems. For example, "b" and "v", which are pronounced the same, or "h", which is not pronounced at all. (See the section on Pronunciation and Spelling, p. xv). In such cases, the question and the answer are usually expressed as follows:
— ¿Cómo se escribe "mujer"?
— Con jota.
— ¿Cómo se escribe "Ribera"? ¿con be o con uve?
— Con be.
— ¿Cómo se escribe "hijo"? ¿con hache o sin hache?
— Con hache.

You will find it useful to learn the names of a few letters from the alphabet:

b: be
v: uve
g: ge
j: jota
c: ce
s: ese
z: zeta
h: hache

12. Listen and answer when you hear the signal.

EN EL HOTEL   IN A HOTEL

 13. Follow the text in the pictures below as you listen to the tape.

A single room.

This is how to ask for a room.

Can I see your passport, please? [i.e. "Will you give me ...?"]

This is how you will be asked to show some identification.

What are you going to have? –A black coffee. –A (fruit) juice.

This is how a barman will ask you for your order and how to reply.

Do you have a telephone? —2.71.56.47.

This is how to ask for someone's telephone number and how to reply.

Learn the following expression by heart, together with the appropriate vocabulary.

To ask for a room in a hotel, say:

Una habitación, por favor.

habitación (f)	= room	habitación con baño	= room
habitación doble	= double room		with a bathroom
habitación individual	= single room	ducha (f)	= shower
		baño (m)	= bathroom

14. Ask for a room in the following circumstances:

1. You are travelling alone.

2. You are travelling with your husband/wife.

3. You are travelling with your husband/wife and one other married couple.

dar (v. i.) = to give

documentación (f) = identification

pasaporte (m) = passport

carné (m) = identity card

When asked for some identification, you will hear:

¿Me da su...?

You may sometimes be asked for identification simply by means of the name of the document in question:

Pasaporte, por favor.

15. Look at the photographs below and indicate what the voice on the tape asks for in each case.

1

2

3

To order something in a bar, reply to the barman's question as in the following example:

—¿Qué va a tomar?

—Un café solo.

<u>un</u> café	=	a coffee
<u>una</u> cerveza	=	a beer
☞ 7		

café (m) = coffee

café solo = black coffee

leche (f) = milk

café con leche = white coffee

cerveza (f) = beer

zumo (m) = (fruit) juice

naranja (f) = orange

zumo de naranja = orange juice

botella (f) = bottle

vaso (m) = glass

agua (f) = water

té (m) = tea

vino (m) = wine

There is more than one way of expressing what is said in the dialogue above. For example: —¿Qué desea? (you already know this)

—Póngame un café con leche.

16. Say in which of these three places —hotel, **bar**, **comisaría**— the following things might be said. For example:

`bar (m)` = bar

`comisaría (f)` = police station

1. *En un bar*
2.
3.
4.

5.
6.
7.
8.

17. Imagine you are the customers in this bar. Give the barman your order.

1   2

18. Imagine you and your partners are in a bar. One person is the barman and asks for your order. You all order what you want.

`tener (v. i.)` = to have

`teléfono (m)` = telephone

Expressions for asking and giving telephone numbers:

—¿Tiene teléfono? —Sí, el 507 12 72.	The person asking the question does not know if the other person has a telephone.
—¿Qué teléfono tiene? —El 56 79 87.	The person who is asking the question assumes that the other person has a telephone.
—¿Teléfono? —El 53 12 24.	For filling in forms and documents.

Telephone numbers are normally given two figures at a time, expressing tens and digits:

     el cincuenta y tres (53) - doce (12) - veinticuatro (24)

     el cinco (5) - cero siete (07) - doce (12) - setenta y dos (72)

20	veinte	25	veinticinco	30	treinta	60	sesenta
21	veintiuno, -a	26	veintiséis	31	treinta y uno, -a	70	setenta
22	veintidós	27	veintisiete	32	treinta y dos	80	ochenta
23	veintitrés	28	veintiocho	40	cuarenta	90	noventa
24	veinticuatro	29	veintinueve	50	cincuenta	100	cien

19. Of the ten numbers which are given below, only five appear on the tape. Listen to the tape and tick which numbers appear.

| 24 | 32 | 89 | 100 | 48 | 73 | 91 | 22 | 47 | 56 |

20. Answer the question you are asked on the tape.

21. Look at the fragment from a telephone directory and answer the questions.

1. ¿Qué teléfono tiene el señor Campo Blanco?
2. ¿Qué teléfono tiene el señor Delgado?
3. ¿Qué teléfono tiene la señora González López?

CABANES GARCÍA, M. - Constitución, 9 302029
CAMPO ANTONIO, F. - Felipe Moratilla, 10 300260
CAMPO BLANCO, J. - Cerro Pelado, 2 301021
CAMPO BUENO, D. - Soto Hidalgo, 6 303445
CASTILLO GONZÁLEZ, V. - Constitución, 5 300022
DELGADO PÉREZ, A. - Constitución, 7 300738
GALÁN JIMÉNEZ, S. - Pico Aneto, 18 322118
GALÁN MARTÍN, P. - Serranilla, 6 500123
GONZÁLEZ LÓPEZ, A. - Soto Hidalgo, 3 300667
GONZÁLEZ SERRANO, V. - La Hiruela, 4 323233
HERNÁNDEZ BOLLO, F.J. - Castilla, 21 301019
HERNÁNDEZ COBO, F. - Av. Madrid, 34 300086
HERNÁNDEZ MARTÍN, J.M. - Jardines, 3 222002

22. Ask your partners their telephone numbers. They should answer.

TRANSCRIPTION OF THE T.V. DIALOGUES
"¿DE QUIÉN ES?"

Presentación. Primera parte

PRESENTADOR: Hola. Buenos días.
RECEPCIONISTA: Buenos días. ¿Qué desea?
PRESENTADOR: Una habitación individual.
RECEPCIONISTA: Un momento, por favor. ¿Con baño?
PRESENTADOR: Sí, sí, con baño completo, por favor.
RECEPCIONISTA: Muy bien. Habitación número 48. ¿Su nombre?
PRESENTADOR: Luis Cánovas.
RECEPCIONISTA: Señor Cánovas. ¿Cómo se escribe, con "b" o con "v"?
PRESENTADOR: Con "v".

Presentation. Part One

PRESENTER: Hello. Good morning.
RECEPTIONIST: Good morning. Can I help you?
PRESENTER: A single room.
RECEPTIONIST: One moment, please. With a bathroom?
PRESENTER: Yes. Yes. With a bathroom, please.
RECEPTIONIST: Very well. Room number 48. Your name?
PRESENTER: Luis Cánovas.
RECEPTIONIST: Mr Cánovas. How do you spell that? With a "b" or a "v"?
PRESENTER: With a "v".

4. ¿De quién es?

RECEPCIONISTA: ¿Me da su carné, por favor? ➡ ①
PRESENTADOR: ¿Dónde está mi carné? Ah, aquí está.
RECEPCIONISTA: Gracias.
PRESENTADOR: Cuarenta y ocho.
TURISTA: ¡Oiga!, ¿son suyas estas gafas?
PRESENTADOR: No, no son mías. Esas gafas no son mías. ¿Son suyas?

Telecomedia. Primera parte

JUAN: Buenas tardes.
RECEPCIONISTA: Sí, dígame. ¿Qué desea?
JUAN: Una habitación individual con baño.
RECEPCIONISTA: ¿Su nombre?
JUAN: Juan Serrano Ribera.
RECEPCIONISTA: ¿Cómo se escribe?
JUAN: ¿Cómo se escribe "Juan"?
RECEPCIONISTA: No. ¿Cómo se escribe "Ribera"? ¿Con "b" o con "v"?
JUAN: Con "b".
RECEPCIONISTA: Espere un momento... ¿Me da su carné, por favor?... Su llave.
JUAN: Gracias... ¿El ascensor?
RECEPCIONISTA: Está allí.
JUAN: Gracias. Buenas tardes.
RECEPCIONISTA: ¡Oiga, por favor!
JUAN: Sí, dígame.
RECEPCIONISTA: ¿Son suyos estos libros?
JUAN: ¡Ah, sí! Son míos. Muchas gracias.
RECEPCIONISTA: ¡Oiga, oiga, por favor! Ese libro es mío.
JUAN: ¡Ah, perdón!

MARÍA: 10, 11, 12, 13, 14, 15, 16, 17, 18...
CARMEN: ¡Hola mamá!
MARÍA: Hola, hija. 21, 22, 23, 24, 25, 26, 27, 28, 29, 30. ¡Ahhh!
DAVID: ¿Cómo se escribe "viaje", con "b" o con "v"?
CARMEN: Con "v".
DAVID: ¿Con "g" o con "j"?
CARMEN: Con "j", David.
DAVID: Gracias, hermana. ¿Y cómo se escribe "carretera"?
CARMEN: Así. "Ca - rre - te - ra".
DAVID: ¿Con dos "erres"?
CARMEN: Sí. Como..., como...
MARÍA: ¡Socorro!
CARMEN: ¡Como socorro!

Presentación. Segunda parte

PRESENTADOR: ¡Dos zumos de naranja, por favor!
CAMARERO: ¿Qué va a tomar?
PRESENTADOR: Póngame dos zumos de naranja.
CAMARERO: ¿Dos zumos?
PRESENTADOR: Sí, dos.
SEÑOR: Mi tarjeta.
PRESENTADOR: Pero...
SEÑOR: Perdón.
PRESENTADOR: Y aquí en Madrid, ¿tiene teléfono?
SEÑOR: ¡Ah, sí! El 224 35 56. ➡ ②
PRESENTADOR: Gracias. Adiós.
SEÑOR: Adiós.
CAMARERO: ¿De quién es este bolígrafo?
PRESENTADOR: No, no, mío no es. ¿De quién es ese bolígrafo?
SEÑOR: ¡Es mío! Gracias.
PRESENTADOR: Hasta luego.

RECEPTIONIST: Can I have your identity card, please? ➡ ①
PRESENTER: Where is my identity card? Ah, here it is.
RECEPTIONIST: Thank you.
PRESENTER: Forty-eight.
TOURIST: Excuse me! Are these your glasses?
PRESENTER: No, they're not mine. Those glasses aren't mine. Are they yours?

TV Comedy. Part One

JUAN: Good afternoon.
RECEPTIONIST: Yes. Can I help you?
JUAN: A single room with a bathroom.
RECEPTIONIST: Your name?
JUAN: Juan Serrano Ribera.
RECEPTIONIST: How do you spell that?
JUAN: How do you spell "Juan"?
RECEPTIONIST: No. How do you spell "Ribera"? With a "b" or a "v"?
JUAN: With a "b".
RECEPTIONIST: Just a moment ... Can I have your identity card, please? Your key.
JUAN: Thank you. The lift?
RECEPTIONIST: It's over there.
JUAN: Thank you. Good afternoon.
RECEPTIONIST: Excuse me, please!
JUAN: Yes. What is it?
RECEPTIONIST: Are these books yours?
JUAN: Ah, yes, they are. They're mine. Thank you very much.
RECEPTIONIST: Excuse me! Excuse me, please! That book is mine.
JUAN: Oh, I'm sorry!

MARÍA: 10, 11, 12, 13, 14, 15, 16, 17, 18, ...
CARMEN: Hello, Mummy.
MARÍA: Hello, dear [i.e. "daughter"]. 21, 22, 23, 24, 25, 26, 27, 28, 29, 30. Ahhhh!
DAVID: How do you spell "viaje"? With a "b" or a "v"?
CARMEN: With a "v".
DAVID: With a "g" or a "j"?
CARMEN: With a "j", David.
DAVID: Thanks, sister. And how do you spell "carretera"?
CARMEN: Like this: "Ca-rre-te-ra".
DAVID: With double "r"?
CARMEN: Yes. As in ... As in ...
MARÍA: Help!
CARMEN: As in "socorro"!

Presentation. Part Two

PRESENTER: Two orange juices, please!
BARMAN: What are you going to have?
PRESENTER: Give me two orange juices.
BARMAN: Two juices?
PRESENTER; Yes, two.
MAN: My card.
PRESENTER: But...
MAN: I'm sorry.
PRESENTER: And do you have a telephone here in Madrid?
MAN: Ah, yes. Number 2 24 35 56. ➡ ②
PRESENTER: Thank you. Goodbye.
MAN: Goodbye.
BARMAN: Whose is this ballpoint pen?
PRESENTER: No, no, it's not mine. Whose is this ballpoint?
MAN: It's mine! Thank you.
PRESENTER: Goodbye.

Telecomedia. Segunda parte

BOTONES: ¿El señor Serrano?

JUAN: Sí, soy yo.

BOTONES: Esto es suyo.

JUAN: ¡Ah, gracias!

BOTONES: ¿Dónde...? Estos billetes de avión son suyos también.

JUAN: ¿Míos?

BOTONES: ¿Son suyos o no?

JUAN: Sí, sí, son míos. Por favor, ¿dónde está la cafetería?

BOTONES: En el primer piso.

JUAN: Gracias.

BOTONES: De nada. Hasta luego.

CAMARERO: ¿Qué va a tomar?

JUAN: Un café con leche. ➡ ③

BOTONES: ¡Señor Rodríguez! ¡Señor Rodríguez!

JUAN: ¡Oiga, por favor!

BOTONES: ¿Es usted el señor Rodríguez?

JUAN: No, no.

BOTONES: Perdón. ¡Señor Rodríguez!

JUAN: ¿Qué teléfono tiene el hotel, por favor?

CAMARERO: El 227 47 54.

JUAN: Dos - veintisiete - cuarenta y siete - cincuenta y cuatro. Dos - cero siete - treinta y dos - sesenta y cinco.

BOTONES: ¡Señor Rodríguez!

RODRÍGUEZ: ¡Soy yo!

BOTONES: ¿Señor Rodríguez?

RODRÍGUEZ: Sí.

JUAN: ¿De quién es este café?

CAMARERO: Suyo.

JUAN: ¿Y esto, de quién es?

DAVID: ¡Dígame! Un momento, Óscar. ¡Carmen, tu novio!

JUAN: ¡Carm...! ¡Pe...!

JUAN: ¡Carmen! Soy Juan.

CARMEN: Perdón.

PRESENTADOR: Sí, sí, sí. ¿A dónde? Otro a Palma de Mallorca. Otro. Sí, otro. Un momento, por favor. Veintiséis - treinta y cuatro - ochenta y dos. Hasta luego. Hasta luego.

TV Comedy. Part Two

BELLBOY: Mr Serrano?

JUAN: Yes. That's me.

BELLBOY: This is yours.

JUAN: Ah, thank you!

BELLBOY: Where...? These plane tickets are yours too.

JUAN: Mine?

BELLBOY: Are they yours or not?

JUAN: Yes, yes, they're mine. Please, where is the cafeteria?

BELLBOY: On the first floor.

JUAN: Thank you.

BELLBOY: Don't mention it. Goodbye.

BARMAN: What are you going to have?

JUAN: A white coffee. ➡ ③

BELLBOY: Mr Rodríguez! Mr Rodríguez!

JUAN: Excuse me, please!

BELLBOY: Are you Mr Rodríguez?

JUAN: No, no.

BELLBOY: I'm sorry. Mr Rodríguez!

JUAN: What is the hotel telephone number, please?

BARMAN: Number 2 27 47 54.

JUAN: Two - twenty-seven - forty-seven - fifty-four. Two - zero seven - thirty-two- sixty-five.

BELLBOY: Mr Rodríguez!

RODRÍGUEZ: That's me! [i.e. "Am I".]

BELLBOY: Mr Rodríguez?

RODRÍGUEZ: Yes.

JUAN: Whose is this coffee?

BARMAN: Yours.

JUAN: And this? Whose is this?

DAVID: Yes! One moment, Oscar. Carmen! Your boyfriend!

JUAN: Carm...! Bu(t)...!

JUAN: Carmen! It's me, Juan!

CARMEN: I'm sorry.

PRESENTER: Yes, yes. Where to? One more to Palma de Mallorca. One more. Yes, one more. One moment, please. Twenty-six - thirty-four - eighty-two. Goodbye. Goodbye.

● **CAJÓN DE SASTRE**

① When registering at a hotel in Spain it is usually not sufficient to give just your name and signature. The receptionist will normally ask for some identification. Identification is usually established by showing your carné identity card (official name: Documento Nacional de Identidad - D.N.I.); your pasaporte passport; or your carné de conducir driving licence (official name: Permiso de conducción or Permiso de conducir).

② Note that the code number for non-local phone calls is referred to as el prefijo in Spanish.

③ In Spanish bars people rarely ask for un vaso de vino a glass of wine or un vaso de cerveza a glass of beer. The most frequent expressions are: un vino a wine, un tinto a red (wine), un blanco a white (wine) to refer to wine, and una cerveza a beer, or una caña a glass (of beer) to ask for beer.

4. ¿De quién es?

● **USTED YA PUEDE...**

ask who something belongs to;	¿De quién es la maleta? ¿Es suya la maleta?
say who something belongs to;	Es mi maleta. La maleta es mía. La maleta es de Luis.
indicate things or people according to how far they are from the speaker;	Esta maleta. Ese coche. Aquél.
ask how a word is spelled;	¿Cómo se escribe?
say how a word is spelled;	Así. Se escribe con "b".
ask for a room in a hotel;	Una habitación individual con baño.
understand when you are asked for some identification;	¿Me da su pasaporte? Pasaporte, por favor.
understand a barman when he asks for your order;	¿Qué va a tomar?
order what you want in a bar;	Un café solo. Póngame dos cervezas.
ask and give telephone numbers.	¿Tiene teléfono? —Sí, el 34 56 78. ¿Qué teléfono tiene? —El 23 56 81. ¿Teléfono? —El 23 45 67.

5 ¿A dónde va Juan?

In this unit you will learn how to ask and say where people or things are going, and to ask and say what there is in a particular place. You will also learn further ways of interacting with other people, by offering people things, by recommending people to do things, and by asking permission to do things.

I

Voy a Salamanca.   I am going to Salamanca.

This is how to say where someone is going.

¿A dónde va?   Where are you going?

And this is how to ask for the same information.

`ir (v. i.)` = to go

1. Listen and repeat when you hear the signal.

To express where someone or something is going, use the verb ir to go followed by a and then the name of a place. The word a precedes dónde if you ask for the same information:

     ¿A dónde?

5. ¿A dónde va Juan?

camping (m) = camping site
playa (f) = beach
cine (m) = cinema
parque (m) = park
pueblo (m) = village

Present tense of the verb IR:

(yo)	voy
(tú)	vas
(usted)	va
(él, ella)	va
(nosotros, -as)	vamos
(vosotros, -as)	vais
(ustedes)	van
(ellos, -as)	van

¿A dónde va usted?

Al camping

A la playa

hombre (m) = man
mujer (f) = woman
chico (m) = boy
chica (f) = girl
tren (m) = train
autobús (m) = bus

Voy a mi hotel

El hombre va al camping, el chico, a la playa, y la mujer, a su hotel

2. Look at the pictures above. Listen to the tape and indicate whether what you hear is true or false.

1. T F   2. T F   3. T F   4. T F
5. T F   6. T F   7. T F

también = too, also

3. Fill the blanks with one word only in each case.

1. A girl asks a railway employee:

   GIRL: Por favor, ¿a dónde _____ este tren?

   EMPLOYEE: _____ Madrid.

   GIRL: Muchas _____ .

   EMPLOYEE: De _____ .

2. A boy and a girl are outside a cinema. They see an old man they know:

   GIRL: Nosotros _____ al cine. ¿Y usted también?

   OLD MAN: No, yo _____ al parque.

3. Two farm labourers working in the fields see a group of cyclists on their way to the village down the road. One says to the other:

LABOURER: Van ▯▯▯ pueblo.

4. A man asks a bus station employee:

MAN: ¡Oiga, por ▯▯▯▯! ¿Este autobús ▯▯▯ a Salamanca?

EMPLOYEE: Sí, señor.

4. Look at this map of Europe. You and your partners each choose a country in which to spend your holidays. Imagine that you come across the other members of the group at the airport, ready to take the plane. Ask them where they are going.

● ●

Ⅱ **Hay una botella en el frigorífico.**   There is a bottle in the fridge.

This is how to say what there is in a particular place.

¿Qué hay en el frigorífico?   What is there in the fridge?

And this is how to ask for the same information.

frigorífico (m) = fridge

5. Listen and repeat.

plátano (m)	= banana
tomate (m)	= tomato
chocolate (m)	= chocolate
fruta (f)	= fruit
aceite (m)	= oil
huevo (m)	= egg
pan (m)	= bread
lata (f)	= tin

The word hay there is/are normally appears in sentences which express what there is in a particular place. Note that hay does not vary with the number of things mentioned:

Hay una naranja.

Hay tres naranjas.

Hay naranjas.

Notice that after hay there may be an indication of the quantity of the thing mentioned: Hay tres naranjas.

Hay muchas naranjas.

or simply the name of the thing:

Hay naranjas.

Hay fruta.

WORDS WHICH EXPRESS QUANTITY:

dos, tres, cuatro... two, three, four...

muchos, -as — many, a lot

pocos, -as — few

un poco de — a little

¿hay algo?

no hay nada

Another way of asking if there is something in a particular place is ¿Hay algo en...?:

¿Hay algo en el frigorífico?

Possible answers:

Sí, hay fruta.   No, no hay nada.

 6. Listen and repeat.

 7. Listen. On the tape a man's voice will answer the questions ¿qué hay ahí?, ¿y allí?, and ¿y qué hay en el frigorífico?. Put a cross against the things which the man says there are in each case.

1. Dos botellas de cerveza
2. Dos tomates
3. Pan
4. Huevos
5. Chocolate
6. Nada
7. Fruta
8. Aceite

8. Look at the map and answer the following questions:

1. ¿Qué hay en la Plaza Mayor?
2. ¿Y en la Gran Vía?
3. ¿Y qué hay en la calle Mayor?
4. ¿Y en la calle de la Libertad?

farmacia (f)	= chemist's
iglesia (f)	= church
banco (m)	= bank
taller (m)	= garage
aparcamiento (m)	= car park
gasolinera (f)	= filling station

 9. Look at the map again. What can you see there? Listen and complete the following sentences.

cerca = near

por aquí = near here, around here

1. En la Plaza Mayor ▓▓▓▓ ▓▓▓▓ ▓▓▓▓ .
2. En la Gran Vía ▓▓▓▓ una ▓▓▓▓ .
3. En la calle Mayor ▓▓▓▓ un ▓▓▓▓ , y en la calle de la Libertad, ▓▓▓▓ ▓▓▓▓ .
4. En la Plaza Nueva ▓▓▓▓ una ▓▓▓▓

MAN: Excuse me, please. Where is there a chemist's?
POLICEMAN: There.

Por favor, ¿dónde hay una farmacia?

Allí

MAN: Excuse me, please. Is there a chemist's near here?
POLICEMAN: Yes, there's one there.

Por favor, ¿hay alguna farmacia cerca?

Sí, hay una allí

To ask where something which you are looking for is, use dónde:

¿Dónde hay una farmacia?

You can also ask where something you are looking for is by using ¿Hay algún (or alguna)...?:

¿Hay alguna farmacia cerca?

¿Hay algún taller por aquí?

¿Hay algún banco en este pueblo?

5. ¿A dónde va Juan?

WOMAN: Excuse me, please. Is there a bank around here?
MAN: No, there isn't one.

The following are the most usual answers to the question ¿Hay algún (or alguna)…?:

—¿Hay algún taller por aquí?   —¿Hay alguna farmacia cerca?
—Sí, hay uno en la plaza.   —No, no hay ninguna.

—¿Hay algo? —No hay nada.
—¿Hay algún banco? —No hay ninguno.   ☞ 7

10. Complete the dialogue.

A: Oiga, ▒▒▒▒▒ favor. ¿Hay ▒▒▒▒▒▒ taller en este pueblo?
B: Sí, ▒▒▒▒ uno ▒▒▒▒▒ la Calle Mayor.
A: ¿Y ▒▒▒▒▒ algún aparcamiento?
B: No, no hay ▒▒▒▒▒▒▒▒ .

11. Imagine you and your partners are in the Plaza Mayor in the map in Exercise 8. Ask them whether the following things exist in or near the square.

alguna farmacia   algún taller   algún aparcamiento
algún banco   algún hospital

● ●

(III)

¿Quiere usted un café?   Would you like a coffee? [i.e. "Do you want…?"]
This is how to offer someone something.
Sí, gracias.   Yes, please. [i. e. "thank you"]
This is how to accept.
No, gracias.   No, thank you.
And this is how to refuse.

querer (v. i.) = to want

To offer someone something, use the verb querer:
¿Quiere un café?
¿Quieren ustedes un café?
You can also offer something simply by mentioning its name:
— ¿Un café?   — No, gracias.

12. Listen and repeat.

13. Offer some of the following things to different members of the group.

una naranja   fruta   chocolate
un tomate   agua   pan

Nouns such as chocolate, fruta, agua and pan, which are normally un-countable, may be preceded by the expression un poco de a little:
¿Quiere un poco de pan?

● ●

IV

¿Puedo sentarme aquí?   May I sit here?

This is how to ask permission to do something.

Sí, claro.   Yes, of course

Bueno.   Yes, O. K.

And this is how to grant permission.

coger = to take	
comer = to eat	
✓ **fumar** = to smoke	
meter = to put in	
✓ **pasar** = to pass by	
✓ **entrar** = to enter	
poner (v. i.) = to put	
sentarse (v. i.) = to sit down	

REFLEXIVE VERBS

sentar**se**

llamar**se**

se llama   ☞ 16

14. Listen and repeat.

To ask permission to do something, use the verb poder:
  ¿Podemos sentarnos?

15. Listen and fill in the blanks with what you hear on the tape.

1. A woman asks if she can take an orange:
  WOMAN: ¿ ▓▓▓▓▓▓ coger esta naranja?

2. A woman wants to smoke on the train. She asks the ticket collector:
  WOMAN: Oiga, ¿ ▓▓▓▓▓▓ fumar aquí?
  TICKET COLLECTOR: No, señora.

3. A young man wants to put his suitcase in the boot of a friend's car:
  YOUNG MAN: ¿ ▓▓▓▓▓▓ meter la maleta aquí?
  FRIEND: Sí, ▓▓▓▓▓▓ .

4. Two students talking to their new landlady. They are carrying a big box of books which they want to put on a table:
  STUDENTS: ¿ ▓▓▓▓▓▓ poner los libros aquí?
  LANDLADY: ▓▓▓▓▓▓ .

5. An office worker wants to enter his boss's office:
  OFFICE WORKER: ¿ ▓▓▓▓▓▓ entrar?

16. Ask permission to do the following things.

coger una naranja   fumar

comer un poco de chocolate   sentarse

Sometimes, the most effective way of achieving something is not to ask permission. Do what you want to and say perdón at the same time.

● ●

V   **Coma una naranja.**   Eat an orange!

No fume.   Don't smoke!

This is how to recommend someone to do something.

Bueno.   O. K.

And this is how to accept the recommendation.

17. Listen and repeat.

√ **subir** = to go/come up

√ **bajar** = to go/come down

probar (v. i.) = to taste, to try

hacer (v. i.) deporte = to practise sport

venir (v. i.) = to come

√ **mirar** = to look

despacio = slowly

deporte (m) = sport

There are some special forms (called imperatives) which are used for making recommendations:

FUMAR: fume - fumen

COMER: coma - coman

These can also be negative, of course:

no fume - no fumen

no coma - no coman

☞ 17

THIS WILL HELP YOU:

FUMAR: fume

SUBIR: suba

BAJAR: baje

IR: vaya

PROBAR: pruebe

HACER: haga

TENER: tenga

VENIR: venga

MIRAR: mire

COMER: coma

18. Listen to the sentences on the tape and indicate which picture is referred to in each case.

> Besides bueno, there are other expressions which can be used to accept a recommendation:
>
> Muy bien.   De acuerdo.   Vale.
>
> Vale is a very frequent, informal expression.

19. Accept the recommendations you hear on the tape.

> The expressions which are used to make recommendations can also be used to ask someone to do something, to order someone to do something, and to prohibit someone doing something. In the next unit you will learn more about this.

20. Look again at Exercise 18. Without listening to the tape, try to write the recommendations you heard there in the space provided under the pictures.

21. What would you say in the following situations?

1. A train is standing at the platform in a station; you want to know where it is going.
2. You want to tell a friend that you are going to Madrid.
3. You are carrying a very heavy parcel for a friend; you want to know what is in the parcel.
4. You want to know where there is a chemist's.
5. You want to know if there is a bank nearby.
6. Someone has come to pay you a visit; you want to offer him/her a coffee.
7. You want to enter your boss's office.
8. You want to recommend someone to try some oranges.
9. You want to recommend someone to stop smoking.

5. ¿A dónde va Juan?

● **TRANSCRIPTION OF THE TV DIALOGUES**
"¿A DÓNDE VA JUAN?"

Presentación. Primera parte

PRESENTADOR: Hola, bienvenidos a Mallorca. ¿Puedo hacerles una foto? Muchas gracias.

JOVEN: Por favor, ¿va usted a Sóller?

PRESENTADOR: Sí, sí.

JOVEN: ¿Puedo ir con usted?

PRESENTADOR: Sí, claro.

JOVEN: ¿Puedo poner esto atrás?

PRESENTADOR: Un momento.

JOVEN: ¿Hay muchos hoteles en Sóller?

PRESENTADOR: Aquí están todos.

JOVEN: Oiga, ¿hay algún camping ➡ ① en Sóller?

PRESENTADOR: Sí, hay uno. Hay un camping en Sóller. Un camping muy bonito. Hasta luego.

Telecomedia. Primera parte

JUAN: ¡Ahora!

CARMEN: ¡No!

JUAN: Un momento. Otra vez, vamos.

CARMEN: Nada, que no.

JUAN: ¿Hay una lata de aceite en el maletero?

CARMEN: Sí, aquí hay una lata de aceite… Pero… ¡Huy! Nada, no hay nada.

JUAN: ¿Puedo coger esto?

CARMEN: ¡Nooo…!

JUAN: Gracias. ¿Puedo meter la ropa aquí?

CARMEN: Bueno.

JUAN: ¡Buff! ¿Y ahora qué hacemos?

CARMEN: Perdón, ¿hay algún taller cerca?

MOTORISTA: Sí, en el pueblo hay uno.

JUAN: ¿Va usted allí?

MOTORISTA: Sí, pero tengo mucha prisa.

JUAN: Yo también.

MOTORISTA: Cuidado, ¿eh?

JUAN: ¡Vaaale!

CARMEN: Vale.

JUAN: Oiga, ¿dónde está el taller?

MOTORISTA: ¡Hombre ➡ ② , allí está el mecánico! ➡ ③

JUAN: Por favor… ¿Puedo pasar?

GUARDIA: ¿A dónde va usted? Ah, pase, pase.

JUAN: ¡Oiga! ¡Pero… ! ¡Oiga, oiga!

Presentación. Segunda parte

JOVEN: Vaya más despacio.

PRESENTADOR: Vale, vale.

JOVEN: ¿Una cerveza? ¿Quiere usted una cerveza? ➡ ④

PRESENTADOR: Bueno, sí. Buena cosa el deporte. Ustedes, ¿hacen deporte? Ah, ¿no? Pues hagan deporte, hombre.

Telecomedia. Segunda parte

JUAN: ¡Por favor, vaya usted más despacio!

MECÁNICO: ¿Qué?

JUAN: ¿Es usted el mecánico?

MECÁNICO: Sí.

JUAN: Mi coche no funciona. Está en la carretera.

MECÁNICO: Espere.

JUAN: Pero…

Presentation. Part One

PRESENTER: Hello. Welcome to Mallorca. Can I take a photo of you? Thank you very much.

YOUNG MAN: Excuse me, please. Are you going to Sóller?

PRESENTER: Yes, yes.

YOUNG MAN: Can I go with you?

PRESENTER: Yes, of course.

YOUNG MAN: Can I put this in the back?

PRESENTER: One moment.

YOUNG MAN: Are there many hotels in Sóller?

PRESENTER: They are all in here.

YOUNG MAN: Excuse me. Is there a camping site in Sóller? ➡ ①

PRESENTER: Yes, there is one. There is a camping site in Sóller. A very nice camping site. See you later.

TV Comedy. Part One

JUAN: Now!

CARMEN: No.

JUAN: One moment. Once again. Come on.

CARMEN: No, it's no use.

JUAN: Is there a can of oil in the boot?

CARMEN: Yes, there's a can of oil here. But … Oh! No, there's nothing (in it).

JUAN: Can I use [i.e. "take"] this?

CARMEN: Noooo!

JUAN: Thank you. Can I put my clothes in here?

CARMEN: Yes. OK.

JUAN: Phew! And now what do we do?

CARMEN: Excuse me. Is there a garage near here?

MOTORCYCLIST: Yes, there is one in the village.

JUAN: Are you going there?

MOTORCYCLIST: Yes, but I'm in a hurry.

JUAN: Me too.

MOTORCYCLIST: Be careful, OK?

JUAN: OK!

CARMEN: OK.

JUAN: Excuse me. Where is the garage?

MOTORCYCLIST: "Hombre" ➡ ② there is the mechanic! ➡ ③

JUAN: Excuse me, please. Can I come by?

POLICEMAN: Where are you going? Ah! Yes, you can come by.

JUAN: Excuse me! But … Excuse me! Excuse me!

Presentation. Part Two

YOUNG MAN: Go more slowly.

PRESENTER: OK. OK.

YOUNG MAN: A beer? Would you like a beer? ➡ ④

PRESENTER: Well, yes. Sport is good for you. Do you practise sport? Ah, don't you? Well, practise sport!

TV Comedy. Part Two

JUAN: Please go more slowly.

MECHANIC: What?

JUAN: Are you the mechanic?

MECHANIC: Yes.

JUAN: My car is out of order. It's (abandoned) on the road.

MECHANIC: Just a moment.

JUAN: But …

MECÁNICO: ¡Espere, hombre, espere!

JUAN: De acuerdo. ¡Buff! Pero vaya más despacio. ¡Que vaya usted más despacio!

MOTORISTA: ¿Quiere?

JUAN: ¿Qué hay en la botella?

MOTORISTA: Agua.

JUAN: ¡Agua! Sí, gracias. ¿Dónde está la meta?

MOTORISTA: Cerca. Muy cerca. A dos kilómetros.

JUAN: ¿A dos kilómetros?

MOTORISTA: ¡Ánimo! ¿Un plátano?

JUAN: No, no, gracias.

CARMEN: ¡Oh, no!

JUAN: ¡Carmen! ¡Carmen! Perdón, perdón… ¡Carmen! ¡Carmen!

CARMEN: ¡Juan!

JUAN: ¡Carmen!

CARMEN: ¡Bravo!

JUAN: ¡Carmen!

PRESENTADOR: ¿Una flor? Hasta otro día. Adiós.

MECHANIC: Wait, man! Wait!

JUAN: OK. Phew! But please slow down a bit. Please slow down, I said.

MOTORCYCLIST: Would you like some?

JUAN: What's in the bottle?

MOTORCYCLIST: Water.

JUAN: Water! Yes, please. Where is the finishing line?

MOTORCYCLIST: Near. Very near. Two kilometres away.

JUAN: Two kilometres?

MOTORCYCLIST: Come on! A banana?

JUAN: No. No, thank you.

CARMEN: Oh, no!

JUAN: Carmen! Carmen! Excuse me. Excuse me. Carmen! Carmen!

CARMEN: Juan!

JUAN: Carmen!

CARMEN: Bravo!

JUAN: Carmen!

PRESENTER: A flower? See you next time. Goodbye.

● **CAJÓN DE SASTRE**

① The word camping comes from English, of course. But note that in Spanish this word means the equivalent of 'camping site' in English. Many English words are used in Spanish. For example, the word parking is used together with the Spanish words aparcamiento (and estacionamiento) for the equivalent of 'car park' in English. The sign to indicate a car park is a white capital "P" on a blue background.

② ¡Hombre! is a very frequent exclamation. It is chiefly used to express surprise or as an affectionate addition to what someone says. Strangely enough, the word hombre may be used when speaking to a woman (though it is also possible to use the word mujer as an exclamation in this case).

③ Note this sentence: allí está el mecánico. You will already have noticed that word order in Spanish is very free. For example, it is also possible to say el mecánico está allí or está allí el mecánico. The part of the sentence which the speaker considers most important is normally placed towards the end. In the sentence here the speaker wishes to emphasise the fact that there is a mechanic there, so the word mecánico comes last. However, do not worry about this question for the moment.

④ Spanish people frequently offer things to others in many situations of everyday life, even to strangers. Do not be surprised if you are offered such things as cigarettes, drinks, food, etc. on public transport, in waiting rooms, and in public generally.

5. ¿A dónde va Juan?

 USTED YA PUEDE...

say where someone or something is going;	Voy a Salamanca.
and ask for the same information;	¿A dónde va usted?
indicate the existence of something in a particular place;	Hay dos naranjas.
ask for the same information;	¿Qué hay ahí?
and reply;	No hay nada.
ask where something which you are looking for is;	¿Dónde hay una farmacia?
ask if there is something in a particular place;	¿Hay algo en el frigorífico? ¿Hay alguna farmacia cerca?
and reply;	No hay nada. No, no hay ninguna.
offer someone something;	¿Un café? ¿Quiere usted un café?
accept an offer and refuse;	Sí, gracias. No, gracias.
ask and grant permission;	¿Puedo entrar? Sí, claro.
excuse yourself for causing some kind of bother;	Perdón.
recommend someone to do something;	Vaya despacio. No fume.
and accept a recommendation.	Bueno. Vale.

In this unit you will learn how to ask what someone is doing, and how to tell someone to do something or not do something. You will also learn how to identify things, and how to use the two alternative forms of address which exist in Spanish.

I USTED / TÚ

FORMS OF ADDRESS:
usted
tú
☞ 19

When speaking to people in Spanish it is necessary to choose between two alternative forms of address: tú and usted. Tú is less formal and less distant; for that reason it is used today to address children, members of the family and friends. It is also the form which is most usual among young people, even if they are strangers. However, in case of doubt use usted.

The form of address chosen affects the forms of the verbs and of other words:
¿Me <u>da</u> <u>su</u> pasaporte? Could you give me your passport?
¿Me <u>das</u> <u>tu</u> pasaporte? Can you give me your passport?
☞ 19

USTED	TÚ
quiere	quier<u>es</u>
va	va<u>s</u>
da	da<u>s</u>
tiene	tiene<u>s</u>
<u>su</u> coche	<u>tu</u> coche
es <u>suyo</u>	es <u>tuyo</u>
<u>se</u> llama	<u>te</u> llamas

6. De "tú", por favor

1. Look at the pictures above. On the tape you will hear five sentences, each of which corresponds to one of the pictures. Indicate the corresponding picture in each case.

2. Look at the pictures again. Cover the text in each of the right-hand pictures and try to write down the sentences you can no longer see.

2

4

6

8

10

3. Now do the same again, this time orally.

4. The words are missing from what the people say in the pictures below. The missing sentences are as follows:

1. ¿Qué van a tomar?
2. ¿Qué vas a tomar?
3. ¿Va usted a Palma?
4. Y tú, ¿a dónde vas?

Indicate which sentence corresponds to each picture.

USTEDES	VOSOTROS
quieren	queréis
van	vais
su coche	vuestro coche
es suyo	es vuestro
se llaman	os llamáis

☞ 19

5. You are speaking to D. Emilio, whom you have just met. You ask him the following questions:

1. Por favor, ¿cómo se llama usted?
2. ¿Dónde vive?
3. ¿Tiene teléfono?

Now say the same things to the following: first to Carlitos; second to Don Antonio and his wife doña Ana; and third to Felipe and Mercedes.

6. Imagine that several people have come to pay you a visit at your home: your mother, a group of friends, your boss and his wife, your child's teacher, and so on. The other members of the group must play these parts. Offer your guests something to drink.

café

zumo de naranja

vino

etc.

FOR EXAMPLE: ¿Queréis un café?

● ●

(II)   **Está jugando.**   He is playing.

This is how to say what someone is doing.

¿Qué está haciendo?   What is he doing?

And this is how to ask for the same information.

¿Qué están haciendo?

Está comiendo.

Están jugando.

7. Listen and repeat when you hear the signal.

hacer (v. i.)	= to do
jugar (v. i.)	= to play
comprar	= to buy
esperar	= to wait
leer (v. i.)	= to read
aparcar	= to park
escuchar	= to listen
hablar	= to speak
abrir (v. i.)	= to open
ver (v. i.)	= to see
radio (f)	= radio
periódico (m)	= newspaper
paquete (m)	= parcel, packet

To express actions which are going on at the present moment, use estar followed by forms such as jugando, comiendo, escribiendo:

Estoy comiendo.

To ask for the same information, use the interrogative word qué and the verb hacer:

¿Qué están haciendo?

jugar	→	jugando
comer	→	comiendo
escribir	→	escribiendo

☞ 18

8. Listen and repeat when you hear the signal.

9. Complete the sentences below with one of the following expressions:

> Qué están haciendo
>
> Estamos
>
> Estoy abriendo
>
> Está hablando
>
> Estoy comprando
>
> Están
>
> Qué está haciendo
>
> Viendo

1. A woman is standing in front of a newsvendor's kiosk. She tells us what she is doing:

WOMAN: el periódico.

2. A married couple are speaking to each other. Their daughter is making a telephone call:

FATHER: ¿   María?

MOTHER: por teléfono.

3. A married couple are speaking to each other. Their two small children are reading a book:

FATHER: ¿   los niños? ¿Están   la televisión?

MOTHER: No,   leyendo.

4. A young couple are at the bus-stop. They tell us what they are doing:

YOUNG PEOPLE: esperando el autobús.

5. A woman is opening a parcel. A man asks:

MAN: ¿Qué estás haciendo?

WOMAN: este paquete.

10. Listen to the tape and join each name in the column on the left with the corresponding action in the column on the right (as shown here for the first sentence on the tape).

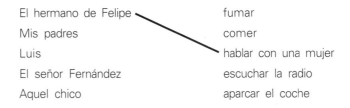

El hermano de Felipe   fumar

Mis padres   comer

Luis   hablar con una mujer

El señor Fernández   escuchar la radio

Aquel chico   aparcar el coche

11. One member of the group (or several together) mimes one of the actions which you have already learned how to express (smoke, listen to the radio, speak to someone, etc.). He then asks: (¿Qué estoy haciendo? **or** ¿Qué estamos haciendo?). **The others reply.**

6. De "tú", por favor

(III)

¡Pare!	Stop!
¡Para!	Stop!

This is how to tell someone to do something.

¡No pare!	Don't stop!
¡No pares!	Don't stop!

And this is how to tell someone not to do something.

PARAR

par<u>a</u>	(tú)
par<u>ad</u>	(vosotros)
par<u>e</u>	(usted)
par<u>en</u>	(ustedes)

☞ 17

 = to stop

Forms such as pare, para, pase, pasa, etc., are used to get someone to do something. Depending on the circumstances and the relationship between the speaker and the hearer, the resulting sentences may express an order, a request, a suggestion or a recommendation (as we saw in the previous unit), and so on. ☞ 17

12. Tell the people below to do certain things by using one of the following words in the appropriate form: mirar, parar, pasar, comprar, esperar, escuchar. Then write each sentence in the space provided.

EXAMPLE:

Your friend Elena wants to know the day's news.

(To Elena): Compra el periódico.

1. D. Carlos and D. Rafael, two of your clients, have come to your office to discuss some business. You open the door and show them in.

(To D. Carlos and D. Rafael):

2. You want your children to listen to what you are going to say.

(To your children):

3. You want to get out of the car which your friend Antonio is driving.

(To Antonio):

4. You are showing a group of tourists round the city. You point to a historic building.

(To the tourists):

5. You are phoning your brother David. Someone rings the doorbell. You want to interrupt the conversation a moment in order to open the door.

(To David):

correr = to run
venir (v. i.) = to come
volver (v. i.) = to return

COMER

come (tú)

comed (vosotros)

coma (usted)

coman (vosotros)

ESCRIBIR

escribe (tú)

escribid (vosotros)

escriba (usted)

escriban (vosotros)

☞ 17

13. Listen and repeat when you hear the signal.

14. Tell the people below to do certain things by using one of the following words in the appropriate form: correr, sentarse, coger, venir. Then write each sentence in the space provided.

THIS WILL HELP YOU:

SENTARSE:

siéntate, siéntese

VENIR:

ven, venga

VOLVER:

vuelve, vuelva

1. D. Felipe has come to see you in your office. You offer him a seat.
(To D. Felipe):

2. Your friend Manuel is taking part in a race and is in second place. You shout to urge him on.
(To Manuel):

3. You want your son Luis to come to you.
(To Luis):

4. You offer some sweets to Isabel and Diego, your young son's classmates.
(To Isabel and Diego):

You have already seen how to tell someone to do something: hable, coma, suba (forms with usted) and habla, come, sube (forms with tú).
Note how to tell someone not to do something -

> with usted the forms remain the same as in the affirmative, except for the presence of no:

no hable   no coma   no suba

> However, with tú there is variation between the affirmative and the negative forms:

habla - no hables

come - no comas

sube - no subas

HABLAR

no hables (tú)

no habléis (vosotros)

COMER

no comas (tú)

no comáis (vosotros)

SUBIR

no subas (tú)

no subáis (vosotros)

☞ 17

15. Look again at the pictures above. Imagine that now it is a colleague of yours who is speaking, not your boss; he says the same things, but he does not use **usted**, he uses **tú**. How would each sentence be expressed in this case?

1:

2:

3:

16. Here are some of the verbs you know already:

fumar

bajar

escribir

jugar

hablar

comer

mirar

leer

subir

entrar

escuchar

venir

Use these verbs to tell one member of the group to do certain things; he should perform the required actions. After that, another member of the group tells him not to do those same things.

EXAMPLE:

YOU: ¡Fuma! (or ¡Fume!)

(the person in question pretends to smoke)

ANOTHER MEMBER OF THE GROUP: ¡No fumes!

(or ¡No fume!)

IV   **¿Qué es eso?**   What is that?

This is how to ask what something is.

Una cámara de vídeo.   A video camera.

And this is how to reply.

¿Qué es una ensalada tropical?

cámara de vídeo (f) = video camera	
máquina de fotos (f) = camera	
reloj (m) = watch	
cosa (f) = thing	

est**o**	= esta cosa
es**o**	= esa cosa
aquell**o**	= aquella cosa

☞ 5

To ask what something is we use one of the following questions:

> ¿Qué es esto?
>
> ¿Qué es eso?
>
> ¿Qué es aquello?

Expressions such as:

> Esto es una cámara.
>
> Eso es un zumo de naranja.
>
> Aquello es un reloj.

are used to identify something which the listener does not know or cannot identify.

If we do not know what a word refers to, we can also ask for this information by using ¿Qué es...?:

> ¿Qué es una ensalada tropical?
>
> ¿Qué es una sangría?

The difference between esto, eso, aquello is the same as that between este, ese and aquel, which you already know i.e. the distinction is related to how far away the object is from the speaker.

17. Draw pictures of certain objects or indicate them by miming, etc. Then ask: ¿Qué es esto? Another member of the group replies.

EN LA MESA

Can you pass me the salt?

Pass me the salt, please.
Here you are. [i.e. "Take!"].

Could you pass me the salt?

Pass me the salt, please.

sal (f) = salt

azúcar (m) = sugar

ensalada (f) = salad

pollo (m) = chicken

cuchara (f) = spoon

tenedor (m) = fork

cuchillo (m) = knife

To ask someone to pass you something (at the table, etc.), use one of the following expressions: ¿me pasas...? (Can you pass me...?), pásame (Pass me...), or the corresponding forms for usted:

¿Me pasas el pan, por favor?

The answer is usually expressed by toma or tome (Here you are).

¿me pasas?

pásame

☞ 10

18. On the tape you will hear the words you have just learned, together with other words, in groups of three. In each group one of the words is the odd one out. Write that word.

Group 1:   Group 3:

Group 2:   Group 4:

19. Draw pictures of the following objects:

un tomate   un tenedor   una botella de vino   pan

una cuchara   un cuchillo   una botella de cerveza   etc.

Imagine they are real. Another member of the group asks you to pass him those things:

EXAMPLE: —Pásame ese tomate, por favor.

                — Toma.

                — Gracias.

Y POR FIN...

20. The text below has been adapted from the PRESENTATIONS from the television unit. Listen to the complete text on the tape and fill in the blanks here.

1

con él

con usted

con nosotros

con vosotros

conmigo

contigo

☞ 10

LUIS: ¡Vengan, vengan ustedes ▨▨ ▨▨▨▨ . Niños, ▨▨▨▨ también vosotros. Despacio, no ▨▨▨▨! Mirad. ▨▨▨▨▨ también ustedes.

NIÑOS: ¿Qué estás ▨▨▨▨▨ ?

LUIS: ▨▨▨▨▨ hablando con ellos.

NIÑO: ¿ ▨▨▨▨ es eso?

LUIS: ¿Esto? Una máquina de fotos. ▨▨▨▨▨ , pero no toques esto.

2

LUIS: ¿Me pasas la sal, por favor?

CHICO: Aquí no hay.

LUIS: ¿ ▨▨▨▨▨ usted la sal, por favor?

SEÑOR: ▨▨▨▨ usted.

LUIS: Gracias.

LUIS: ¿ ▨▨▨▨ ▨▨▨▨ una ensalada tropical?

CAMARERO: Mire, ▨▨▨▨ ▨▨▨▨ una ensalada tropical.

● **TRANSCRIPTION OF THE TV DIALOGUES "DE TÚ, POR FAVOR"**

Presentación. Primera parte

PRESENTADOR: ¿Qué tal? Bonita Mallorca, ¿eh? Vengan conmigo. Vengan ustedes. ¡Eh, vosotros! Venid conmigo. ¡Despacio, no corráis! Mirad. Miren también ustedes.

NIÑO: ¿Qué estás haciendo?

PRESENTADOR: Estoy hablando con ellos.

NIÑO: ¿Qué es eso?

PRESENTADOR: ¿Esto? Una máquina de fotos. No toques esto.

NIÑO: Hay unos niños en esa playa.

PRESENTADOR: ¿Ah, sí? ¿Y qué están haciendo?

NIÑO: Están jugando.

Telecomedia. Primera parte

JUAN: ¡Qué bien!

CARMEN: Sí. Es muy bonito.

JUAN: ¡Ven! ¡Mira, Carmen!

CARMEN: ¡Escucha!

JUAN: ¡Ay!

CARMEN: ¡Juan!

NIÑO 1: Perdone usted.

JUAN: Toma.

NIÑO 1: Gracias.

NIÑOS: ¡Eh, tú! ¡Ven!

CARMEN: ¿Qué estáis haciendo?

NIÑO 1: Estamos jugando.

Presentation. Part One

PRESENTER: How are you? Mallorca is very pretty, isn't it? Come with me. Come along. Hey, children! Come with me. Slowly. Don't be in such a hurry. Look! You look too.

CHILD: What are you doing?

PRESENTER: I am talking to them.

CHILD: What is that?

PRESENTER: This? A camera. Don't touch this.

CHILD: There are some children on that beach.

PRESENTER: Are there? [i.e. "Ah, yes?"] And what are they doing?

CHILD: They are playing.

TV Comedy. Part One

JUAN: This is nice!

CARMEN: Yes, it's very nice.

JUAN: Come here! Look, Carmen!

CARMEN: Listen!

JUAN: Ow!

CARMEN: Juan!

1ST CHILD: I'm sorry.

JUAN: Here. [i.e. "Take!"]

1ST CHILD: Thank you.

CHILDREN: Hey, you! Come on!

CARMEN: What are you doing?

1ST CHILD: We're playing.

JUAN: ¿Y vuestros papás?
NIÑO 1: No están aquí. Estamos con mi hermano Álvaro.
CARMEN: ¿Con tu hermano?
NIÑO 1: Sí. Mire.
ÁLVARO: Hola, buenos días.
CARMEN: Buenos días.
JUAN: Hola.
NIÑO 2: ¿Qué es eso?
NIÑA 1: ¡Antonio, no toques!
NIÑO 2: Vale, vale.
CARMEN: Es una cámara de vídeo.
NIÑO 3: ¿Sí?
JUAN: Sí, sí.
NIÑOS: ¡Qué bien!
ÁLVARO: Hola. Soy Álvaro.
CARMEN: Encantada.
JUAN: ¿Qué tal?
ÁLVARO: Voy al pueblo. Al médico con la niña.
JUAN: ¿Qué es eso?
CARMEN: Pobrecita.
JUAN: ¿Y los niños?
ÁLVARO: ¿Ustedes van a…?
CARMEN: No nos hables de usted, hombre.
ÁLVARO: Vale. ¿Vosotros ➡ ① vais a…?
CARMEN: No te preocupes, nosotros nos quedamos con ellos.
ÁLVARO: Muchas gracias. ¡No molestéis a estos señores! Vuelvo enseguida, hasta luego.
CARMEN, NIÑOS, JUAN: Adiós, hasta luego.
NIÑOS: Vengan, vengan con nosotros.
CARMEN: De tú, por favor.
NIÑOS: Bueno, pues venid.
CARMEN: Vamos, Juan.
JUAN: ¿Y el trabajo?
CARMEN: ¿El trabajo?
JUAN: Mira, Carmen.
NIÑO 1: ¿Qué estoy haciendo?
JUAN: Estás comiendo un helado.
NIÑO 1: Sí.
JUAN: ¿Qué estoy haciendo?
NIÑA 2: Estás pelando un plátano.
JUAN: ¡No hagáis eso! ¡Vamos al agua! ¡Vamos! ¡Carmen, ven!
CARMEN: ¡No!
CARMEN: ¡No, no! ¡No hagáis eso! ¡Por favor, no!
JUAN: ¡Cuidado!

JUAN: And your parents?
1ST CHILD: They aren't here. We are with my brother Álvaro.
CARMEN: With your brother?
1ST CHILD: Yes. Look.
ÁLVARO: Hello. Good morning.
CARMEN: Good morning.
JUAN: Hello.
2ND CHILD: What's that?
1ST GIRL: Antonio! Don't touch that!
2ND CHILD: OK. OK.
CARMEN: It's a video camera.
3RD BOY: Is it? [i.e. "Yes?"]
JUAN: Yes. Yes (it is).
CHILDREN: Great!
ÁLVARO: Hello. I'm Álvaro.
CARMEN: Pleased to meet you.
JUAN: Hello.
ÁLVARO: I'm going into the village. To take the girl to the doctor.
JUAN: What's that?
CARMEN: Poor girl.
JUAN: And the children?
ÁLVARO: Are you going to …?
CARMEN: Don't use "usted" with us, "hombre".
ÁLVARO: OK. Are you ➡ ① going to …?
CARMEN: Don't worry. We'll stay here with them.
ÁLVARO: Thank you very much. Don't be a nuisance to these people! I'll be right back. See you in a while.
CARMEN, CHILDREN, JUAN: Goodbye. See you later.
CHILDREN: Come along with us.
CARMEN: Use "tú" with us, please.
CHILDREN: OK. Come along.
CARMEN: Come on, Juan.
JUAN: And work?
CARMEN: Work?
JUAN: Look, Carmen.
1ST CHILD: What am I doing?
JUAN: You're eating an ice cream.
1ST CHILD: Yes.
JUAN: What am I doing?
2ND CHILD: You're peeling a banana.
JUAN: Don't do that! Let's go into the water! Come on! Carmen, come on!
CARMEN: No!
CARMEN: Don't do that! Please don't do that!
JUAN: Careful!

Presentación. Segunda parte
PRESENTADOR: Oye, ¿me pasas la sal, por favor?
CHICO: Aquí no hay.
PRESENTADOR: Oiga, ¿me pasa usted la sal, por favor?
SEÑOR MAYOR: Toma.
CHICO: Tome usted.
PRESENTADOR: Gracias.
CHICA: Una ensalada tropical.
CAMARERO: ¡Marchando! ➡ ② ¡Una ensalada tropical!
PRESENTADOR: ¿Qué es una ensalada tropical? Oye, ¿qué es una ensalada tropical?
CHICA: Lechuga, manzana, piña, jamón y arroz.
CAMARERO: Mire, esto es una ensalada tropical.
CHICA: ¿Quiere un poco?
PRESENTADOR: Y ustedes, ¿quieren?

Presentation. Part Two
PRESENTER: Can you pass me the salt, please?
BOY: There isn't any here.
PRESENTER: Excuse me. Can you pass me the salt, please?
OLD MAN: Here you are.
BOY: Here you are.
PRESENTER: Thank you.
GIRL: A tropical salad!
WAITER: Right away! ➡ ② A tropical salad!
PRESENTER: What is a tropical salad? Excuse me. What is a tropical salad?
GIRL: Lettuce, apple, pineapple, ham and rice.
WAITER: Look, this is a tropical salad.
GIRL: Would you like a little?
PRESENTER: And would you like some?

Telecomedia. Segunda parte

Niño: Tengo hambre.

Niño 2: Yo también tengo hambre.

Niña 2: Y yo.

Niño 1: Y yo. ¡Vamos a casa! ➡ ③

Juan: ¿A casa?

Niño 1: Sí. Es aquélla.

Carmen: ¿Y tus padres?

Niño 1: No están.

Carmen: ¿Y la comida entonces?

Niño 1: La hacemos nosotros. ¡Vamos!

Niña 2: Éstas son demasiado pequeñas y ésas, demasiado grandes.

Niño 2: Es verdad. Toma.

Niña 2: ¡Jo!

Carmen: Dame dos tomates.

Niño 1: ¿Verdes o rojos?

Carmen: Rojos, rojos.

Niño 1: ¿Éstos?

Todos: ¡Bien! ¡Bravo!

Niña 1: No, no, siéntate.

Carmen: Bueno.

Niño 3: No, no. Trae.
   ¿Quieres agua?

Juan: Sí, gracias.

Carmen: ¿Me pasas el apio?

Niño 1: ¿Qué es eso?

Niña 1: Mira. Esto es el apio.

Juan: Pásame la sal.

Niño 2: Sí, sí, toma.

Juan: ¡Toma!

Carmen: ¡Cuidado!

Álvaro: Buenas noches.

Juan: Hola.

Carmen: Hola, buenas noches. ¿Qué te pasa?

Álvaro: Mira.

Juan: Huy, ¿qué es eso?

Álvaro: Alergia.

Niña 3: ¿Qué es alergia?

Álvaro: Esto es alergia. ¿Y eso qué es?

Carmen: ¿Esto? Ven.

Presentador: ¡Shhhh!

TV Comedy. Part Two

Boy: I'm hungry.

2nd Boy: I'm hungry, too.

2nd Girl: So am I.

1st Boy: So am I. Let's go home! ➡ ③

Juan: Home ?

1st Boy: Yes. That's our house over there.

Carmen: And your parents?

1st Boy: They aren't here.

Carmen: So what about the meal?

1st Boy: We make it. Let's go.

2nd Girl: These are too small and those are too big.

2nd Boy: It's true. Here.

2nd Girl: Oh!

Carmen: Give me two tomatoes.

1st Boy: Green ones or red ones?

Carmen: Red ones, red ones.

1st Boy: These?

All: Great! Bravo!

1st Girl: No, no. Sit down.

Carmen: OK.

3rd Boy: No, no. Let me do it. [i.e. "Bring!"]
   Would you like some water?

Juan: Yes, please.

Carmen: Can you pass me the celery?

1st Boy: What's that?

1st Girl: Look. This is "celery".

Juan: Pass me the salt.

2nd Boy: Yes, yes. Here you are.

Juan: Here.

Carmen: Be careful!

Álvaro: Good evening.

Juan: Hello.

Carmen: Hello. Good evening. What's the matter?

Álvaro: Look.

Juan: Phew! What's that?

Álvaro: An allergy.

3rd Girl: What's "allergy"?

Álvaro: This is an allergy. And what's that?

Carmen: This? Come (with me)!

Presenter: Shhhh!

● **CAJÓN DE SASTRE**

① In many varieties of Spanish, including those spoken in Latin America, either tú or usted may be used for addressing a single person, but only ustedes for more than one person i.e. vosotros and its corresponding forms do not exist in these varieties.

② Marchando! This is a word used by a waiter to indicate that he has noted the order and is telling the kitchen staff to get it ready right away.

③ The word casa expresses meaning equivalent to both 'house' and 'home' in English. When the meaning is equivalent to 'home' the definite article is absent, exactly the same as in English. Compare:

   Estoy en la oficina.
   Estoy en la primera casa.
   Estoy en casa.

6. De "tú", por favor

● **USTED YA PUEDE...**

use the two forms of address in Spanish;	Y tú ¿dónde vives? - Y usted, ¿dónde vive? ¿Me das tu pasaporte? - ¿Me da su pasaporte?
ask what someone is doing;	¿Qué está haciendo?
say what someone is doing;	Está jugando.
ask or tell someone to do something;	¡Para! ¡Pare usted!
ask or tell someone not to do something;	¡No pares! ¡No pare usted!
ask what something is;	¿Qué es eso?
say what something is;	Esto es una cámara.
ask what object a word refers to;	¿Qué es una ensalada tropical?
ask someone to pass you something.	Páseme la sal, por favor. ¿Me pasa la sal?

7 ¿De dónde vienes?

In this unit you will learn how to express where people and things have been or where they have come from; to ask and say whether something is permitted in a particular place; to ask what is going on; to ask someone to repeat what he has said; and also to point things out and identify them.

(I) **Ese barco viene de Valencia.**   That ship has come [i.e. "is coming"] from Valencia.

This is how to say where someone or something has been or has come from.

¿De dónde viene ese barco?   Where has that ship come from?

And this is how to ask for the same information.

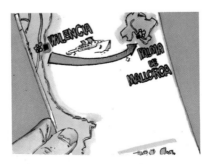

barco (m) = ship, boat

1. Listen and repeat when you hear the signal.

To indicate that someone or something is coming or has come from a particular point towards the speaker, use the verb venir to come followed by the word de. To ask for the same information, place de before dónde i.e. ¿de dónde? from where?

7. ¿De dónde vienes?

Viene   Va

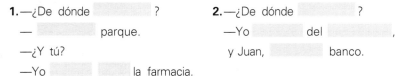

IR   ¿a dónde?   VENIR   ¿de dónde?

The verb VENIR: Present tense

(yo)	vengo	(nosotros/as)	venimos
(tú)	vienes	(vosotros/as)	venís
(usted) —⌐ viene		(ustedes) —⌐ vienen	
(él, ella) —⌐		(ellos, ellas) —⌐	

2. Listen and fill in the blanks.

1.—¿De dónde _____ ?

— _____ parque.

—¿Y tú?

—Yo _____ la farmacia.

2.—¿De dónde _____ ?

—Yo _____ del _____,

y Juan, _____ banco.

¿De dónde viene usted?

Del camping

La mujer viene del camping; el chico, de la playa, y el hombre, del hospital

De la playa

Vengo del hospital

3. Look at the pictures above. Listen and indicate whether what you hear is true or false.

médico (m. y f.) = doctor

dentista (m. y f.) = dentist

1. [T] [F]
2. [T] [F]
3. [T] [F]
4. [T] [F]
5. [T] [F]
6. [T] [F]
7. [T] [F]

It is possible to express where you have been (or where you have come from) with the names of some professions: médico, dentista, and so on:

Vengo del dentista.

I've been to the dentist's.

The same words may be used to refer to where you are going:

Voy al dentista.

I am going to the dentist's.

4. Look at the pictures and fill in the blanks.

¿A dónde?

Voy al médico.

¿De dónde?

Vengo ___ médico

¿A dónde?

¿De dónde?

___ ___ dentista.

5. Look at this map of the centre of Spain. You all choose one of the cities which appear on the map and keep your choice secret for the moment. You have all just returned from your holidays in those cities. Ask other members of the group where they have been. As they reply, they should point to the place they are referring to on the map.

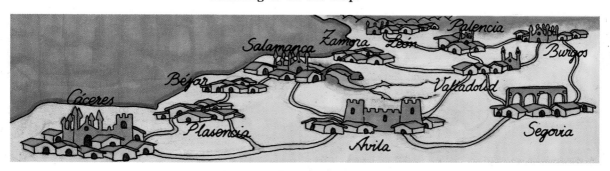

● ●

Ⅱ **¿Se puede fumar aquí?**   Can you smoke here?

This is how to ask for permission to do something or whether or not something is permitted in a particular place.

No se puede fumar.   You can't smoke.

And this is how to give the same information.

todavía = still

beber = to drink

6. Listen and repeat when you hear the signal.

If you are not certain whether something is permitted in a particular place, ask by using ¿se puede...?:

> ¿Se puede pasar?

7. Look at the signs below and say what they indicate. Use one of the following words to do this:

fumar	hablar	pasar
beber	aparcar	

se   ☞ 11

EXAMPLE: No se puede fumar.

1   2   3   4   5   6

8. What questions would you ask in the situations below? The following table will help you: each question is formed by combining one element from each column.

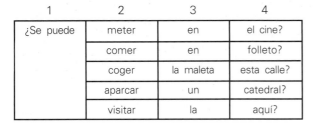

1	2	3	4
¿Se puede	meter	en	el cine?
	comer	en	folleto?
	coger	la maleta	esta calle?
	aparcar	un	catedral?
	visitar	la	aquí?

folleto (m) = brochure

visitar = to visit

1. You are visiting a historic building. You see some tourist brochures but you don't know whether you are allowed to take one.

2. You have bought a cheese roll. You go into the cinema. You don't know whether you can eat in the cinema or not.

3. You are boarding a plane, and you have a medium-sized suitcase with you. You want to put it in the compartment over the passenger seats, but you don't know whether this is allowed.

4. You drive into a strange city in your car. You want to park. You find an available space but you see a series of blue marks painted on the ground and you don't know whether it is possible to park there.

5. You are a tourist in a strange city. You arrive at the cathedral. You want to know whether it is possible to visit it at that moment.

Now try to repeat the exercise without the help of the table.

9. The other members of the group each write on a slip of paper something which they would like to do. For example, comer naranjas**. Imagine that you are the mayor of your town and you have the power to decide what is permitted and what is not permitted. Read the pieces of paper and decide whether or not you will permit what the others want to do. Tell them your decision in each case.**

¿Qué pasa?

What is going on?

This is how to ask what is going on in a particular place.

Que el Rey está aquí.

The King is here.

And this is how to reply.

rey, reina = king, queen

dinero (m) = money

encontrar (v. i.) = to find

avería (f) = breakdown

gasolina (f) = petrol

When you notice something strange is going on in a particular place and you want to know the cause, use the following question: ¿Qué pasa?

The answer will usually begin with the word que before the description of the situation:

Que no encuentro mi dinero.

Que Juan está fumando.

The answer may be shortened, as in the following

—¿Qué pasa?

—No encuentro mi dinero.

—¿Qué pasa?

—¡Mi dinero!

The word nada may be placed at the beginning of the reply in order to indicate that the situation is not serious:

—¿Qué pasa?

—Nada, que Juan está fumando.

10. Look at the pictures below. Listen to the tape and fill in the blanks.

A noisy situation may make communication difficult. People may also slur their words in speaking. Do not worry if you do not always understand; the same happens in your own language. When you do not understand, ask the person to repeat what he said by using:

¿Cómo? - ¿Cómo dice?

You can also say just ¿qué?, although this is more informal.

The answer to such questions usually begins with que, in exactly the same way as we saw above with ¿qué pasa?:

Que estoy escuchando la radio.

Que qué pasa.

● ●

Ⅳ

To indicate something and say what it is, use the verb ser after éste, ése and aquél and their various forms. Note that this structure is the same as that which is used for identifying people:

Ése es el Hotel Real.

Ése es el profesor Serrano.

In this structure, the verb ser is normally followed by the articles el, la, los and las , or by words which are used to indicate possession: mi, tu, su, etc.:

Ésa es la cocina.

Ésa es tu habitación.

Éste es mi perro, "Canelo".

cocina (f) = kitchen

cuarto de estar (m) = living room, sitting room

cuarto de baño (m) = bath-room

ciudad (f) = city

policía (f) = policeman, -woman

REMEMBER:

ése es el Hotel Real

ésa es la catedral

ésos son los libros

ésas son las duchas

11. Fill the blanks with one of these words:

el   la   los   las   es   son

1. Ésa es   Plaza Mayor.
2. Mira, éste   aeropuerto de la ciudad.
3. Éste es   cuarto de estar, ésa   cocina, y aquélla,   habitación de los niños.
4. Éste es   aparcamiento del hotel.
5. Ésa es   comisaría de policía, y ése   Hotel Real.
6. Ésta   mi habitación.
7. Aquélla   maleta del profesor.
8. Mire, ésta   calle de Alcalá.
9. Éstas   sus gafas, señora.
10. Éstos   periódicos de la ciudad.

12. Imagine that you have rented this apartment for your holidays. A friend comes to pay you a visit. Go round the apartment, stopping at points 1, 2, 3, 4 and 5. From those points, show your friend each room and say what room it is.

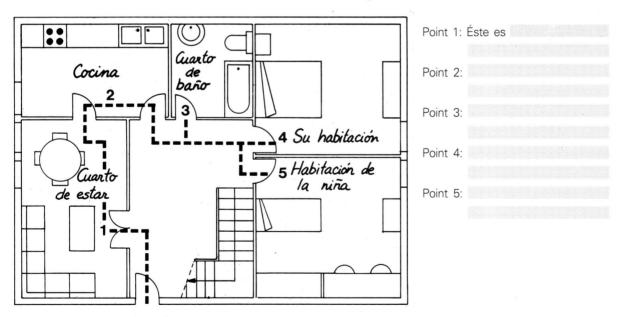

Point 1: Éste es

Point 2:

Point 3:

Point 4:

Point 5:

13. Write the names of some places of interest in your city on slips of paper. Pin them on the wall. Go round the room pointing out and identifying those places for a friend who is visiting you. For example: Éste es el parque.

100 = cien			500 = quinientos, -as		
101 = ciento uno, -a			600 = seiscientos, -as		
200 = doscientos, -as			700 = setecientos, -as		
201 = doscientos uno, doscientas una			800 = ochocientos, -as		
300 = trescientos, -as			900 = novecientos, -as		
301 = trescientos uno, trescientas una			1000 = mil		
400 = cuatrocientos, -as			☞ 8		

14. Cross out the numbers as you hear them.

100	222	301	500	601	775
121	243	350	555	625	803
169	300	499	600	765	901

15. Look at the following menu. Read each item aloud and say the price in pesetas, **as follows:** sopa de pescado, doscientas cincuenta pesetas.

Casa Ramón

Platos del día

	PTAS.		PTAS.		PTAS.
Sopa de pescado / Soupe de poissons	250			Queso / Fromage	325
Ensalada de lechuga y tomate / Salade verte aux tomates	100	Calamares a la romana (fritos) / Calmars à la romaine	450	Fruta del día / Fruits de saison	175
Huevos fritos con patatas / Oeufs frits et pommes frites	210	Gambas a la plancha / Crevettes roses grillées	500	Fresas con leche / Fraises au lait	250
Tortilla francesa / Omelette	175	Pescado del día / Poisson du jour	680	Zumo de Naranja / Jus d'orange	125
Tortilla española / Tortilla	275	Pollo asado / Poulet rôti	425		
Jamón / Jambon	760	Ternera asada / Veau rôti	575		

16. Choose one of the three set menus below. Add up the prices of the three items on the bill. Then add tax and say how much the total meal costs.

1.

Ensalada	100 ptas.
Pescado del día	680 ptas.
Zumo de naranja	125 ptas.
Total before tax	
Tax	91 ptas.
Total after tax	

2.

Huevos fritos con patatas	210 ptas.
Pollo asado	425 ptas.
Fruta del día	175 ptas.
Total before tax	
Tax	81 ptas.
Total after tax	

3.

Ensalada	100 ptas.
Ternera asada	575 ptas.
Fruta del día	175 ptas.
Total before tax	
Tax	76 ptas.
Total after tax	

Y POR FIN...

17. Do as instructed in the following:

1. You are in the bus station in Salamanca. A bus has just arrived. Ask where it has come from.

2. You are in the bus station in Salamanca. A bus is just about to leave. Ask where it is going.

3. It is 8.00pm. You want to eat in a restaurant. It is probably too early for the evening meal in Spain and you don't know whether you can eat or not. Ask a waiter who is standing at the door.

4. You are in the street. You see a lot of people gathering round a woman who is very white in the face. You want to know what is going on. Ask someone.

5. Someone says something to you, but you don't understand. Ask the person to repeat what he/she said.

6. You are in a crowd of people waiting to see Pepe Gómez, a famous singer, who is visiting the city. One of the people there does not know what is going on and asks you ¿qué pasa?. Answer him.

7. You are acting as a guide for a person who is visiting your city. Point out the following places and identify them as you go from one to the other: the station, your house, your office, the park, the cathedral, and other places in the city.

TRANSCRIPTION OF THE TV DIALOGUES
"¿DE DÓNDE VIENES?"

Presentación. Primera parte

PRESENTADOR: Hola. ¿Qué tal? Estamos todavía en Palma de Mallorca. Vengan conmigo. Miren, ésa es la catedral. Y aquél es... ¿Qué pasa? Oiga, ¿qué pasa?
GUÍA: Que el Rey está aquí. ➡ ①
PRESENTADOR: ¿Cómo? ¿Qué?
GUÍA: Que el Rey está en Palma.
TURISTA: ¿Cómo dice?
PRESENTADOR: Que el Rey está aquí, en Palma.
TURISTA: Gracias, muchas gracias.

Telecomedia. Primera parte

TERESITA: ¡Oiga, oiga, joven!
JUAN: Sí, dígame.
TERESITA: Oiga, ¿dónde está mi grupo?
JUAN: ¿Cómo dice?
TERESITA: Sí, mi grupo.
JUAN: ¡Ah, su grupo!
CARMEN: ¿Qué pasa?
TERESITA: Que no encuentro a mi grupo.
CARMEN: Señora, ¿dónde está su hotel?
TERESITA: ¿Cómo?

Presentation. Part One

PRESENTER: Hello. How are you? We are still in Palma de Mallorca. Come with me. Look, that's the cathedral. And that's the ... What's going on? Excuse me; what's going on?
GUIDE: The King is here. ➡ ①
PRESENTER: Sorry? What?
GUIDE: The King is here in Palma.
TOURIST: What's that?
PRESENTER: The King is here in Palma.
TOURIST: Thank you. Thank you very much.

TV Comedy. Part One

TERESITA: Excuse me. Excuse me, young man.
JUAN: Yes? Can I help you?
TERESITA: Excuse me. Where is my group?
JUAN: What's that?
TERESITA: Yes, my group.
JUAN: Ah, your group!
CARMEN: What's wrong?
TERESITA: I can't find my group.
CARMEN: Madam, where is your hotel?
TERESITA: What?

CARMEN: Que dónde está su hotel. ➡ ②
TERESITA: ¡Ah! Cerca de la catedral.
JUAN: ¿Y cómo se llama?
TERESITA: ¿Qué?
JUAN: Que cómo se llama.
TERESITA: Teresita. ➡ ③
CARMEN: No, el hotel. Que cómo se llama el hotel.
TERESITA: No me acuerdo.
JUAN: ¿Y ahora qué hacemos?
CARMEN: Esperad un momento. Por favor, ¿dónde está la catedral?
TURISTA: Perdón. No hablo español.
JUAN: ¿Qué dice?
CARMEN: "Perdón, no hablo español."
JUAN: ¡Señora, cuidado!
CARMEN: Buenos días.
GUARDIA: Buenos días.
CARMEN: Por favor, ¿dónde está la catedral?
GUARDIA: Mire, aquélla es la catedral.
TERESITA: ¡No, no, aquél no es mi hotel! Mi hotel es más moderno.
GUARDIA: ¿Qué pasa?
CARMEN: Que esta señora no encuentra a su grupo.
GUARDIA: Esperen un momento.
CARMEN: ¡Oiga!
JUAN: ¡Señora! ¡Venga aquí!
CARMEN: ¡No se vaya, Teresita!
GUARDIA: ¡Oigan! ¡Oigan!
TERESITA: Es muy grande esta ciudad, ¿verdad?
JUAN: Sí, muy grande.
TERESITA: Y muy bonita, ¿verdad, señorita?
CARMEN: Sí, preciosa.
TERESITA: ¿Es usted su novia?
CARMEN: ¡No!
TERESITA: Felicidades. Es muy guapa.
JUAN: ¡No es mi novia!

Presentación. Segunda parte

PRESENTADOR: Ese barco viene de Barcelona. ¿Ah, no? ¿De dónde viene?
VENDEDOR: De Valencia.
PRESENTADOR: Ese barco viene de Valencia.
VENDEDOR: Su helado. Doscientas, trescientas, cuatrocientas, quinientas. Y quinientas, mil.
Gracias.
PRESENTADOR: Miren. Cien pesetas. Doscientas. Quinientas. Mil pesetas.
POLICÍA: Mil pesetas.
PRESENTADOR: ¿Cómo?
POLICÍA: Aquí no se puede aparcar.
PRESENTADOR: ¡Vaya, hombre! ¡Oiga! ¿Y allí se puede aparcar?
POLICÍA: Allí, sí.
PRESENTADOR: Allí sí se puede.

Telecomedia. Segunda parte

CARMEN: ¿Qué está haciendo ahora?
JUAN: Está comprando.
CARMEN: ¿Se puede beber aquí?
JUAN: No, no se puede.
TERESITA: Hace mucho calor. ¡Tengan! ¿Les puedo hacer una foto? Sonrían. ¿Qué pasa? Son ustedes novios, ¿no?

CARMEN: Where is your hotel? ➡ ②
TERESITA: Ah! Near the cathedral.
JUAN: And what's the name of it?
TERESITA: What?
JUAN: What is the name of it?
TERESITA: Teresita. ➡ ③
CARMEN: No, the hotel. What's the name of your hotel?
TERESITA: I can't remember.
JUAN: So what do we do now?
CARMEN: Wait a moment. Excuse me, please. Where is the cathedral?
TOURIST: I'm sorry. I don't speak Spanish.
JUAN: What did [i.e. "does"] she say?
CARMEN: "I'm sorry. I don't speak Spanish."
JUAN: Be careful, madam!
CARMEN: Good morning.
POLICEMAN: Good morning.
CARMEN: Please, where is the cathedral?
POLICEMAN: Look, that's the cathedral.
TERESITA: No, no, that's not my hotel! My hotel is more modern.
POLICEMAN: What's wrong?
CARMEN: This lady can't find her group.
POLICEMAN: Just a moment.
CARMEN: Excuse me!
JUAN: Come here, madam!
CARMEN: Don't go away, Teresita!
POLICEMAN: Excuse me! Excuse me!
TERESITA: This city is very big, isn't it [i.e. "true?"]?
JUAN: Yes, very big.
TERESITA: And it's very pretty, isn't it, miss?
CARMEN: Yes, lovely.
TERESITA: Are you his girl friend?
CARMEN: No!
TERESITA: Congratulations. She is very pretty.
JUAN: She's not my girl friend!

Presentation. Part Two

PRESENTER: That boat comes from Barcelona. Ah, doesn't it? [i.e. "Ah, no?"] Where is it from?
VENDOR: From Valencia.
PRESENTER: That boat is from Valencia.
VENDOR: Your ice-cream. Two hundred, three hundred, four hundred, five hundred. And five hundred, (makes) a thousand. Thank you.
PRESENTER: Look. A hundred pesetas. Two hundred. Five hundred. A thousand pesetas.
POLICEMAN: A thousand pesetas.
PRESENTER: What?
POLICEMAN: You can't park here.
PRESENTER: Well, I never! Excuse me! And over there? Can you park over there?
POLICEMAN: Over there, yes.
PRESENTER: You can park over there.

TV. Comedy. Part Two.

CARMEN: What is she doing now?
JUAN: She is doing some shopping.
CARMEN: Can you drink here?
JUAN: No. No, you can't.
TERESITA: It's very hot here. Take this. Can I take a photo of you? Smile! What's wrong? You are going out together [i.e. "you are boy/girl-friends"], aren't you?

CARMEN Y JUAN: ¡No!

TERESITA: Claro. Novios.

CARMEN: ¡Oh, no, por favor!

TERESITA: ¿Cómo dice?

CARMEN: Nada, nada.

TERESITA: Huy, aquél es mi grupo. Sí, sí, aquél es el autobús.

SEÑORA: ¡Teresita! ¡Teresita!

TERESITA: ¿De dónde venís?

SEÑORA: ¿De dónde vienes tú?

TERESITA: ¿Qué?

SEÑORA: Que de dónde vienes.

TERESITA: De visitar Palma. Es preciosa y muy grande.

SEÑORA: ¿Tú sola?

TERESITA: No, con estos dos jóvenes. Son novios y muy simpáticos. ¡Huy, no están! ¿Dónde están los novios?

CARMEN: Una noche preciosa, ¿no?

JUAN: Sí, todo es precioso... contigo.

CARMEN: Gracias.

JUAN: Llevas un vestido muy bonito.

CARMEN: Es un regalo... de mi novio. ¿Qué pasa?

JUAN: Nada, la garganta.

CARMEN: Perdona. Vuelvo enseguida.

TERESITA: ¿Qué vas a comer?

JUAN: No sé. ¡Madre mía, otra vez!

TERESITA: Sopa de pescado, cuatrocientas cincuenta; tortilla, trescientas setenta y cinco; calamares, novecientas cincuenta; gambas... ¡mil pesetas!

CARMEN: No te preocupes, su grupo está allí.

JUAN: Están llamándola.

TERESITA: ¡Oh! ¡Los novios!

SEÑORA: ¿Nos podemos sentar con usted?

TERESITA: Sí, sí. Son muy simpáticos.

JUAN: Sí, claro. Muy simpáticos.

CAMARERO: Su plato, señor.

PRESENTADOR: Perdón, ¿cómo dice?

CAMARERO: Su plato.

PRESENTADOR: ¡Ah! Gracias. Adiós. Hasta el próximo programa.

CARMEN AND JUAN: No!

TERESITA: Yes, you are obviously going out together.

CARMEN: Oh, no, please!

TERESITA: What did [i.e. "do"] you say?

CARMEN: No, no. Nothing.

TERESITA: Ah! That's my group. Yes, yes, that's the coach.

WOMAN: Teresita! Teresita!

TERESITA: Where have you been?

WOMAN: Where have you been?

TERESITA: What?

WOMAN: Where have you been?

TERESITA: I've been visiting Palma. It's lovely. And it's very big.

WOMAN: Alone?

TERESITA: No, with these two young people. They are going out together and they are very nice. Oh, they aren't here! Where is that young couple?

CARMEN: It's a beautiful night, isn't it?

JUAN: Yes, everything is beautiful ... with you.

CARMEN: Thank you.

JUAN: You are wearing a very pretty dress.

CARMEN: It was [i.e. "is"] a present ... from my boyfriend. What's the matter?

JUAN: No, nothing. It's my throat.

CARMEN: Excuse me a moment. I'll be right back.

TERESITA: What are you going to eat?

JUAN: I don't know. Oh dear! Again!

TERESITA: Fish soup, four hundred and fifty; omelette, three hundred and seventy-five; squid, nine hundred and fifty; prawns... a thousand pesetas!

CARMEN: Don't worry. Her group is over there.

JUAN: They are calling you.

TERESITA: Oh, the young couple!

WOMAN: Can we sit with you?

TERESITA: Yes, yes. They are very nice.

JUAN: Yes, of course. Very nice.

WAITER: Your order, sir.

PRESENTER: Sorry. What did [i.e. "do"] you say?

WAITER: Your order.

PRESENTER: Ah! Thank you. Goodbye. See you in the next programme.

● CAJÓN DE SASTRE

(1) Spain is a constitutional monarchy. The present king is don Juan Carlos I. Executive power is held by a democratic government elected every four years.

(2) Note that question marks are absent in the repetition of a question: ¿Dónde está su hotel? becomes Que dónde está su hotel.

(3) Short or familiar forms of forenames are frequent in Spain. For example, Juan - Juanito; Teresa - Teresita; Dolores - Lola; Concepción - Concha, Conchita; and José - Pepe; Francisco - Paco, etc. Note that there is sometimes very little phonetic relation between the original and the derived form. You should also note that these familiar names are not normally used in formal situations. It would be very strange for the president of the government, for example, to publicly use a name such as Pepe Martín, and even more so for him to sign his name that way.

7. ¿De dónde vienes?

● **USTED YA PUEDE...**

say where someone or something has been or has come from;	Ese barco viene de Valencia. Vengo del dentista.
and ask for the same information;	¿De dónde viene ese barco?
say whether or not something is permitted in a particular place;	Aquí no se puede fumar.
and ask for the same information;	¿Se puede fumar aquí?
ask what is going on in a particular situation;	¿Qué pasa?
and reply;	Que viene el tren.
ask someone to repeat what they say;	¿Cómo dice?
and repeat what you say;	Que vengo del dentista.
point something out and identify it;	Ésa es la catedral.
use numbers from 100 to 1000.	Cien, ciento uno, ciento una, doscientos, doscientas... mil.

8 Van a llegar

In this unit you will learn how to express what is going to happen in the immediate future; to indicate what you need and to ask for it; to ask how much something is when you want to pay; and to ask someone to speak up or to speak more slowly, and so on. You will also learn further expressions for interacting with other people.

I   **Voy a leer el periódico.**   I am going to read the newspaper.

This is how to express what is going to happen or what someone is going to do in the immediate future.

voy		
vas		**llamar**
va	a	com**er**
vamos		escrib**ir**
vais		
van		

REMEMBER:

The base form of verbs (i.e. the infinitive) ends in:

-ar: llamar

 -er: comer

 -ir: escribir

☞ 13

The most usual way to express what is going to happen or what someone is going to do in the more or less immediate future is to use a form of the verb ir followed by a:

Voy a escuchar la radio.

Van a venir mañana.

8. Van a llegar

llamar = to call, to make a phone call

salir (v. i.) = to go/come out

llegar = to arrive

1. Listen and repeat when you hear the signal.

2. Look at the pictures and fill in the blanks.

¿Qué pasa?

Que ____ venir el Rey

Señores, el autobús ____ salir

El tren de Madrid ____ llegar

ir a + -r

Van a comer.

estar + -ndo

Están comiendo.

<u>el</u> lunes

<u>el</u> jueves

These sentences with a ... -r are especially useful for indicating what someone intends to do. They are used frequently to express more or less immediate plans.

To ask someone about their immediate plans, use:

¿Qué vas a hacer...?

¿Qué va a hacer usted mañana?

¿Qué vais a hacer el martes?

3. The people in the pictures below intend to do certain things. Say what those intentions are.

EXAMPLE: Van a hacer deporte.

Use these words: llegar   sentarse   entrar.

TERCERO

1   2   3   4

4. Here is a page from Luis Cánovas's diary, with his plans for each day of next week. Say what his plans are.

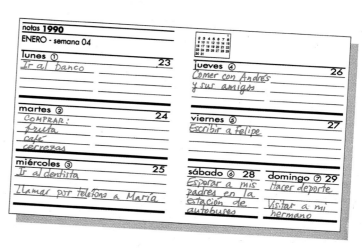

EXAMPLE: El lunes va a ir al banco.

El martes… El viernes…

El miércoles… El sábado…

El jueves… El domingo…

5. Now we are going to focus on you yourself. Tell your partners what your plans are for each day of next week. Then ask them what they are going to do tomorrow.

● ●

Ⅱ

Necesito un café. I need a coffee.

This is how to express what you need.

necesitar = to need

zapato (m) = shoe

fuego (m) = a light (for cigarette)

cigarro (m) = cigarette

llave (f) = key

papel (m) = paper

pañuelo (m) = handkerchief

nuevo, -a = new

To express what someone needs, use the word necesitar followed by a noun phrase:

Necesito un café.

Necesitan un cuchillo.

6. Indicate what things the people on the tape say they need, in the order in which you hear them.

un cigarro papel

unos zapatos nuevos un coche

libros nuevos un pañuelo

las llaves

7. Say what things the people in the pictures below need.

EXAMPLE: Necesita un abrigo.

Choose from the following words:

un pañuelo	un bolígrafo
un libro	una cámara de vídeo
una cuchara	un cajón
un tenedor	un abrigo
agua	unos zapatos

1

2

3

4

5

8. What would you say if you found yourself in the following situations? Remember to begin your sentences with Necesito…

1. You are in a restaurant. You are about to start eating but you see that the waiter has forgotten to give you a knife.
2. You would like to film your child's first attempts to walk, but you don't have a video camera.
3. You want to cross the border in order to enter a foreign country.
4. You want to read the news.
5. You want to spend the night in a hotel with your husband/wife.

● ●

(III) **¿Me da el periódico?**   Could you give me the newspaper?

This is how to ask for something.

¿Me da el periódico?

1

¿Qué?

2

Déme el periódico, por favor

3

> me da
> nos da   ☞ 10.4

The words me and nos indicate the person or the persons who receive what is asked for. They are alternative forms of the personal pronouns yo and nosotros, which you already know. Do not worry about the exact uses of these words for the moment. Nevertheless, if you want more information, go to the grammar appendix.   ☞ 10

¿me da?	¿nos da?
déme	dénos
¿me das?	¿nos das?
dame	danos

☞ 10.7

To ask for something, use a sentence with dar and the name of the thing you wish to obtain:
¿Me das el periódico?
Dame el periódico.
Note that you can ask for something in two different ways. One way is to phrase your request as a question: ¿me das…?, ¿me da…?:
¿Me das tu pasaporte, por favor?
¿Nos da dos cafés con leche?
This structure is slightly more formal. Another way (which you learned in Unit 6) is to say: dame, danos, déme, dénos:
Dénos dos cervezas, por favor.
Dame un cigarro.
This structure is more informal.

9. Listen and repeat when you hear the signal.

10. Read the Spanish transcription of the TV Comedy from this unit. Underline all those cases in which someone says what he needs or asks for something. This will help you to practise understanding these structures.

11. Look again at the pictures from Exercise 7. Imagine that those people are with you now. What things would they ask you for and how would they express this?

EXAMPLE: Déme un abrigo.   or   ¿Me da un abrigo?

12. What would you say if you found yourself in the following situations? Remember to begin your sentences with Dame… **or with** ¿Me das…?

1. You want to read the news and you ask your friend for the newspaper which is on the table.
2. You want to smoke but you do not have any cigarettes. Ask a friend.
3. You have some cigarettes, but you do not have a light. Ask a friend.
4. You want to go for a drive in the car; your husband/wife has the keys.

13. Ask the others in the group for things which they have and which you need.

● ●

⊘ **MÁS BAJO, POR FAVOR**   (COULD YOU) LOWER (YOUR VOICE), PLEASE?

14. Follow the text in the pictures below as you listen to the tape.

After you. [i.e. "Pass."]

No, no. After you, please. [i.e. "You first"]

This is how to give someone preference in doorways.

Can you speak up [i.e. "louder"]?

(Could you) lower (your voice), please.

How much is it?

This is how to ask someone to raise or to lower his voice.

This is how to ask how much something is when you want to pay.

Note the following:

To give someone preference in doorways, use one of the following expressions: pase, pase or usted primero.

15. Give preference to the people in the following situations:

1. You and a friend are about to board a train on the underground.

2. When you are leaving a restaurant, a woman is about to come in through the same doorway.

3. When you are leaving work, your boss is about to leave through the same doorway.

16. Dramatise the situations from the previous exercise with a partner.

Sometimes you may not understand what people say to you because they speak too quietly or too quickly, or slur their words, and so on. In these circumstances, use expressions such as the following:

¿Puede hablar más alto?	Could you speak up?
Más despacio, por favor.	More slowly, please.
¿Puede hablar más bajo?	Could you speak more quietly?
No hable tan rápido.	Don't speak so quickly.

17. Listen to the woman's voice on the tape. When you hear the signal, ask her to modify the way she is speaking. (She will comply with your wish and repeat her message a second time.)

In order to pay for something in a shop, bar, restaurant or similar service encounter, ask how much it is by saying:

> ¿Cuánto es?
>
> ¿Cuánto es esto? (at the same time as you point to what you have bought or consumed)

If you have bought or consumed several things, you can say:

> ¿Cuánto es todo?

In the reply, the verb ser may appear or not:

> Son 250 pesetas.
>
> 250 pesetas.

18. What are you asked on the tape? Write each sentence.

19. Imagine that you want to buy the things in the picture below. When you hear the signal, ask the person on the tape how much it is. When you hear the answer, point to which object is referred to.

20. Imagine that your partners are the following: a waiter, a mechanic, a newsvendor, a plumber, a shop assistant. Ask each one how much you owe him/her. They should reply to your questions.

Y POR FIN...

Look at the questions below. In what follows you will be asked to carry out a series of operations with them.

1.	¿Cómo se...	... gafas?
2.	¿Es suyo este...	... por favor?
3.	¿Dónde...	... aquí?
4.	¿Cómo se escribe su...	... coche?
5.	¿De quién son estas...	... viene David?
6.	¿A dónde va...	... este tren?
7.	¿Quiere...	... llama usted?
8.	¿Hay alguna farmacia por...	... es todo?
9.	¿Qué es...	... pasa?
10.	¿Me pasas el tenedor,...	... están los cigarros?
11.	¿Qué...	... fumar aquí?
12.	¿De dónde...	...eso?
13.	¿Cuánto...	... usted una cerveza?
14.	¿Se puede...	...apellido?

21. Join each element in the column on the left to the corresponding element in the column on the right and write each full question in the spaces provided below and on the following page. For the moment, do not worry about the answers to the questions.

1.—¿   ?
 —

2.—¿   ?
 —

3.—¿   ?
 —

4.—¿   ?
 —

5.—¿   ?
 —

6.—¿   ?
 —

7.—¿   ?
 —

8.—¿ ?
— .

9.—¿ ?
— .

10.—¿ ?
— .

11.—¿ ?
— .

12.—¿ ?
— .

13.—¿ ?
— .

14.—¿ ?
— .

22. Here are the answers to the questions. Decide which one corresponds to each question and complete the dialogues in Exercise 21.

ANSWERS:

a) No, no hay ninguna.

b) Felipe García Sánchez.

c) No, no se puede.

d) Son suyas.

e) No, no es mío.

f) Esto es un zumo de naranja.

g) Toma.

h) ¿García? Con ce.

i) Que no se puede fumar aquí.

j) 1.450 pesetas.

k) En el cajón de la mesa.

l) A Barcelona.

m) Sí, gracias.

n) De la calle.

23. Now listen to the questions on the tape. When you hear the signal, give the appropriate answer to each one.

TRANSCRIPTION OF THE TV DIALOGUES
"VAN A LLEGAR"

Presentación. Primera parte

PRESENTADOR: Hola. ¿Cuánto es?

QUIOSQUERO: Setecientas diez.

PRESENTADOR: ¿Cuánto es? ¿Cuánto? Más alto, por favor. ¡Ah!, gracias.

SEÑORA: ¡Socorro! ¡Socorro! ¡Socorro! ¡Socorro!

PRESENTADOR: ¿Qué pasa? Más despacio, por favor... ¿Puede hablar más alto?

SEÑORA: ¡Socorro!

PRESENTADOR: Perdón, ¿qué le pasa?

SEÑORA: ¿Me da el periódico?

PRESENTADOR: ¿Qué?

SEÑORA: Déme el periódico, por favor.

Presentation. Part One

PRESENTER: Hello. How much is it?

NEWSVENDOR: Seven hundred and ten.

PRESENTER: How much is it? How much? Can you speak up, please? Ah, thank you.

WOMAN: Help! Help! Help! Help!

PRESENTER: What's the matter? More slowly, please ... Can you speak up?

WOMAN: Help!

PRESENTER: I'm sorry. What's the matter?

WOMAN: Can you give me the newspaper?

PRESENTER: What?

WOMAN: Give me the newspaper, please.

Telecomedia. Primera parte

CARMEN: ¿Me das una cebolla? ¿Me das el limón?
DAVID: ¿Qué te pasa? ➡ ①
MARÍA: ¿De dónde vienes?
DAVID: Del parque. ¿Qué está haciendo?
MARÍA: Está haciendo la comida.
CARMEN: ¡David! ¡Las aceitunas!
DAVID: ¿Qué aceitunas?

SEÑORA: ¿Me da una revista?
PELUQUERA: ¿Puede hablar más alto, por favor?
SEÑORA: ¿Me da una revista?
JUAN: ¿Cuánto es?
PELUQUERO: "Mil entas". ➡ ②
JUAN: ¿Cómo?
PELUQUERO: "Mil entas".
JUAN: ¿Puede hablar más despacio, por favor?
PELUQUERO: Mil quinientas, señor.
JUAN: ¿Puedo pagar con tarjeta?
PELUQUERO: "Pende jeta".
JUAN: Perdón, no entiendo. ¿Puede hablar más…?
PELUQUERO: Ya. Que depende de la tarjeta. ¡Vale! ¡Cobrando "mil entas" con "jeta"!

CARMEN: ¡Ay! ¡Ya está!
MARÍA: Carmen, ¿me das un pañuelo? ¿Qué pasa? ¿Qué estás haciendo?
CARMEN: ¿Dónde está la…?
MARÍA: Ahí debajo.
CARMEN: ¿Dónde está la caja de herramientas?
MARÍA: No sé.
CARMEN: ¡Socorro! ¿Dónde está David? ➡ ③
MARÍA: ¡David! ¡Socorro!
DAVID: ¿Qué pasa?

Presentación. Segunda parte

SEÑORA: ¿Va a llamar por teléfono?
PRESENTADOR: ¡No, pase, pase!
SEÑORA: Gracias.
PRESENTADOR: Adiós. Así…
SEÑORA: ¡Ya, ya! Gracias. Necesito monedas. Muchas gracias. Voy a llamar.
PRESENTADOR: De nada. Hasta luego.
SEÑORA: ¡Eh!, ¡oiga!
PRESENTADOR: ¡Socorro!

Telecomedia. Segunda parte

SEÑORA: ¿Cuánto es?
DEPENDIENTA: Mil trescientas.
SEÑORA: Mil, cien, doscientas, mil trescientas.
DEPENDIENTA: Gracias. Adiós. ¿Qué desea?
JUAN: Una tarta.
DEPENDIENTA: Tenemos de chocolate, trufa, fresa, limón, nata, kiwi, naranja, moka…
JUAN: ¿Puede hablar más despacio, por favor?
DEPENDIENTA: Cho - co - la - te, tru - fa, fre - sa, li - món…
JUAN: De cho - co - la - te, gra - cias.
DEPENDIENTA: ¡De na - da!

CARMEN: Necesito un martillo.
DAVID: Toma.
CARMEN: Voy a probar con esto.

TV Comedy. Part One

CARMEN: Can you give me an onion? Can you give me the lemon?
DAVID: What's the matter? ➡ ①
MARÍA: Where have you been?
DAVID: In the park. What is she doing?
MARÍA: She's making lunch.
CARMEN: David! The olives!
DAVID: What olives?

WOMAN: Could you give me a magazine?
HAIRDRESSER: Could you speak up, please?
WOMAN: Could you give me a magazine?
JUAN: How much is it?
HAIRDRESSER: "Thousandundred". ➡ ②
JUAN: Sorry?
HAIRDRESSER: "Thousandundred".
JUAN: Can you speak more slowly, please?
HAIRDRESSER: One thousand five hundred, sir.
JUAN: Can I pay by credit card?
HAIRDRESSER: "Iddependard".
JUAN: I'm sorry, I can't understand. Can you speak more…?
HAIRDRESSER: OK. It depends which credit card. OK. Charge "thousandundred crecard".

CARMEN: Phew! That's it! [i.e. "Already it is."]
MARÍA: Carmen, can you give me a handkerchief? What's the matter? What are you doing?
CARMEN: Where is the …?
MARÍA: Down under there.
CARMEN: Where is the toolbox?
MARÍA: I don't know.
CARMEN: Help! Where is David? ➡ ③
MARÍA: David! Help!
DAVID: What's the matter?

Presentation. Part Two

YOUNG WOMAN: Are you going to make a phone call?
PRESENTER: Go ahead. [i.e. "Pass."]
YOUNG WOMAN: Thank you.
PRESENTER: Goodbye. Like this.
YOUNG WOMAN: Yes, yes! Thank you. I need some coins. Thank you very much. I'm going to make a call.
PRESENTER: Don't mention it. Goodbye.
YOUNG WOMAN: Excuse me! Excuse me!
PRESENTER: Help!

TV Comedy. Part Two

WOMAN: How much is it?
ASSISTANT: One thousand three hundred.
WOMAN: One thousand, one hundred, two hundred, one thousand three hundred.
ASSISTANT: Thank you. Goodbye. What would you like?
JUAN: A gateau.
ASSISTANT: We have chocolate, strawberry, lemon, cream, kiwi, orange, mocha …
JUAN: Could you speak more slowly, please?
ASSISTANT: Choc - o - late, straw - ber - ry, lem - on…
JUAN: Choc - o - late, please.
ASSISTANT: Don't men - tion it!

CARMEN: I need a hammer.
DAVID: Here.
CARMEN: I'm going to try with this.

MARÍA: Lo vas a romper.
CARMEN: Mamá…
MARÍA: Hija, necesitamos un fontanero.
CARMEN: No. Voy a hacerlo yo. Dame la llave inglesa.
DAVID: ¿Dónde está?
CARMEN: Allí.
MARÍA: Van a llegar los invitados.
CARMEN: Ya lo sé, mamá.
DAVID: ¿Necesitas el destornillador?
CARMEN: No, no.

DAVID: ¿Sí?
JUAN: ¿Está Carmen?
DAVID: Sí, sí.

DAVID: ¿Sí?
ÓSCAR: Soy Óscar. ¿Está tu hermana?
DAVID: Sí.

JUAN: ¡Pasa, pasa!
ÓSCAR: Tú primero, por favor.

ÓSCAR: Hola, ¿qué tal?
JUAN: Buenos días.
MARÍA: Buenos días, ¿qué tal?
CARMEN: ¡Socorro!
JUAN: ¿Qué pasa?
ÓSCAR: ¿Qué es eso?
MARÍA: ¡Pasad, pasad!
ÓSCAR: Tú primero.
JUAN: No, no, tú primero, por favor.

PRESENTADOR: Adiós.

MARÍA: You're going to break it.
CARMEN: Mummy…
MARÍA: We need a plumber, dear [i.e. "daughter"].
CARMEN: No, I'm going to do it. Give me the adjustable spanner.
DAVID: Where is it?
CARMEN: Over there.
MARÍA: The guests are going to arrive.
CARMEN: I know, Mummy.
DAVID: Do you need the screwdriver?
CARMEN: No, no.

DAVID: Yes?
JUAN: Is Carmen in?
DAVID: Yes. Yes, she is.

DAVID: Yes?
ÓSCAR: It's Óscar. Is your sister in?
DAVID: Yes, she is.

JUAN: After you! After you!
ÓSCAR: No. After you, please.

ÓSCAR: Hello. How are you?
JUAN: Good morning.
MARÍA: Good morning. How are you?
CARMEN: Help!
JUAN: What's the matter?
ÓSCAR: What's that?
MARÍA: Come in! Come in!
ÓSCAR: After you.
JUAN: No, no. After you, please.

PRESENTER: Goodbye.

● CAJÓN DE SASTRE

(1) In the previous unit you learned that the expression ¿qué pasa? (What is going on?) is used to ask what is happening in a particular situation. We use the questions ¿qué le pasa?, ¿qué te pasa? (What is the matter with you?) in order to inquire about someone's physical and emotional state, especially when we notice something unusual in their attitude or behaviour.

(2) Note that the hairdresser in the TV Comedy speaks very quickly and slurs his words (so much so that Juan Serrano does not understand). The hairdresser misses out many syllables:

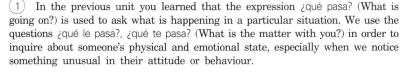

HAIRDRESSER: "Mil entas" for "mil quinientas".
"Pende jeta" for "depende de la tarjeta".

If you find yourself in a similar situation, do not be afraid to ask people to speak more clearly or more slowly, and so on.

(3) ¡Socorro! (Help!) and ¡Auxilio! (Help!) are the most frequent ways of shouting for help in the face of some immediate danger, or of an emergency, and so on. Learn them, for you never know when you might need them.

USTED YA PUEDE...

say what is going to happen in the more or less immediate future;	Va a llover mañana.
express what you intend to do and what you plan to do;	Voy a comprar un coche. Vamos a ir a Salamanca.
say what you need;	Necesito un pasaporte nuevo.
ask for something;	¿Me da un pañuelo? Déme fuego, por favor.
give preference to someone in doorways;	¡Pase, pase! Usted primero.
ask someone to speak up, to speak more slowly, and so on;	¿Puede hablar más despacio? Más alto, por favor.
ask how much something is when you want to pay.	¿Cuánto es?

9 ¿Quién es ése?

In this unit you will learn how to establish the identity of people and things by their appearance, situation, family relationship, and so on. You will also learn how to express nationality.

I **¿Quién es ése?** — Who is that?

This is how to ask who someone is.

¿quién?
¿quiénes?

☞ 12

 1. Listen and repeat when you hear the signal.

papá (m) = Daddy

mamá (f) = Mummy

abuelo, -a = grandfather, -mother

nieto, -a = grandson, -daughter

tío (m) = uncle

tía (f) = aunt

sobrino (m) = nephew

sobrina (f) = niece

primo (m) = cousin

prima (f) = cousin

mecánico (m) = mechanic

cartero (m) = postman

To ask who someone is, use quién or quiénes and the appropriate form of the verb ser:

> ¿Quién es esta niña?
>
> ¿Quiénes son ésos?

To say who someone is, again use a form of the verb ser, followed by the respective name, profession, family relationship, or some other identifying characteristic:

> Ésa es Carmen.
>
> Aquél es el profesor.
>
> Éstos son mis padres.

Answers to questions with ¿quién? or ¿quiénes? are formed in the same way: —¿Quién es esa chica?

> —Es mi hermana.
>
> —Mi hermana.

¿QUIÉN ES QUIÉN?   WHO'S WHO?

2. Look at the photographs above. They belong to a young man called Carlos and they have been dedicated to him by different members of his family. Listen to the tape and indicate whether what you hear is true or false.

1. T F   2. T F   3. T F
4. T F   5. T F   6. T F

3. On the tape someone rings your doorbell. Before opening, ask who it is. You will then hear the answer to your question. Indicate who is at the door in each case in the list below.

la policía

el médico

el profesor de su hijo

tu padre

el mecánico

el cartero

¿Cuál es su vestido?   Which one is your dress?

¿Cuál es la madre del novio?   Which one is the groom's mother?

This is another way of establishing the identity of people and things.

4. Listen and repeat when you hear the signal.

In order to establish the identity of one or more particular things in a group of several similar things, ask by using cuál or cuáles and an appropriate form of the verb ser:

          ¿Cuál es tu vestido?

          ¿Cuáles son tus zapatos?

The same structure can be used in order to establish the identity of one or more particular person in a group of several people:

          ¿Cuáles son los padres del novio?

Note the following: to ask about things, use cuál; to ask about people, use quién (although cuál can also be used for people):

          ¿Cuál es tu bolígrafo?

          ¿Quiénes son los padres del novio?

          ¿Cuáles son los padres del novio?

¿cuál?

¿cuáles?

☞ 12

5. Try to establish the identity of the people and the things in the following situations.

1. Juan, a friend of yours, has left his bolígrafo on a desk somewhere and has asked you to fetch it for him. When you go to get it, you see there are two more on the desk. Ask an office colleague in order to find out which one is el bolígrafo de Juan.

2. You have left your new gafas de sol sun-glasses on a table somewhere. When you go to get them there are some very similar ones beside them, belonging to your friend; they are so similar that you don't really know which are yours. Ask your friend.

3. There is a group of people standing across the room from you. Try to establish which one is Pepe.

4. In the same group of people, there is also a girl called María whom you want to identify. Ask a friend.

¿Qué bolígrafo?
¿Qué gafas?
☞ 12

Instead of cuál it is also possible to use qué followed by a noun:

—Dame el bolígrafo.

—¿Qué bolígrafo?

—El azul.

6. On the tape a voice will ask you for certain things. Reply to what the voice says by asking a further question, as shown in the following example:

TAPE: —Dame el bolígrafo.

YOU: —¿Qué bolígrafo?

arriba = above
abajo = below
dentro = inside
fuera = outside
último, -a = last

In replying to questions with ¿cuál? or ¿quién? you will frequently need to refer to where people and things are situated:

—¿Cuál es el novio?

—El chico de la derecha.

Notice also that words such as chico, señora, and so on, can be freely omitted in the replies to such questions:

—¿Cuál es el novio?

—El de la derecha.

7. Look at the pictures below and indicate which person or object is referred to in each case on the tape.

REMEMBER THE FOLLOWING WORDS: primero, segundo, tercero, …, izquierda, derecha. NOTE ALSO: el primero por la derecha = the first from the right, el cuarto por la izquierda = the fourth from the left.

8. Look at the pictures again and reply to the questions below by using the information from the previous exercise. You may listen to the tape again if you find this helps.

pelo (m) = hair
barba (f) = beard
corbata (f) = tie
falda (f) = skirt
camisa (f) = shirt
pantalones (m. pl.) = trousers
vestido (m) = dress

1. ¿Cuál es la chica?
2. ¿Cuál es el coche de Juan?
3. ¿Cuál es el bolígrafo de Ana?
4. ¿Quién es el chico?
5. ¿Cuáles son tus gafas?

rojo, -a = red	**verde (m. y f.)** = green
blanco, -a = white	**azul (m. y f.)** = blue
negro, -a = black	**gris (m. y f.)** = grey
amarillo, -a = yellow	**moreno, -a** = dark-haired
marrón (m. y f.) = brown	**rubio, -a** = fair-haired

> In answering questions with ¿cuál? or ¿quién?, you may also need
> to refer to people and things by their physical characteristics:
>> —¿Quién es la madre?
>>
>> —La señora rubia.
>
> You already know that words such as chico, señora, and so on, may
> be freely omitted if they are obvious in the particular context:
>> —¿Quién es la madre?
>>
>> —La rubia.

9. Look at the picture below. Juan Serrano is somewhere among these people in fancy dress. Which one is he? Indicate each person which the voice on the tape tells you is not Juan.

pequeño, -a = small	**gordo, -a** = fat	**guapo, -a** = good-looking, pretty
grande (m. y f.) = big	**delgado, -a** = thin	**feo, -a** = ugly
alto, -a = tall	**nuevo, -a** = new	**bonito, -a** = nice, pretty
bajo, -a = short	**viejo, -a** = old	

It is also possible to establish the identity of people and things in statements where there is no previous question:

> La señora rubia es la madre.

> La rubia es la madre.

Notice that here also words such as chico, señora, and so on may sometimes be omitted if they are obvious in the particular context:

> La chaqueta grande es mía.

> La grande es mía.

 10. In the picture here there are some people you know. They are some of the characters from the TV Comedy. Identify each one by means of the characteristics which are indicated below:

Carmen (falda)
Juan (camisa)
Luis Cánovas (corbata)
El novio de Carmen (zapatos)
David (pantalones)

EXAMPLE: Carmen es la de la falda marrón.

 11. Look again at the picture above and write answers to the following questions:

EXAMPLE: ¿Quién es Carmen? La de la falda marrón.

1. ¿Quién es Juan?

2. ¿Quién es Luis Cánovas?

3. ¿Cuál es el novio de Carmen?

4. ¿Quién es David?

12. Look at the pictures and ask a partner to identify the people and the things in each pair of pictures. Your partner should reply.

EXAMPLE:

—¿Quién es Diego?

—El gordo.

1

El coche de Juan (pequeño)   El coche de Carmen (grande).

2

Diego (gordo)   José (delgado)

3

La madre (baja)   La hija (alta)

4

Los zapatos de Óscar (nuevos)   Los zapatos de David (viejos)

5

Julio (guapo)   Víctor (feo)

6

La corbata de Emilio (bonita)   La corbata de Pepe (fea)

13. Look at the pictures again and complete the following sentences:

El coche de Juan ⬚⬚⬚⬚ ⬚⬚⬚⬚ pequeño.

La hija ⬚⬚⬚⬚ ⬚⬚⬚⬚ alta.

Los zapatos de David ⬚⬚⬚⬚ ⬚⬚⬚⬚ viejos.

14. Look at the pictures once more and identify the people and the things in pairs.

EXAMPLE:

El coche de Juan es el pequeño y el de Carmen es el grande.

El coche de Juan es el pequeño y el de Carmen, el grande.

9. ¿Quién es ése?

Es inglesa.   She is English.

This is how to express someone's nationality, or where someone is from.

¿De dónde es?   Where is she from?

And this is how to ask for the same information.

> To ask someone's nationality or where someone is from, use the expression ¿de dónde? and the corresponding form of the verb ser:
>
> ¿De dónde eres?
>
> ¿De dónde es Juan?

15. Listen and complete the following sentences:

1. ¿De dónde   ustedes?
2. Y tú ¿de dónde   ?
3. ¿De dónde   vosotros?
4. Y usted ¿de dónde   ?

> To express someone's nationality or where someone is from, use the verb ser followed by either 1) de and the name of the city or country, or 2) an adjective of nationality:
>
> Soy de París.
>
> Carla es de Italia.
>
> Somos alemanes.

español, -a = Spanish	**alemán, -a** = German
Francia = France	**Japón** = Japan
francés, -a = French	**japonés, -a** = Japanese
Inglaterra = England	**Brasil** = Brazil
inglés, -a = English	**brasileño, -a** = Brazilian
Italia = Italy	**Marruecos** = Morocco
italiano, -a = Italian	**marroquí (m. y f.)** = Moroccan
Alemania = Germany	

16. Look at the pictures and say where the people are from.

EXAMPLE: Es de España. Es española.

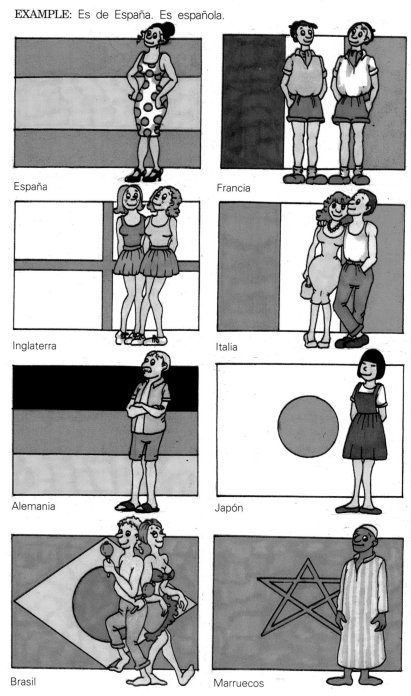

España

Francia

Inglaterra

Italia

Alemania

Japón

Brasil

Marruecos

17. You and the other members of the group each draw the flag of a particular country on a slip of paper and keep it hidden until you are asked about your 'new' nationality. When your turn comes, show the flag and at the same time say which country you are from.

Y POR FIN...

18. The following text is adapted from the PRESENTATIONS from the television unit. Listen to the tape and fill in the blanks.

LUIS: Oiga, ¿⬚⬚⬚ es ese señor?

FOTÓGRAFO: Es el ⬚⬚⬚ de la novia, y ⬚⬚ ⬚⬚ ⬚⬚ derecha es su ⬚⬚⬚ , la madre de la novia.

LUIS: ¿Y ésa de la izquierda, ⬚⬚ ⬚⬚ vestido ⬚⬚ ?

FOTÓGRAFO: Elisabeth, la ⬚⬚⬚ del novio.

LUIS: ¿Elisabeth? ¿De ⬚⬚⬚ es?

FOTÓGRAFO: Inglesa.

JOVEN: ¡Qué bonito es el ⬚⬚⬚ !

LUIS: ¿⬚⬚⬚ ?

JOVEN: El de la ⬚⬚⬚ , hombre.

LUIS: Ah, sí, sí, muy ⬚⬚⬚ ... Oye, ¿⬚⬚ ⬚⬚ ese señor?

JOVEN: ¿⬚⬚⬚ ?

LUIS: Ése, ⬚⬚⬚ gris.

JOVEN: El cura.

● **TRANSCRIPTION OF THE TV DIALOGUES**
"¿QUIÉN ES ÉSE?"

Presentación. Primera parte

PRESENTADOR: ¿Qué tal? Miren. Esto es una boda ➡ ① española. La novia... el novio... y ése es... Oiga, ¿quién es ése?

FOTÓGRAFO: Es el padre de la novia, y la de la derecha es su mujer. La madre de la novia.

PRESENTADOR: Ya ven ustedes...

FOTÓGRAFO: ¡Oye, Carlos!

NOVIO: ¿Qué?

FOTÓGRAFO: ¡La corbata! ¡Un momento...!

PRESENTADOR: ¿Y ésa de la izquierda, la del vestido azul?

FOTÓGRAFO: Elisabeth, la madre del novio.

PRESENTADOR: ¿Elisabeth? ¿De dónde es?

FOTÓGRAFO: Inglesa.

PRESENTADOR: Es inglesa. Y usted, ¿de dónde es?

FOTÓGRAFO: ¡Don Julián! Mire aquí, por favor. Una, dos y...

JOVEN: ¡Un momento!

FOTÓGRAFO: Una, dos y... ¡tres!

Telecomedia. Primera parte

ANDRÉS: "Conocer España". Tres, uno, uno.

CARMEN: ¡Un momento! La señora rubia. Sí, usted, por favor. A la derecha. El niño alto, un poco más a tu izquierda. ¡Oye, Andrés! ➡ ② ¡Pon eso al fondo!

ANDRÉS: ¿Puedo pasar por aquí?

CARMEN: Sí, sí.

AYUDANTE: ¡Oye, tú! ¿A dónde vas?

Presentation. Part One

PRESENTER: How are you? Look. This is a Spanish wedding. ➡ ① The bride ... the groom ... and that man is ... Excuse me, who is that man?

PHOTOGRAPHER: It's the bride's father, and the woman on the right is his wife. The bride's mother.

PRESENTER: So you see (how things are).

PHOTOGRAPHER: Hey! Carlos!

GROOM: What?

PHOTOGRAPHER: Your tie! One moment ...!

PRESENTER: And that woman on the left, the one in the blue dress?

PHOTOGRAPHER: Elisabeth, the groom's mother.

PRESENTER: Elisabeth? Where is she from?

PHOTOGRAPHER: (She's) English.

PRESENTER: She's English. And you? Where are you from?

PHOTOGRAPHER: Don Julián! Look this way, please. One, two, [and] ...

YOUNG WOMAN: One moment!

PHOTOGRAPHER: One, two [and] ... three!

TV Comedy. Part One

ANDRÉS: "Getting to know Spain". Three, one, one.

CARMEN: One moment! The fair-haired lady. Yes, you, please. To the right. The tall boy, a little more to your left. Hey, Andrés! ➡ ② Put that back there.

ANDRÉS: Can I come by?

CARMEN: Yes. Yes.

ASSISTANT: Hey, you! Where are you going?

EXTRA: A los servicios. ➡ ③
AYUDANTE: Espera un momento.
CARMEN: ¡Ven aquí!
AYUDANTE: ¡Veinte minutos de descanso!
CARMEN: Hola, buenos días.
DIEGO: Hola, ¿qué tal?
JUAN: Buenos días.
GUITARRISTA: Perdón, con permiso.
JUAN: ¿Quién es ese?
CARMEN: El guitarrista.
EXTRA 1: Ése es mi marido y aquél es mi hijo. Se llama Ángel.
EXTRA 3: *¡Mamma mía!* ¡Qué calor!
EXTRA 2: ¿De dónde es usted?
EXTRA 3: De Italia. Soy italiano. Y usted, ¿de dónde es?
EXTRA 2: De Madrid.
EXTRA 3: Mi mujer también es de Madrid.
EXTRA 2: ¡Ángel! ¡No cojas eso!
AYUDANTE: Bueno, vamos a empezar. ¡Niño!

Presentación. Segunda parte
JOVEN: ¡Qué bonito es el vestido!
PRESENTADOR: ¿Cuál?
JOVEN: El de la novia, hombre.
PRESENTADOR: Ah, sí, sí, muy bonito. Oye, ¿quién es ese señor?
JOVEN: ¿Qué señor?
PRESENTADOR: Ése, el de gris.
JOVEN: Ah, ése es el cura. ➡ ④
NOVIA: Papá, ¿dónde está el cura?
DON JULIÁN: ¿El cura? Pero, ¿quién es el cura?
PRESENTADOR: El de gris, don Julián, el de gris. Allí está. ¡Buen viaje! Hasta luego.

Telecomedia. Segunda parte
EXTRA 4: ¿Dónde está mi madre?
JUAN: ¿Quién es su madre?
DIEGO: ¿Quién es la madre de este niño?
CARMEN: Aquella señora del fondo.
DIEGO: ¿Qué señora?
CARMEN: La del vestido verde.
EXTRA 2: ¡Angel!
CARMEN: Vamos a empezar.
ANDRÉS: *"Conocer España".* Tres, uno, dos.
CARMEN: ¡Acción!
ENCARGADO SONIDO: ¡Un momento! No...
ANDRÉS: *"Conocer España".* Tres, uno, tres.
CARMEN: ¡Ese cable!
EXTRA 3: *¡Mamma mía!*
CARMEN: ¿Y ahora, qué hacemos?
EXTRA 1: Mi marido es músico.
CARMEN: ¿Es usted músico?
MARIDO: Sí.
CARMEN: Lo siento pero no... ¿Quién está tocando la guitarra? ➡ ⑤
PRESENTADOR: Adiós. Hasta luego.

EXTRA: To the toilet. ➡ ③
ASSISTANT: Just a moment.
CARMEN: Come here!
ASSISTANT: Twenty minutes' break!
CARMEN: Hello. Good morning.
DIEGO: Hello. How are you?
JUAN: Good morning.
GUITARIST: Excuse me. May I come by?
JUAN: Who's that?
CARMEN: The guitarist.
1ST EXTRA: That's my husband and that's my son. His name is Ángel.
3RD EXTRA: *Mamma mía!* Isn't it hot!
2ND EXTRA: Where are you from?
3RD EXTRA: From Italy. I'm Italian. And you? Where are you from?
2ND EXTRA: From Madrid.
3RD EXTRA: My wife is from Madrid too.
2ND EXTRA: Ángel! Leave that alone! [i.e. "Don't pick up that!"]
ASSISTANT: OK, we are going to start. Child!

Presentation. Part Two
YOUNG WOMAN: Isn't the dress pretty!
PRESENTER: Which one?
YOUNG WOMAN: The bride's, "hombre".
PRESENTER: Ah, yes, yes, very pretty. Hey; who is that man?
YOUNG WOMAN: Which man?
PRESENTER: That one; the one in grey.
YOUNG WOMAN: Ah; that's the priest. ➡ ④
BRIDE: Daddy, where is the priest?
DON JULIÁN: The priest? ["But"], who is the priest?
PRESENTER: The man in grey, don Julián, the man in grey. There he is. Have a good journey! See you later.

TV Comedy. Part Two
ÁNGEL: Where is my mother?
JUAN: Who is his mother?
DIEGO: Who is this boy's mother?
CARMEN: That woman back there.
DIEGO: Which woman?
CARMEN: The one in the green dress.
2ND EXTRA: Ángel!
CARMEN: We are going to start.
ANDRÉS: *"Getting to know Spain".* Three, one, two.
CARMEN: Action!
SOUND TECHNICIAN: One moment. (There is) no (sound).
ANDRÉS: *"Getting to know Spain".* Three, one, three.
CARMEN: That wire!
3RD EXTRA: *Mamma mía!*
CARMEN: And what do we do now?
1ST EXTRA: My husband is a musician.
CARMEN: Are you a musician?
HUSBAND: Yes.
CARMEN: I'm sorry but ... (I'm afraid) not. Who's playing the guitar? ➡ ⑤
PRESENTER: Goodbye. See you soon.

CAJÓN DE SASTRE

 Since the coming of democracy to Spain it is quite common for Spanish couples to get married in court before a judge (casarse por lo civil). However, most people still get married in church (casarse por la Iglesia). The religious or civil ceremony is called boda (wedding) and is usually followed by a banquet to which the couple invite their guests.

(2) You already know the form oiga which is used to call someone's attention. Oye is the equivalent for the tú form of address.

(3) In Spanish, as in other languages, there are various euphemisms for referring to things such as toilets. Use the words, baño or cuarto de baño, which you already know, for the toilet in a private home, and servicios in public places. Public toilets may be indicated by the letters W.C. or by the word ASEOS.

(4) To refer to priests of the Catholic church, use the words sacerdote (more formal) or cura (less formal). The second of these is more frequent.

(5) It is true that the guitar is the most characteristic Spanish musical instrument. It is also true that there is a guitar in many Spanish homes. But don't expect every Spaniard to play it, nor to sing and dance flamenco. Similarly, very few Spaniards are in fact bullfighters.

USTED YA PUEDE...

ask who someone is;	¿Quién es ése?
say who someone is;	Ésa es Carmen.
identify someone by expressing their family relationship;	Aquéllos son mis padres.
ask the identity of particular persons and things when there are several together;	¿Quién es la madre del novio? ¿Cuál es la madre del novio? ¿Cuál es tu bolígrafo?
identify people and things by referring to where they are;	El chico de la derecha. El de la derecha.
identify people and things by referring to their appearance and physical characteristics;	La señora rubia. La rubia. El bolígrafo azul. El azul. El chico de la camisa roja. El de la camisa roja.
ask someone's nationality or where someone is from;	¿De dónde es usted?
and express the same information.	Soy de Madrid. Soy italiano. Es de Francia.

10 ¿Qué día es hoy?

In this unit you will learn how to ask and express the days of the week, the date, and the time. You will also learn how to express suggestions and invitations.

I **Hoy es jueves.**   Today is Thursday.

Hoy es veinticinco   Today is the twenty-fifth [i.e. "twenty-five"]

This is how to express the day of the week and the date.

¿Qué día es hoy?   What day/date is it today?

And this is how to ask for the same information.

1. The voices on the tape mention various dates and days of the week. Listen and indicate the respective days and dates which you hear for the last week on the calendar.

hoy = today

10. ¿Qué día es hoy?

REMEMBER:

lunes
martes
miércoles
jueves
viernes
sábado
domingo

To express the day of the week and the date, use the form es followed by the respective day or date:

> Hoy es jueves.
>
> Hoy es catorce.

To ask for the same information, use a question beginning with ¿qué día es...?, or simply with ¿qué es...?:

> ¿Qué día es hoy?
>
> ¿Qué es hoy?
>
> ¿Qué es mañana?

2. Answer the questions in the pictures below, taking into account the day on which each person is situated.

3. Read the following dialogue as you listen to the tape:

> HOMBRE: Elena, ¿qué día es hoy?
>
> ELENA: Pues domingo.
>
> HOMBRE: Ya, mujer, ya. Pero ¿a qué estamos?
>
> NIÑO: A veintidós.
>
> ELENA: No, hijo, no. Estamos a veintitrés.

It is also possible to express the date by using the form estamos and the word a:

> Estamos a veintitrés.
>
> ¿A qué estamos?
>
> A veintitrés.

4. Read the dialogue in Exercise 3 again and answer sí **or** no**:**

    1. Is it Sunday in the dialogue?

    2. Does the man ask the date?

    3. Does the child say that it is the twenty-third?

Now imagine that you are Elena. Answer the man by writing the date:

    4. HOMBRE: ¿Qué es hoy?

       USTED:

● ●

(II)   **Son las cinco.**   It is five o'clock.

This is how to express the time.

¿Qué hora es?   What time is it?

And this is how to ask for the same information.

5. Listen and repeat when you hear the signal.

y diez = ten past
y cuarto = a quarter past
y media = half-past
menos veinte = twenty to
menos cuarto = a quarter to

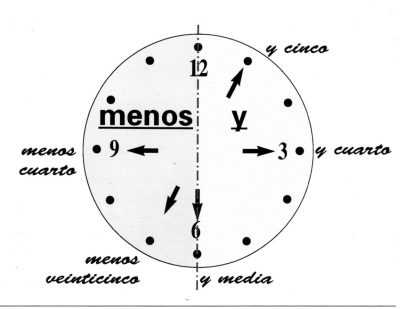

10. ¿Qué día es hoy?

The verb ser is also used to express the time. Use the form es for la una (one o'clock) (Es la una. It is one o'clock) and the form son for other times (Son las cinco. It is five o'clock). The question is always formed with es.

6. Which clock does each of the following sentences correspond to?

1. Son las dos menos diez.   RELOJ NÚMERO
2. Las nueve y veinticinco.   RELOJ NÚMERO
3. Es la una y media.   RELOJ NÚMERO
4. Son las nueve y cuarto.   RELOJ NÚMERO
5. Las diez menos cinco.   RELOJ NÚMERO

7. Look again at the clocks above. What time is it by each one?

Note that the questions
    ¿Tiene hora, por favor?
    ¿Tienes hora?
mean the same as ¿Qué hora es?:
    —¿Tienes hora, por favor?
    —Las once y diez.

Sentences such as:

> Son las veintitrés horas.

are only used in restricted situations in Spanish. If you wish to be more specific, use the words mañana, tarde, and noche:

> Son las once de la mañana.

> Son las tres de la tarde.

> Son las once de la noche.

The approximate times of reference for these words are as follows:

mañana	➡	until 1.00pm
tarde	➡	until 8.00 or 9.00pm
noche	➡	until 1.00am

Notice that these divisions do not coincide exactly with those which govern the use of buenos días, buenas tardes, and buenas noches.

mañana (f) = morning

tarde (f) = afternoon

noche (f) = night

8. Listen to the tape and write the following times in the space for each respective city: 14.00, 22.00, 13.00, 10.00, 8.00, 16.00, 21.00.

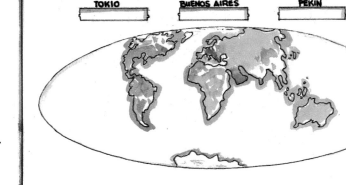

hora (f) = hour

media hora (f) = half an hour

cuarto de hora (m) = quarter of an hour

minuto (m) = minute

Note that the words hora, media and cuarto, which are used for expressing the time, may also be used to indicate a period of time:

> una hora = 60 minutos

> media hora = 30 minutos

> un cuarto de hora = 15 minutos

> hora y media = 90 minutos

	but:
una hora	
un cuarto de hora	media hora
un minuto	hora y media

10. ¿Qué día es hoy?

9. What time is it in each of the above pictures?

10. What period of time has passed between each pair of pictures?

Between 1 and 2

Between 3 and 4

Between 5 and 6

11. Read the following notes for a brief detective report on the activities of Alberto López (A.L. in the text.) True or false? Indicate your choice.

THE FOLLOWING WORDS WILL HELP YOU:

tarde = late

pronto = early

más = more

ahora = now

pero = but

muy = very

otro,-a = another

irse (v. i.) = to go, to leave

> Martes, 21
>
> Ahora A.L. está dentro, en el bar, esperando a Rosi. Todavía es pronto: las siete menos cuarto.
>
> Las siete. Llega una mujer, pero no es Rosi. Es la rubia de la falda azul. Entra en el bar. Están hablando. La rubia le da un paquete y se va. Son las siete y cinco.
>
> Treinta minutos más y Rosi no viene. A.L. mira el reloj y toma otra cerveza. La novena. ¿Va a venir Rosi o no?
>
> Es muy tarde. Las diez menos diez. Rosi no va a venir. A.L. se va.

1. Las siete menos cuarto. Un cuarto de hora más tarde llega la rubia de la falda azul. ☐T ☐F
2. La rubia está en el bar diez minutos. ☐T ☐F
3. Alberto toma la novena cerveza media hora más tarde. ☐T ☐F
4. Rosi llega a las diez menos diez. ☐T ☐F

12. Mime something which you or people in general do at a fixed time (for example, put your pyjamas on). Ask your partners ¿Qué hora es?. They should reply.

UNA COPA   A DRINK

13. Follow the text in the pictures below as you listen to the tape.

— Half-past eight. Shall we go?
— OK.
— OK. Fine.

This is how to express a suggestion, and how to reply.

— I invite you to a drink.
— OK.

This is how to express an invitation, and how to reply.

Thanks for the drink.

This is how to thank someone for something.

Questions such as

¿Nos <u>vamos</u>?

¿Toma<u>mos</u> un café?

¿Ve<u>mos</u> la televisión?

¿Va<u>mos</u> al cine?

may be used to express suggestions. However, they become invitations if the suggested activity costs money (eg. having a coffee in a bar, going to the cinema, etc.) and the person who suggests doing so indicates that he is willing to pay for everyone. The same is also true of expressions which you have already learned for offering things:

¿Queréis una copa?

¿Una cerveza?

invitar = to invite, to treat

tomar una copa = to have a drink

descansar = to rest

llevar = to take

bailar = to dance

película (f) = film

helado (m) = ice cream

rato (m) = short while

momento (m) = moment

In order to make it clear that you are inviting or treating someone, use the verb invitar a:

     Os invito a una copa.

     Te invito a un café.

     La invito a usted al cine.

PRONOUNS: <u>te</u> invito

               <u>la</u> invito a usted

               <u>os</u> invito   ☞ 10.3

You can accept or reject the invitation by using expressions which you already know:

      —¿Vemos la televisión?   —Os invito a un café.

      —De acuerdo.   —Muy bien.

                                     —No, yo no puedo. Gracias.

14. Complete each dialogue with one of the suggestions on the left.

A. ¿Las llevamos?

B. ¿Nos vamos?

C. ¿Entramos?

D. ¿Descansamos un rato?

E. ¿Vemos una película?

F. ¿Salimos un momento?

1. —Mira, esa es la iglesia del pueblo.

   —

2. —¿Se puede fumar aquí dentro?

   —No, dentro no.

   —

3. —Ese es el vídeo nuevo de mi padre.

   —

4. —

   —No, yo no puedo irme todavía.

5. —

   —Bueno, descansa un poco.

6. —Mira, las amigas de Felipe.

   —

   —Sí, para.

15. Now cover what you wrote in Exercise 14 and try to reproduce what you put.

16. On the tape you will hear several invitations. Say which of the following situations is the result of each invitation.

1   2   3   4

flor (f) = flower

regalo (m) = present

Sentence 1 Picture   Sentence 3 Picture

Sentence 2 Picture   Sentence 4 Picture

Gracias por las flores

GRACIAS POR SU VISITA.

In order to thank someone explicitly for something, use por:

Gracias por las flores.

Gracias por el regalo.

Gracias por su visita.

17. Listen to the tape, and answer the questions in Spanish.

1. What does the girl thank the young man for?

2. What does the young man suggest?

3. Does the girl accept?

Y POR FIN...

18. Listen to the tape, and answer the questions in Spanish.

1. What day of the week is it in the dialogue?

2. What date is it? (Write it in full.)

3. What does Luis invite his colleague to?

4. What time is it in the dialogue? (Write it in full.)

19. Read the Spanish transcription of the TV Comedy again. Then fill in the blanks below.

Hoy ⬚⬚⬚ jueves, veinticinco, el cumpleaños de Diego. Su ⬚⬚⬚ sale deprisa de la oficina: son ⬚⬚⬚ menos diez y tiene una cita. Juan, Rosi, Carmen le dan a ⬚⬚⬚ un regalo, y él los invita. Comen, beben y ⬚⬚⬚. En ese momento, ⬚⬚⬚ el jefe con otro regalo.

TRANSCRIPTION OF THE TV DIALOGUES
¿QUÉ DÍA ES HOY?

Presentación. Primera parte
PRESENTADOR: ¿Qué tal? Estamos viendo una película.
JOVEN DE LA PELÍCULA: ¿Qué hora es?
OTRO: Las siete y cuarto.
CHICA DE LA PELÍCULA: ¡Son las siete y cuarto!
JOVEN: Ya, ya, perdona.
MONTADOR: ¿Tienes hora, Luis?
PRESENTADOR: Sí, son las seis menos veinte. ¿Quieres un café?
MONTADOR: ¿Qué?
PRESENTADOR: Que te invito a un café.
MONTADOR: ¡Ah! Muy bien. Vamos. ¿Qué día es hoy?
PRESENTADOR: Jueves.
MONTADOR: Ya, pero ¿a qué estamos?
PRESENTADOR: A doce.
MONTADOR: ¡Anda! ¡El cumpleaños de mi mujer!
PRESENTADOR: Hoy es jueves, doce: el cumpleaños de su mujer.

Presentation. Part One
PRESENTER: How are you? We are watching a film.
YOUNG MAN IN FILM: What time is it?
2ND MAN: A quarter past seven.
GIRL IN FILM: It's a quarter past seven!
YOUNG MAN: Yes. Yes. I know. I'm sorry.
EDITOR: Have you got the time, Luis?
PRESENTER: Yes, it's twenty to six. Would you like a coffee?
EDITOR: What?
PRESENTER: I invite you to a coffee.
EDITOR: Ah! Fine. Let's go. What day is it?
PRESENTER: Thursday.
EDITOR: Yes. But what date is it?
PRESENTER: The twelfth.
EDITOR: Oh, dear! My wife's birthday!
PRESENTER: Today is Thursday, the twelfth; his wife's birthday.

Telecomedia. Primera parte
JEFE: Oye, ¿qué es hoy?
DIEGO: Viernes.
JEFE: Ya, ya, pero ¿a qué estamos?
DIEGO: A veinticinco.
ROSI: ¡Su cita!
JEFE: ¡Ahí va! ¡Las cinco menos cuarto! Me voy ➡ ① enseguida.
JEFE: Rosi, ¿quién es ése?
ROSI: ¿Quién?
JEFE: El del casco.
ROSI: Es... Alberto.

TV Comedy. Part One
BOSS: What day is it?
DIEGO: Friday.
BOSS: Yes, I know. But what date is it?
DIEGO: The twenty-fifth.
ROSI: Your appointment!
BOSS: Oh, dear. A quarter to five! I'm leaving right away. ➡ ①
BOSS: Rosi, who is that?
ROSI: Who?
BOSS: The one with the helmet.
ROSI: It's Alberto.

JEFE: Ah. ¿Y quién es Alberto?

ROSI: Pues... Alberto.

JEFE: Ah. Pues no le conozco.

ROSI: ¡Es nuevo!

JEFE: ¡Ah!

ROSI: Las cinco menos diez... Va a llegar tarde. ➡ ②

JEFE: Sí, sí, ya me voy. Hasta luego. Adiós, Diego.

DIEGO: Hasta luego, jefe.

ROSI: ¡Ya! ¡Ya!

DIEGO: ¿Qué te pasa?

ROSI: ¿A mí? Nada.

CARMEN: Diego, ¿qué día es hoy?

DIEGO: Veinticinco.

TODOS: Cumpleaños feliz... ➡ ③

DIEGO: ¡Pero bueno!

TODOS: ¡Felicidades! ¡Feliz cumpleaños, Diego! ¡Que cumplas muchos!

CARMEN: Ya tienes treinta años, ¿eh?

DIEGO: ¡Si, treinta! Ya soy un viejo.

TODOS: Uno, dos, tres, cuatro...

DIEGO: ¿Queréis tomar una copa? ➡ ④

TODOS: Sí, sí.

JUAN: ¿Una copa? Aquí no hay nada...

DIEGO: Sí, sí...

JUAN: ¿Dónde?

DIEGO: ¡Aquí! ¡Tatacháááán! Os invito a comer, os invito a beber y... ¡os invito a bailar!

Presentación. Segunda parte

MONTADOR: ¿Vamos?

PRESENTADOR: Vamos. ¿Entramos?

JOVEN DE LA PELÍCULA: Ya, ya, perdona. Toma; ¿lo abres?

CHICA DE LA PELÍCULA: No, ahora no. Muchas gracias por el regalo.

JOVEN DE LA PELÍCULA: De nada. ¿Bailamos?

CHICA DE LA PELÍCULA: Sí, muy bien.

PRESENTADOR: ¿Bailamos? Gracias. Hasta luego.

Telecomedia. Segunda parte

JUAN: Gracias.

ROSI: Toma.

JUAN: Gracias, ya tengo.

DIEGO: ¿Bailamos, Rosi? Venga.

ROSI: No, ahora no, estoy con...

DIEGO: ¿Con quién?

ROSI: Con... con... Huy, con la tarta.

DIEGO: Vamos, venga.

CARMEN: ¡Juan! ¡Ven!

JUAN: ¡Espera!

CARMEN: ¿Vamos...?

JUAN: ¿A dónde?

CARMEN: Allí.

JUAN: ¿Solos?

CARMEN: Sí, solos.

JUAN: Ah... Vale.

ROSI: ¡Ay!

DIEGO: ¿Qué pasa?

ROSI: ¡Mi pie! ¡Ay!

DIEGO: ¿Qué pasa ahora?

ROSI: ¡La cabeza!

CARMEN: ¡Diego...!

DIEGO: ¡No...!

JUAN: Sí, sí.

BOSS: Ah. And who is Alberto?

ROSI: Well, ... Alberto.

BOSS: Ah. Well, I don't know him.

ROSI: He's new!

BOSS: Ah!

ROSI: Ten to five ... You are going to arrive late. ➡ ②

BOSS: Yes, yes. I'm leaving right away. See you later. Bye, Diego.

DIEGO: See you later, sir [i.e. "boss"].

ROSI: Now! Now!

DIEGO: What's the matter?

ROSI: With me? Nothing.

CARMEN: Diego, what day is today?

DIEGO: The twenty-fifth.

ALL: Happy birthday to you ➡ ③

DIEGO: Well, really!

ALL: Many happy returns! Happy birthday, Diego! Many happy returns!

CARMEN: You're thirty now, aren't you?

DIEGO: Yes, thirty. I'm an old man already.

ALL: One, two, three, four, ...

DIEGO: Would you like a drink? ➡ ④

ALL: Yes, yes.

JUAN: A drink? There's nothing here ...

DIEGO: Yes, there is.

JUAN: Where?

DIEGO: Here! "Tatacháááán!" I invite you to eat, I invite you to drink and ... I invite you to dance!

Presentation. Part Two

EDITOR: Shall we go?

PRESENTER: Yes, let's go. Shall we go in?

YOUNG MAN IN FILM: Yes, yes. I'm sorry. Here. Will you open it?

GIRL IN FILM: No, not now. Thank you very much for the present.

YOUNG MAN IN FILM: Not at all. Shall we dance?

GIRL IN FILM: Yes, O.K.

PRESENTER: Shall we dance? Thank you. See you later.

TV Comedy. Part Two.

JUAN: Thank you.

ROSI: Here.

JUAN: No, thank you. I already have some.

DIEGO: Shall we dance, Rosi? Come on.

ROSI: No, not now. I'm with ...

DIEGO: With whom?

ROSI: With ... with ... Oh, ... with the gateau.

DIEGO: Come on, come on.

CARMEN: Juan! Come here!

JUAN: Just a moment!

CARMEN: Let's go.

JUAN: Where?

CARMEN: In there.

JUAN: Just the two of us? [i.e. "Alone?"]

CARMEN: Yes, just the two of us.

JUAN: Ah! OK.

ROSI: Ow!

DIEGO: What's the matter?

ROSI: My foot! Ow!

DIEGO: What's the matter now?

ROSI: My head!

CARMEN: Diego ... !

DIEGO: No!!!

JUAN: Yes, yes.

CARMEN: ¿Lo abres?
DIEGO: ¡Muchas gracias por el regalo!
JUAN: De nada.
DIEGO: ¡Gracias…!
ROSI: ¿Bailamos?
JUAN: ¿Perdón?
ROSI: Que si bailamos.
JUAN: No, ahora no.
ROSI: Ahora sí. Vamos.
JUAN: No sé… ¿qué hora es?
ROSI: Las seis y media.
JUAN: Es muy tarde.
ROSI: Buena hora para bailar, las seis y media de la tarde. Vamos.
JUAN: ¡Muy bien! ¡Diego, un rock por favor!
COMPAÑERO: ¡El jefe! ¡Viene el jefe!
JUAN: ¿El jefe?
DIEGO: ¡El jefe!
ROSI: ¡Olé, olé, el jefe! Buenas tardes, Sr. Irízar, ¿qué tal?
JEFE: ¿Qué?, ¿celebramos el cumpleaños de Diego?
TODOS: ¿Quéééé?
JEFE: ¡Feliz cumpleaños, Diego!
DIEGO: Gracias, jefe.
PRESENTADOR: Buenas tardes. Adiós, buenas tardes.

CARMEN: Will you open it?
DIEGO: Thank you very much for the present!
JUAN: Not at all.
DIEGO: Thank you!
ROSI: Shall we dance?
JUAN: Sorry?
ROSI: Shall we dance?
JUAN: No, not now.
ROSI: Yes. Now. Come on.
JUAN: I don't know. What time is it?
ROSI: Half-past six.
JUAN: It's very late.
ROSI: A good time to dance, half past six in the evening. Come on.
JUAN: Very well! Diego, some rock please!
COLLEAGUE: The boss! The boss is coming!
JUAN: The boss?
DIEGO: The boss!
ROSI: "Olé! Olé!" The boss! Good evening, Mr. Irízar. How are you?
BOSS: What (is going on)? Are we celebrating Diego's birthday?
ALL: What?
BOSS: Happy birthday, Diego!
DIEGO: Thank you, sir [i.e. "boss"].
PRESENTER: Good night. Goodbye. Good night.

CAJÓN DE SASTRE

(1) You will already have observed that the verb ir is frequent in Spanish and is used with several different meanings. For example:

Voy al cine. I am going to the cinema.
Me voy. I'm going, I'm leaving (pronominal verb. ☞ 16.2, 16.3. This means 'to go' or 'to leave', when the destination itself is immaterial.)
Van a venir. They are going to come. (future meaning)
¡Vamos! Come on! (expression of encouragement)
¡Ahí va! Really! (exclamation of surprise)

(2) Note the following expressions:
llegar tarde   to arrive late
llegar pronto   to arrive early

(3) Note the following:

Hoy es 25.   Today is the twenty-fifth.
Hoy es el cumpleaños de Diego.   Today is Diego's birthday.
Mañana es Navidad.   Tomorrow is Christmas Day.

The structure which is used to express the date can also be used to refer to a special event, such as a party or a birthday, the same as in English.
Note also that surprise birthday parties, such as that in the TV Comedy, are a recent imported custom in Spain. The traditional procedure is for the one whose birthday it is to treat his friends to a drink, to receive some presents, and to have his ear pulled. (Compare the 'bumps' in Britain.)

(4) Invitations are subject to different conventions in different cultures. For the moment, it will be sufficient for you to note that in a bar in Spain the normal practice is for one person alone to pay for what the rest have had to drink, each person taking turns to pay for everyone. Remember also that if you offer to take people for a drink or suggest going for a drink, your companions will probably interpret it as an invitation. Make sure you pay!

10. ¿Qué día es hoy?

● **USTED YA PUEDE...**

express the day of the week and the date;	Hoy es jueves. Estamos a veinticinco.
and ask for the same information;	¿Qué es hoy? ¿A qué estamos hoy?
express the time;	Es la una. Son las cinco de la tarde.
and ask for the same information;	¿Qué hora es? ¿Tiene hora?
express a suggestion;	¿Nos vamos?
and reply;	Muy bien. No, yo no.
invite someone to something;	¿Un café? Te invito a un café.
and accept or reject an invitation;	Muy bien. No, gracias, ahora no puedo.
thank someone for something.	Gracias por el regalo.

In this unit you will learn how to go shopping: to order different articles, to ask how much they cost, where they are from, and what they are called.

DE TIENDAS

GOING SHOPPING

¿Qué precio tiene esta camisa?

How much is this shirt?

This is how to ask the price of something.

Before buying something we normally ask its price. Use the following expression: ¿qué precio tiene...?

> ¿Qué precio tiene esta camisa?
>
> ¿Qué precio tienen las naranjas?
>
> ¿Qué precio tienen los huevos?

Answers to such questions (for example, for the price of a shirt) are expressed as follows:

> Siete mil quinientas pesetas.

or   Son siete mil quinientas pesetas.

tienda (f) = shop
precio (m) = price

11. ¿Cuánto cuesta éste?

In other situations you may be given the price of the characteristic quantity of the article in question:

> Ciento setenta y cinco <u>el kilo</u>.
> Ochenta y nueve pesetas <u>el litro</u>.
> Doscientas pesetas <u>la docena</u>.

jersey (m) = jersey	**vino tinto (m)** = red wine
calcetín (m) = sock	**vino blanco (m)** = white wine
bolso (m) = handbag	**tarta (f)** = cake, gateau
fresa (f) = strawberry	**pastel (m)** = small cake
manzana (f) = apple	**kilo (m): Kg.** = kilo
pescado (m) = fish	**gramo (m): g.** = gram
atún (m) = tuna fish	**litro (m): l.** = litre
merluza (f) = hake	**docena (f)** = dozen
carne (f) = meat	**medio, -a** = half
bocadillo (m) = roll	**trozo (m)** = piece

1. Look at the photographs below. When you hear the number of each photograph, ask the price of the respective article(s). You will then hear the answer to your question.

EXAMPLE:

> TAPE: Uno.
> YOU: ¿Qué precio tiene el jersey?
> TAPE: ¿El jersey? Ocho mil seiscientas.

| 1 jersey | 2 bolso | 3 postales | 4 merluza |

2. Listen again to the prices which you were given in Exercise 1. Now write them down:

el jersey, _____ pesetas.

el bolso, _____ pesetas.

las postales, _____ pesetas.

la merluza, _____ pesetas el kilo.

3. Write some of the following words on separate slips of paper:

> camisa, chaqueta, falda, pantalones, jersey, calcetines, zapatos, bolso, postales, fresas, manzanas, pescado, atún, merluza, carne, huevos, vino tinto, tarta, pasteles, sellos, colonia, jabón, champú, dentífrico, cepillo de dientes.

Write an appropriate price for these articles on the back of each slip of paper. Then place the pieces of paper in front of you with the names of the articles face up. Imagine that they are products which you are selling in your tienda **shop. Your partners ask the price of each article. Look at the price on the back and reply.**

jabón (m) = soap
champú (m) = shampoo
dentífrico (m) = toothpaste
cepillo de dientes (m) = toothbrush
colonia (f) = eau de cologne
postal (f) = postcard
sello (m) = stamp

> There are other ways of asking the price of something; one of these is ¿cuánto cuesta?:
>
> ¿Cuánto cuesta la gasolina en España?
>
> ¿Cuánto cuestan estos calcetines?
>
> The expression ¿a cuánto está...? (or ¿a cómo está...?) is normally used to ask the price of articles which frequently vary in price (especially foodstuffs). Note that the reply also begins with a:
>
> —¿A cuánto están las fresas?
>
> —A trescientas diez el kilo.
>
> —¿A cómo está la merluza?
>
> —A dos mil.

costar (v.i.) = to cost
barato, -a = cheap
caro, -a = expensive

Es muy barato. = ¡Qué barato!
Es muy caro. = ¡Qué caro!

> Note how both the question and the answer refer to the price of the characteristic quantity in which those articles are sold: un kilo, un litro, una docena...

4. Use one of the following expressions, in the appropriate form, to give your opinion about the prices you hear:

es barato – es muy barato es caro – es muy caro

FOR EXAMPLE:

—Las postales, doscientas pesetas. —Son muy caras.

5. Listen again to the prices from the previous exercise. This time give your opinion by using one of the following expressions in the appropriate form:

¡Qué barato!   ¡Qué caro!

FOR EXAMPLE: —Las postales, doscientas pesetas.   —¡Qué caras!

● ●

(II)

Una botella de agua mineral, por favor .

A bottle of mineral water, please.

Déme un sello, por favor.

Could I have [i.e. "Give me"] a stamp, please?

This is how to ask for things in shops.

NOTE:

un kilo	– medio kilo
un litro	– medio litro
una docena	– media docena

jamón (m) = ham
queso (m) = cheese

The expressions for asking for things in shops are the same as those you already know from Unit 8 for asking for things in general: un…, por favor or déme un…, por favor:

> Un kilo de tomates, por favor.
> Déme una botella de vino tinto, por favor.

Remember that it is also possible to ask for something by using a question:

> ¿Me da un sello de 25 pesetas?

6. Answer the greeting which you hear, and then ask the shop-keeper for the articles detailed below. For example:

> TAPE: —Buenos días. ¿Qué desea?
> YOU: —Buenos días. Doscientos gramos de jamón, por favor.
> OR —Buenos días. Déme doscientos gramos de jamón.
> OR —Buenos días. ¿Me da doscientos gramos de jamón?
> 1. Doscientos gramos de jamón.
> 2. Una lata de atún.
> 3. Un kilo de merluza.
> 4. Una docena de huevos.
> 5. Un trozo de tarta de chocolate.
> 6. Media docena de pasteles.
> 7. Un sobre y dos sellos de 30 pesetas.

In some service encounters (food shops, bars, cafés, filling stations) you can ask for things by using the expression póngame (or pónganos if there is more than one person):

> Póngame medio kilo de naranjas.
>
> Pónganos dos cafés solos.
>
> Póngame dos mil pesetas de gasolina.

You can also use the corresponding question:

> ¿Me pone doscientos gramos de jamón?
>
> ¿Nos pone una cerveza?

Remember that in these situations it is also possible to ask for things simply by giving the name of the article in question:

> Medio kilo de naranjas.
>
> Dos cafés solos.
>
> Dos mil pesetas de gasolina.
>
> Doscientos gramos de jamón.

REMEMBER:

póngame	➙	¿me pone?
pónganos	➙	¿nos pone?

☞ 10.7

7. Answer the greeting you hear, and then ask the shopkeeper for the articles below. For example:

> TAPE: —Buenos días. ¿Qué desea?
>
> YOU: —Buenos días. Póngame doscientos gramos de jamón, por favor.
>
> OR —Buenos días. ¿Me pone doscientos gramos de jamón?

1. Doscientos gramos de jamón.
2. Una lata de atún.
3. Una botella de vino tinto.
4. Un bocadillo de queso.
5. Dos kilos de naranjas.

N.B. In shops which sell articles other than food (clothes shops, shoe shops, jewellers', travel agencies, bookshops, record shops, and so on), begin your request with quería:

> Quería unos pantalones blancos.
>
> Quería un reloj.

8. We would not normally ask for some of the following things by using póngame. Put a cross against those things which would not normally be asked for in this way:

- una camisa
- una chaqueta
- un kilo de pescado
- un bocadillo de jamón
- una docena de huevos
- un trozo de tarta
- unos zapatos
- un bolso
- una botella de agua
- tres sellos
- un cepillo de dientes

SUMMARY:

Un café con leche.
Déme una merluza.
¿Me da una docena de huevos?
Póngame una merluza.
¿Me pone unas manzanas?

Quería una camisa blanca.
Quería un reloj.

Dos sellos.
Déme un cepillo de dientes.
¿Me da unas postales?

9. Use the slips of paper from Exercise 3 again. Imagine you are a shop assistant and that your partners are customers who want to buy various articles.

You can also ask for articles in shops, etc. by quoting the commercial brand name. Many everyday products of this kind are international. But bear in mind that commercial brand names may be pronounced differently in your own language and in Spanish even though they are spelled the same.

Note also that in filling stations we normally ask the attendant to fill the tank. Use the following:

> —¿Cuánto?
>
> —Lleno, por favor.   Fill the tank [i.e. "Full"], please.

YOU WILL FIND THE FOLLOWING USEFUL:

You already know how to ask permission to do something: ¿Puedo...?

Before buying an article of clothing you can ask to try it on:

probarse (v. i.) = to try on

¿Puedo probarme la camisa?   Can I try this shirt on?

WHEN YOU ARE SHOPPING YOU MAY HEAR THE FOLLOWING EXPRESSIONS:

¡Tome!	Here. [i.e. "Take."]
¿Para llevar?	To take away?
¿Se lo envuelvo?	Shall I wrap it for you?
¿Al contado?	In cash?
¿Al contado, o con tarjeta?	In cash or by credit card?

● ●

¿Cuántos sellos?   How many stamps?

This is how to ask the quantity of something.

Dos.   Two.

And this is how to reply.

10. Answer the questions you hear by giving a number from 1 to 10.

¿cuánto aceite?

¿cuánta leche?

¿cuántos libros?

¿cuántas botellas?

To ask the quantity of something, use cuánto, cuánta, cuántos or cuántas:

> ¿Cuánto dinero?
>
> ¿Cuántos sellos?

Note that it is not necessary to repeat the name of the article if it has already been mentioned. In the reply to the following question the word sellos does not appear:

> ¿Me da unos sellos?
>
> ¿Cuántos quiere?

You can answer questions with ¿cuánto? by using a number (dos, cinco, etc.) and words such as docena, kilo, gramo, litro, etc.:

> —¿Cuántos huevos?
>
> —Dos docenas.
>
> —¿Cuántas fresas quiere?
>
> —Medio kilo.

11. Listen to the tape and ask the quantity of each thing you hear. For example:

> TAPE: —Necesito naranjas.
>
> You: —¿Cuántas?

12. Imagine that you want to cook the following two dishes for four people. Look at the ingredients and then go and buy the ones you need. A partner should pretend to be the shopkeeper.

Meat and tomatoes:
  1 Kg. de carne
  1/2 Kg. de patatas
  tres tomates
  1/2 l. de agua
  medio vaso de aceite
  un poco de sal

Caramel custard:
  1/2 docena de huevos
  1 l. de leche
  80 g. de azúcar
  un limón

patata (f) = potato
limón (m) = lemon

13. Look again at the ingredients for the dishes in the previous exercise. Imagine that you are preparing them in the kitchen and a partner is helping you. Ask him/her for the things you need by saying:

> You: —Necesito huevos.
>
> PARTNER: —¿Cuántos quieres?
>
> You: —Media docena.

todo = everything

Remember that in Unit 8 you learned how to ask how much something is when you want to pay:

> —¿Cuánto es?
>
> —Mil pesetas.

If you have bought several articles, ask in the following way:

> ¿Cuánto es todo?

IV EN LA CAFETERíA IN A CAFÉ

14. Follow the text in the pictures below as you listen to the tape.

saber (v. i.) = to know

If you do not know the name of something, ask by using ¿cómo se llama?:

¿Cómo se llama eso?

If you do not know the answer to a question you are asked, say so by using one of the following expressions:

No sé.

No lo sé.

Remember also how to ask and express where a product comes from. Use ¿de dónde? followed by the verb ser:

—¿De dónde es esta camisa?

—Italiana.

—¿De dónde son estas fresas?

—De Huelva.

QUESTION WORDS:

¿qué?	¿cuánto?
¿quién?	¿cómo?
¿cuál?	¿dónde? ☞ 12

What is that called?

This is how to ask what something is called.

I don't know.

This is how to say you do not know the answer to a question.

Where are the baby cuttle fish from?
(They are) Andalusian. From Málaga.

This is how to express where a product is from.

15. Your partners ask you the names of the following things in Spanish. Answer by giving the names. If you do not know the name, say so by using one of the expressions which you have already learned.

1   2   3   4   5   6

Solutions: 1. Kiwi 2. Paella 3. Jamón 4. Botón charro 5. Palillos 6. Bota

16. Look at the solutions to the previous exercise. Now ask your partners where those things are from. If they do not know, they should say so.

They are from the following places:

6. España   5. China   (España) Salamanca .4

3. España   2. Valencia (España)   1. Nueva Zelanda

Y POR FIN...

17. Listen to the dialogue on the tape before reading the text below. Then try to fill in the blanks. Finally, listen to the tape again to see whether what you have put is correct.

ASSISTANT: —Buenos días.

CUSTOMER: —Buenos días. ¿⬚⬚⬚ da unas fresas?

ASSISTANT: —Sí, señor. ¿⬚⬚⬚⬚ quiere?

CUSTOMER: —¿A cuánto ⬚⬚⬚⬚⬚⬚ ?

ASSISTANT: —A trescientas cincuenta el kilo.

CUSTOMER: —¡Qué ⬚⬚⬚⬚⬚⬚ !

ASSISTANT: —¿Cómo dice?

CUSTOMER: —⬚⬚⬚ son muy caras. Bueno, póngame ⬚⬚⬚⬚ kilo.

ASSISTANT: —Muy bien. Medio ⬚⬚⬚ de fresas.

CUSTOMER: —Póngame también naranjas.

ASSISTANT: —¿Cuántas quiere?

CUSTOMER: —Dos kilos ⬚⬚⬚ medio.

ASSISTANT: —De acuerdo.

CUSTOMER: —Oiga, ¿cómo se ⬚⬚⬚⬚ eso?

ASSISTANT: —¿Esto? Chirimoyas.

CUSTOMER: —Déme una, por favor.

ASSISTANT: —Tome.

CUSTOMER: —Gracias. ¿⬚⬚⬚⬚⬚ es todo?

ASSISTANT: —Quinientas veinticinco pesetas, señor.

CUSTOMER: —Tome. Muchas gracias. Adiós.

ASSISTANT: —Adiós, hasta luego.

18. Listen to this excerpt from the TV Comedy in which Óscar goes shopping. Then answer the following questions.

1. Write here the names of the fruits which Oscar asks the price of.

2. Oscar asks for a certain quantity of one kind of fruit. Write that quantity here.

3. Write here, in figures, the prices you heard on the tape.

● **TRANSCRIPTION OF THE TV DIALOGUES**
¿CUÁNTO CUESTA ÉSTE?

Presentación. Primera parte

PRESENTADOR: Un kilo de fresas, por favor. Hola, ¿qué tal? Estoy haciendo compras. ¿Quieren una fresa?
¡Qué buenas! ¿A cuánto están las naranjas?
DEPENDIENTA: A 120 pesetas el kilo.
PRESENTADOR: ¿A cuánto están las naranjas? ¡Muy bien! A 120 pesetas el kilo. Póngame tres kilos. Y déme también dos limones.
MADRE: ¡Niño! ¡No toques eso!

Telecomedia. Primera parte

JUAN: ¿Cómo se llama eso?
DEPENDIENTA: Tarta de Santiago. ➡
JUAN: ¿Quieres?
CARMEN: Sí.
JUAN: Déme dos trozos.
CARMEN: ¡Ahhhh!
JUAN: ¿Qué pasa?
CARMEN: Mira. Necesito un regalo para Óscar.
DEPENDIENTA: ¿Quieren ustedes una tarta?
JUAN: ¿Cuánto...?
DEPENDIENTA: Dos mil doscientas.
JUAN: ¿Dos mil doscientas? Qué caro, ¿no?
DEPENDIENTA: Es el día de los enamorados, hombre...
JUAN: Ah, no, no. Las tartas no, esto. ¿Cuánto es esto?
DEPENDIENTA: Perdón. Son doscientas veinte pesetas.
CARMEN: ¿Qué hora es?
JUAN: La una menos cuarto.
CARMEN: Es muy tarde. Van a cerrar las tiendas.
➡ Vamos.
JUAN: ¿A dónde? ¿Qué vas a comprar?
CARMEN: El regalo.
JUAN: ¿El regalo?
CARMEN: Sí, hombre, el regalo para Óscar.
JUAN: Ah, claro, el día de los enamorados.
DEPENDIENTE: Buenos días. ¿Qué desea?
ÓSCAR: Un libro de cocina.

Presentation. Part One

PRESENTER: A kilo of strawberries, please. Hello. How are you? I'm doing some shopping. Would you like a strawberry? They are delicious! How much are the oranges?
ASSISTANT: 120 pesetas a kilo.
PRESENTER: How much are the oranges? Very good! 120 pesetas a kilo. Give me three kilos, please. And give me two lemons as well, please.
MOTHER: Child! Don't touch that!

TV Comedy. Part One

JUAN: What is that called?
ASSISTANT: Santiago tart. ➡
JUAN: Would you like some?
CARMEN: Yes.
JUAN: Give me two pieces, please.
CARMEN: Oh!
JUAN: What's the matter?
CARMEN: Look. I need a present for Óscar.
ASSISTANT: Do you want a gateau?
JUAN: How much ...?
ASSISTANT: Two thousand two hundred.
JUAN: Two thousand two hundred? That's expensive, isn't it?
ASSISTANT: It's Valentine's Day [i.e. "the day of those in love"], you know.
JUAN: Ah, no, no. Not the gateaux. This. How much is this?
ASSISTANT: I'm sorry. That's two hundred and twenty pesetas.
CARMEN: What time is it?
JUAN: A quarter to one.
CARMEN: It's very late. The shops are going to close.
➡ Come on.
JUAN: Where to? What are you going to buy?
CARMEN: The present.
JUAN: The present?
CARMEN: Yes, of course, the present for Óscar.
JUAN: Ah, of course. St. Valentine's Day.
ASSISTANT: Good morning? Can I help you?
ÓSCAR: A cookery book.

11. ¿Cuánto cuesta éste?

DEPENDIENTE: Enseguida. Venga, por favor... Aquí están. Éste es muy bueno.

ÓSCAR: "Cocina fácil".

DEPENDIENTE: Y éste es de cocina italiana.

ÓSCAR: ¿Cuánto cuesta éste?

DEPENDIENTE: Ése, 1300 pesetas.

ÓSCAR: Me lo llevo.

DEPENDIENTE: Muy bien. ¿Algo más, señor?

ÓSCAR: No, no, gracias.

SEÑOR: Este libro no...

ÓSCAR: Déme el otro libro, por favor. Por favor, ¿a cuánto están las fresas?

DEPENDIENTE: A 175 pesetas el kilo.

ÓSCAR: Póngame kilo y medio. Y las manzanas, ¿qué precio tienen?

DEPENDIENTE: Éstas 110, éstas, 130 y aquéllas, 160.

NIÑO: Mamá, quiero manzanas.

MADRE: Espera un momento.

NIÑO: Mamá, quiero manzanas.

MADRE: ¡Vale! Espera.

DEPENDIENTE: ¿Cuántas quiere?

NIÑO: Quiero una.

MADRE: ¡Niño!

Presentación. Segunda parte

PRESENTADOR: ¿De dónde es ese queso? ¿Es francés?

DEPENDIENTE: No, es de Cabrales. ➡ ③

SEÑORA: Quería unos pantalones para este niño.

DEPENDIENTA: ¿Qué niño?

SEÑORA: ¿Dónde está?

NIÑO: ¿Qué es esto?

PRESENTADOR: Queso.

NIÑO: ¿Y esto qué es?

PRESENTADOR: No sé.

NIÑO: ¿Es colonia?

PRESENTADOR: No lo sé...

NIÑO: Sí, sí. Es colonia.

Telecomedia. Segunda parte

ÓSCAR: Póngame medio kilo de almejas.

PESCADERO: ¿Éstas o ésas?

ÓSCAR: Éstas. No, no. Ésas...

PESCADERO: ¿Algo más?

ÓSCAR: Dos kilos de mejillones.

PESCADERO: Son estupendos.

ÓSCAR: No, no, no, sólo un kilo, por favor.

PESCADERO: ¿Algo más?

ÓSCAR: Sí, dos kilos de langostinos. ¿De dónde son?

PESCADERO: De Galicia. ➡ ④

ÓSCAR: ¿De Galicia? ¿De verdad?

PESCADERO: Sí, señor.

ÓSCAR: ¿Cuánto es todo?

PESCADERO: Ocho mil setecientas cincuenta.

ÓSCAR: Muy barato.

PESCADERO: ¿Qué le pongo, señora?

DEPENDIENTE: Buenos días, ¿qué desean?

CARMEN: Por favor, ¿dónde está la ropa de deportes?

DEPENDIENTE: Por aquí... Aquí está.

CARMEN: Quería un chándal de caballero ➡ ⑤ pero...

DEPENDIENTE: ¿Para usted?

JUAN: No, no. Es para su novio.

DEPENDIENTE: Ah, ya...

CARMEN: Toma, pruébatelos, por favor.

ASSISTANT: Right away. Come this way, please. Here they are. This one is very good.

ÓSCAR: "Cooking made easy".

ASSISTANT: And this one is on Italian cooking.

ÓSCAR: How much is this one?

ASSISTANT: That one (is) 1300 pesetas.

ÓSCAR: I'll take it.

ASSISTANT: Very well. Anything else, sir?

ÓSCAR: No, no thank you.

MAN: This book isn't ...

ÓSCAR: Give me the other book, please. Excuse me, please. How much are the strawberries?

ASSISTANT: 175 pesetas a kilo.

ÓSCAR: Give me a kilo and a half, please. And the apples? How much are they?

ASSISTANT: These (are) 110, these (are) 130, and those (are) 160.

CHILD: Mummy, I want some apples.

MOTHER: Wait a moment.

CHILD: Mummy, I want some apples.

MOTHER: OK! Wait a moment.

ASSISTANT: How many does he want?

CHILD: I want one.

MOTHER: Child!

Presentation. Part Two

PRESENTER: Where is that cheese from? Is it French?

ASSISTANT: No, it's from Cabrales. ➡ ③

WOMAN: I want(ed) some trousers for this boy.

ASSISTANT: What boy?

WOMAN: Where is he?

BOY: What's this?

PRESENTER: It's cheese.

BOY: And what's this?

PRESENTER: I don't know.

BOY: Is it eau de cologne?

PRESENTER: I don't know.

BOY: Yes. Yes. It's cologne.

TV Comedy. Part Two

ÓSCAR: Give me half a kilo of clams.

FISHMONGER: These or those?

ÓSCAR: These. No, no. Those ...

FISHMONGER: Anything else?

ÓSCAR: Two kilos of mussels.

FISHMONGER: They are delicious.

ÓSCAR: No, no. Just one kilo, please.

FISHMONGER: Anything else?

ÓSCAR: Yes, two kilos of king prawns. Where are they from?

FISHMONGER: From Galicia. ➡ ④

ÓSCAR: From Galicia? Really?

FISHMONGER: Yes, sir.

ÓSCAR: How much is everything?

FISHMONGER: Eight thousand seven hundred and fifty.

ÓSCAR: Very cheap.

FISHMONGER: What would you like, madam?

ASSISTANT: Good morning. Can I help you?

CARMEN: Where is the sports wear, please?

ASSISTANT: This way ... Here it is.

CARMEN: I want(ed) a man's track suit ➡ ⑤ but ...

ASSISTANT: For you?

JUAN: No, no. It's for her boyfriend.

ASSISTANT: Ah, I see.

CARMEN: Here. Try them on, please.

JUAN: ¿Yo?

CARMEN: Sí... ¡por favor!

DEPENDIENTE: El probador ➡ ⑥ está allí. Bonito, ¿verdad? Es italiano.

CARMEN: ¿Italiano?

DEPENDIENTE: Sí, mire.

CARMEN: ¡Es feísimo! Toma éstos también.

DEPENDIENTA: ¿Qué desea?

ÓSCAR: Mmmm... no lo sé.

DEPENDIENTA: Este traje es estupendo. Muy barato. Y estas gafas también son muy baratas. Y esto, y esto... El probador está allí. Venga, por favor.

CARMEN: Ése es muy bonito, pero... pruébate éste.

JUAN: Carmen, por favor...

CARMEN: Un momento. Es el último, de verdad.

DEPENDIENTE: ¿Éste?

CARMEN: Sí, sí. Ése. Ése es estupendo para Óscar. Sí, sí, sí. Para Óscar, estupendo. Sí, sí.

ÓSCAR: ¡No, no, no, no, no! Ése no. Es feísimo.

CARMEN: ¡Óscar!

JUAN: ¡Óscar!

DEPENDIENTE: ¿Óscar?

DEPENDIENTA: ¿Óscar?

ÓSCAR: ¡Óscar!

PRESENTADOR: Adiós. Hasta luego.

JUAN: Me?

CARMEN: Yes. Please!

ASSISTANT: The fitting room ➡ ⑥ is over there. It's nice, isn't it? It's Italian.

CARMEN: Italian?

ASSISTANT: Yes. Look.

CARMEN: It's horrible! Take these too.

ASSISTANT: Can I help you?

ÓSCAR: Um ... I don't know.

ASSISTANT: This suit is very nice. Very cheap. And these goggles are very cheap too. And this, and this ... The fitting room is over there. This way, please.

CARMEN: That one is very nice but ... try this one on.

JUAN: Carmen, please ...

CARMEN: Just a moment. This is the last one, really.

ASSISTANT: This one?

CARMEN: Yes, yes. That one. That one is just right for Óscar. Yes, yes, yes. For Óscar, very nice. Yes, yes.

ÓSCAR: No, no, no! Not that one. It's horrible.

CARMEN: Óscar!

JUAN: Óscar!

ASSISTANT: Óscar?

ASSISTANT: Óscar?

ÓSCAR: Óscar!

PRESENTER: Goodbye. See you soon.

● **CAJÓN DE SASTRE**

① Pastelerías (cake shops) are very common in Spain. There is great variety in the names of tartas and pasteles. You will soon learn the most common ones if you travel round the country and have a sweet tooth.

② Both the times of meals and opening hours for shops are peculiar to Spain. Although there are variations according to season, kind of establishment and region, normal opening hours are as follows: from 10.00am to 1.30pm, and from 4.30pm to 8.00pm. But many shops now have all-day opening, and there are some which stay open all night.

③ There is a great variety of cheeses in Spain. Those made with sheep's milk are characteristic of many parts of the country. Queso de Cabrales, made with cow's milk, is an excellent cheese from the north of Spain. It is a strong cheese both in taste and smell.

④ Galicia is an autonomous region in the north-west of Spain. It has a mountainous green landscape and wet climate. The people speak their own language, gallego, which is closely related to Portuguese. Among other things, it is famous for its mariscos (sea food).

⑤ The word caballero, meaning 'man' or 'gentleman' in English, is not very frequent in modern Spanish. However, it can be seen in the expression ropa de caballero (as against ropa de señora). It is also used to indicate men's toilets.

⑥ You will often come across this word or the plural in large shops and department stores. It is obviously related to the word probarse, which you already know.

11. ¿Cuánto cuesta éste?

● **USTED YA PUEDE...**

ask the price of something;	¿Qué precio tiene esta camisa? ¿Cuánto cuesta el billete? ¿A cuánto están las fresas?
and understand the reply;	Cuatro mil quinientas. Ochocientas pesetas. A doscientas el kilo.
ask for something in a shop;	Una botella de leche, por favor. Déme dos sellos. ¿Me da dos postales? Póngame medio kilo de fresas. ¿Me pone unas naranjas? Quería una camisa blanca.
ask and express the **quantity of** something;	—¿Cuántos huevos? —Media docena. —¿Cuánto jamón? —Doscientos gramos. —¿Cuántos? —Doce.
ask the name of something;	¿Cómo se llama eso?
say that you do not know **the an-**swer to a question;	No sé. No lo sé.
ask where something is **from;**	¿De dónde son esas fresas?
and reply.	Son de Huelva. Es italiana.

In this unit you will learn how to express someone's occupation, age, marital status, possessions, and so on. You will also learn a new way of asking others to do things.

Ⅰ

profesión (f) = profession, occupation	
enfermero, -a = nurse	
camarero, -a = waiter, waitress	
recepcionista (m. y f.) = receptionist	
policía (m. y f.) = policeman, -woman	
periodista (m. y f.) = journalist	
vendedor, -a = vendor	
empleado, -a = employee	
abogado, -a = lawyer	

Mi papá es policía. My father is a policeman.

This is how to express someone's occupation.

¿Qué es tu mamá? What is your mother?

And this is how to ask for the same information.

¿Quién es?: is used to ask someone's identity.

¿Qué es?: is used to ask someone's occupation. ☞ 12

To ask someone's occupation, use the expression ¿qué es?:

¿Qué es tu padre?

¿Qué es su novia?

To express someone's occupation, use the appropriate form of the verb ser followed immediately by the name of the occupation:

Elena es médico.

Son mecánicos.

1. Listen and repeat when you hear the signal.

2. Listen to the tape and number the following occupations according to the order in which you hear them.

cartero   enfermero

periodista   camarera

vendedora   profesora

empleado de banco

3. Look at the pictures below. Say what occupations these people have. EXAMPLE: Antonio es médico.

4. Mime typical activities of some occupations. Ask your partners: ¿Qué soy? **They should try to guess the answer.**

● ●

 (II)

Tiene dos coches, pero no tiene casa.

He has two cars, but he hasn't got a house.

This is how to express someone's possessions.

casete (m) = cassette recorder

pelota (f) = ball

5. Listen and repeat when you hear the signal.

TENER: Present tense

tengo

tienes

tiene

tenemos

tenéis

tienen

☞ 16.3

To express someone's possessions, use a form of tener followed immediately by the name of the thing possessed. If you want to indicate the quantity, add words such as un, dos, tres, cinco, muchos, etc.:

¿Tienes dinero?	Have you got any money?
Tienen un barco.	They have a boat.
Tiene muchos relojes.	He has a lot of clocks / watches.

Tengo un libro. → Tengo uno.   ☞ 7.1

6. In each picture below there are two people. One has something which the other does not have. Say what each person has or does not have. Then write the sentences in the spaces provided below.

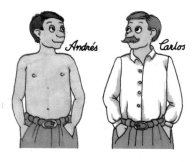

Andrés no tiene

Carlos tiene

7. The voice on the tape will ask if you have certain things. Give a true answer.

EXAMPLE: ¿Tiene usted coche?

Sí, sí tengo. / No, no tengo.

8. Ask your partners about their possessions (for example, ¿tienes coche?). They should reply.

The verb tener can also be used to express natural properties and characteristics rather than strictly material possessions:

—¿Tiene usted hijos?

—Sí, tengo dos.

La habitación no tiene baño.

garaje (m) = garage

jardín (m) = garden

pila (f) = battery

puerta (f) = door

ventana (f) = window

año (m) = year

mes (m) = month

9. Look at the pictures here. Listen to the tape and indicate whether what you hear is true or false.

1. T F   2. T F   3. T F

4. T F   5. T F

10. Do as shown in the following example:

EXAMPLE: una hora - minutos ➡ Una hora tiene sesenta minutos.

Un año semanas.	Un mes días.
Un año meses.	Una semana días.
Un año días.	Un día horas.

11. The voice on the tape will ask you some questions about yourself. Give true answers.

● ●

¿Vienen ustedes conmigo?   Will you come with me?

This is how to ask someone to do something.

¿Vienen conmigo?

You already know (from Unit 6) that there are some forms of the verb (para, pare, parad, paren i. e. imperative forms) which are used to get people to do things:

    Vengan conmigo.

    Compra el periódico.

You can achieve the same effect in a more polite, tentative way by phrasing what you say as a question:

    ¿Vienen conmigo?

    ¿Compras el periódico?

    ¿Traes unas cervezas?

cerrar (v. i.) = to close   **traer (v. i.)** = to bring   **encender (v. i.)** = to turn/switch

luz (f) = light   **apagar** = to turn/switch off   on

12. Listen and repeat when you hear the signal.

13. Imagine that you want the people in the situations below to do certain things.

FOR EXAMPLE:

Your son is going out. You want him to buy the newspaper.

To your son: ¿Compras el periódico?

First give the sentences orally. Then write them in the spaces provided. The basic expressions you need are as follows:

apagar la radio	coger el paquete
encender la luz	traer la maleta
cerrar la puerta	llevar los niños a casa
abrir la ventana	

1. You want a friend from work to take your children home. Ask him/her.

To your friend:

2. You are in a room in a hotel. Phone the receptionist and ask him to bring you your suitcase.

To the receptionist:

3. You are trying to speak to someone on the phone, but your children have the radio on. Ask them to turn it off.

To your children:

4. You are in a shop. There is a parcel on the counter. Ask your husband/wife to pick it up.

To your husband/wife:

5. You enter your house, and the light is off. Ask your friend to switch it on.

To your friend:

6. The room where you are having a meeting with some colleagues is full of smoke. You need some fresh air.

To a colleague sitting near the window:

7. Someone has left the door of your office open. Ask your secretary to close it.

To your secretary:

14. Revise your vocabulary. Use the verbs which you already know to ask or tell your partners to do various things. They should do what you tell them.

EXAMPLE: JUGAR

Juega conmigo.

Jugad conmigo.

¿Juegas conmigo?

¿Jugáis conmigo?

12. Pero, ¿qué es usted?

EN UN CUMPLEAÑOS AT A BIRTHDAY PARTY

15. Follow the text in the pictures below as you listen to the tape.

—And how old is he?
—Twenty-three. He's only 23 years old.

—Is he married?
—No, he's single.

edad (f) = age

This is how to express someone's age.

This is how to express someone's marital status.

To ask someone's age, use the expression ¿cuántos años...? with the corresponding form of the verb tener:

    ¿Cuántos años tienes?

You can answer the question simply by giving the number of years:

    Veinticinco.

    Dieciocho.

To express someone's age, use a form of the verb tener followed by the number of years:

    Tengo treinta y siete años.

    Julia tiene doce años.

16. Listen and repeat when you hear the signal.

17. Look at these identity cards and write how old each person is.

estado civil (m)	= marital status
casado, -a	= married
soltero, -a	= single
viudo, -a	= widower, widow
divorciado, -a	= divorced

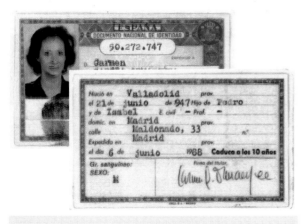

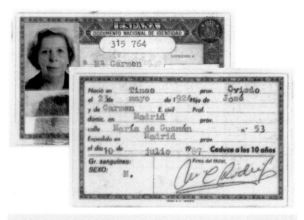

18. Now say how old each person is.

19. Imagine that your partners have become children again. Ask them how old they are. (Remember to use the tú forms of the verb.) They should answer. Then your partners become old people. Again, ask them how old they are (using the usted forms of the verb). They should answer.

To ask and express someone's marital status, use the verb estar followed by one of the expressions from the vocabulary list at the top of this page:

> Están divorciados.
>
> —¿Está usted casado?   —No, no. Estoy soltero.

12. Pero, ¿qué es usted?

20. Express the marital status of the following people:

1. Elena. Her husband died last year.
2. Lali and Pepe. They got married in 1981.
3. Alfonso. His wife left him and he got a divorce.
4. Luisa. She has just met her first boy-friend.
5. Ana and Andrés. They got married yesterday.

21. Ask your partners their marital status. They should answer.

REMEMBER: ¿nombre?
¿apellidos?
¿dirección?
¿teléfono?

To fill in forms and official documents you will be asked the following questions:
Occupation: ¿profesión?
Age: ¿edad?
Marital status: ¿estado civil?

22. Fill in the form with your personal details:

datos personales

NOMBRE
APELLIDOS
DIRECCIÓN
TELÉFONO
PROFESIÓN
EDAD
ESTADO CIVIL

23. Listen to the official on the tape. Answer with your personal details.

Y POR FIN...

24. Answer the following questions about the Presentations and the TV Comedy from the television unit.

1. ¿Tiene hijos Luis Cánovas?
2. Luis Cánovas habla con dos niños.
   ¿Qué es la mamá de los niños?
3. Carmen y Juan están comprando algo. ¿Qué es?
4. Juan y Carmen miran un libro. ¿Qué tiene el libro?
5. ¿Cuánto cuesta el libro?
6. ¿Qué tiene Carmen en el bolso?
7. ¿Luis Cánovas está soltero?
8. ¿Cuántos años tiene Luis Cánovas?

● **TRANSCRIPTION OF THE TV DIALOGUES**
"PERO, ¿QUÉ ES USTED?"

Presentación. Primera parte

PRESENTADOR: Hola, ¿qué tal? ¿Vienen conmigo? Hoy estamos en Granada. ¿Vamos? ¿Me cobras este libro ➡ ① , por favor?
VENDEDOR: ¿Tiene usted casete?
PRESENTADOR: Sí.
VENDEDOR: Tome. Un regalo.
PRESENTADOR: Muchas gracias.
VENDEDOR: ¿Tiene usted hijos?
PRESENTADOR: No, no tengo. No tengo hijos.
VENDEDOR: Pues tome.
SEÑORA: Oiga, yo sí tengo hijos. Estos dos.
VENDEDOR: ¿Qué es tu papá?
NIÑO 1: Es policía.
VENDEDOR: Toma.
NIÑO 2: Mi mamá es enfermera.
VENDEDOR: Tooooma…
SEÑORA: Gracias.
NIÑO 1: Y mi abuelo es…
SEÑORA: ¡Niiiño!
PRESENTADOR: Su papá es policía. Su mamá es enfermera… Y usted, ¿qué es? ¿Qué profesión tiene? ➡ ② Ah, muy bien.

Telecomedia. Primera parte

CARMEN: ¿Me enseña algún libro sobre la Alhambra? ➡ ③
DEPENDIENTE: Sí, un momento. Mire.
JUAN: ¿Tiene fotos?
CARMEN: Sí. Mira.
JUAN: ¿Tiene más libros?
DEPENDIENTE: Sí, sí, un momento. Mire éstos.
JUAN: Éste es estupendo.
CARMEN: Es verdad. Bueno, pues nos llevamos éste.
JUAN: ¿Cuánto es?
DEPENDIENTE: Mil seiscientas pesetas.
JUAN: Por favor, ¿dónde está la entrada?
DEPENDIENTE: Allí al fondo.
JUAN: Muchas gracias.
DEPENDIENTE: De nada. Adiós.
CARMEN: Hasta luego. ¿Compras tú las entradas? ➡ ④
JUAN: Sí.
CARMEN: ¿Tienes dinero?
JUAN: Sí, sí, tengo. Sí, sí, tengo…
CARMEN: Toma. Ahora sí tienes dinero.
JUAN: Mira, Carmen.
CARMEN: ¿Quién es ése?
JUAN: Es un rey de la Alhambra.
CARMEN: ¿Cómo se llama?
JUAN: Yúsuf. Y éste es su hijo. Muhammad.
GUÍA: Buenos días. ¿Es usted el profesor Serrano?
JUAN: Sí, sí. Soy yo.
GUÍA: Yo soy su guía.
CARMEN: Huy, ¿ya son las cuatro?
JUAN: Mi compañera, Carmen Alonso.
CARMEN: Encantada.
GUÍA: ¿Qué tal? ¿Es usted profesora también?
CARMEN: No, no, soy de televisión.
GUÍA: Bueno, ¿empezamos la visita?

Presentation. Part One

PRESENTER: Hello. How are you? Would you like to come with me? Today we are in Granada. Shall we go? Would you charge me for this book, ➡ ① please?
VENDOR: Have you got a cassette recorder?
PRESENTER: Yes.
VENDOR: Here. A present (for you).
PRESENTER: Thank you very much.
VENDOR: Have you any children?
PRESENTER: No, I haven't. I haven't any children.
VENDOR: Well, here you are.
WOMAN: Excuse me. I have children. These two.
VENDOR: What is your father?
1ST CHILD: He's a policeman.
VENDOR: Here.
2ND CHILD: My mother is a nurse.
VENDOR: Here; take this.
WOMAN: Thank you.
1ST CHILD: And my grandfather is …
WOMAN: Child!
PRESENTER: His father is a policeman. His mother is a nurse. And you? What are you? What is your occupation? ➡ ② Ah! Very good.

TV Comedy. Part One

CARMEN: Could you show me some book on the Alhambra? ➡ ③
ASSISTANT: Yes, one moment. Look.
JUAN: Has it any photographs?
CARMEN: Yes. Look.
JUAN: Have you any more books?
ASSISTANT: Yes, yes. One moment. Look at these.
JUAN: This one is very good.
CARMEN: That's true. Good. Well, we'll take this one.
JUAN: How much is it?
ASSISTANT: One thousand six hundred pesetas.
JUAN: Please, where is the entrance?
ASSISTANT: Over there.
JUAN: Thank you very much.
ASSISTANT: Not at all. Goodbye.
CARMEN: Goodbye. Can you buy the tickets? ➡ ④
JUAN: Yes.
CARMEN: Have you got any money?
JUAN: Yes. Yes, I have. Yes. Yes, I have.
CARMEN: Here. Now you do have some money.
JUAN: Look, Carmen.
CARMEN: Who is that?
JUAN: It's a king of the Alhambra.
CARMEN: What's his name?
JUAN: Yúsuf. And this is his son, Muhammad.
GUIDE: Good morning. Are you Mr Serrano, the teacher?
JUAN: Yes, yes. That's me [i.e. "Am I"].
GUIDE: I am your guide.
CARMEN: Oh! Is it already four o'clock?
JUAN: My colleague, Carmen Alonso.
CARMEN: How do you do.
GUIDE: Hello. How are you? Are you a teacher too?
CARMEN: No. No. I work in television.
GUIDE: Well, shall we begin the visit?

JUAN: Sí, sí, vamos.
GUÍA: ¿Tiene usted máquina de fotos?
CARMEN: Sí, tengo una en el bolso.
GUÍA: Va a necesitarla.
CARMEN: Parece Yúsuf, el rey.
GUÍA: Vamos a la Sala de los Reyes.

Presentación. Segunda parte

NIÑO 1: ¿Estás casado?
PRESENTADOR: No, no. Estoy soltero.
NIÑO 1: Mi mamá sí está casada.
NIÑO 2: Mi papá también está casado.
NIÑO 1: Claro.
NIÑO 2: ¿Cuántos años tienes?
PRESENTADOR: Treinta y seis.
NIÑO 1: Yo tengo siete años. Y mi hermano, cuatro.
NIÑO 2: Cuatro.
PRESENTADOR: Cuatro. Yo tengo…, treinta y seis años. ¿Y usted, cuántos tiene?

Telecomedia. Segunda parte

GUÍA: Tengo recuerdos muy agradables de esta sala.
CARMEN: ¡Qué bonita! Pero hay mucha gente, ¿no?
GUÍA: Sí, demasiada.
JUAN:: Bueno, pero éste es su trabajo, ¿no? Es usted guía.
GUÍA: A veces.
CARMEN: Pero, ¿no es usted guía de la Alhambra?
GUÍA: Bueno. La Alhambra es como mi casa.
JUAN: ¿Qué te pasa?
CARMEN: No sé, tengo algo en los ojos.
JUAN: ¿Quieres un pañuelo?
CARMEN: Gracias.
JUAN: ¿Ya?
CARMEN: Sí, sí, vamos.
GUÍA: Esta sala se llama "Sala de los Reyes" por las pinturas del techo.
CARMEN: ¿Me das el libro?
JUAN: ¿Qué vas a mirar?
CARMEN: La foto del rey. Son iguales.
JUAN: Iguales, iguales, no… éste tiene barba y el guía no.
CARMEN: Pero mira los ojos. Son los mismos. ¿Cuántos años tiene el rey en el libro?
JUAN: Treinta y cinco años.
GUÍA: Vamos a visitar otra sala.
CARMEN: ¿Cuántos años tiene usted?
GUÍA: Treinta y cinco. Esta es la sala de "Las dos Hermanas". Es la preferida de Yasmina.
CARMEN: ¿Yasmina? ¿Su mujer? ¿Está usted casado?
GUÍA: Sí, estoy casado.
CARMEN: ¡Ya está! Mira. Lee esto.
JUAN: "El Rey y Yasmina…"
CARMEN: ¿Ves? La mujer del rey también se llama Yasmina, como la del guía.
JUAN: ¡Dame el libro!
GUÍA: ¡Profesor!
CARMEN: ¡Juan! ¡Juan!
JUAN: ¿Dónde estás?
CARMEN: ¡Estamos aquí!
GUÍA: La escalera está allí.
CARMEN: ¿Qué te pasa?
JUAN: Nada.

JUAN: Yes, let's go.
GUIDE: Have you got a camera?
CARMEN: Yes, I have one in my handbag.
GUIDE: You will need it.
CARMEN: He looks like Yúsuf, the king.
GUIDE: Let's go to the Room of the Kings.

Presentation. Part Two

1ST CHILD: Are you married?
PRESENTER: No, no. I'm single.
1ST CHILD: My mother is married.
2ND CHILD: My father is married too.
1ST CHILD: Of course he is.
2ND CHILD: How old are you?
PRESENTER: Thirty-six.
1ST CHILD: I'm seven years old. And my brother is four.
2ND CHILD: Four.
PRESENTER: Four. I am thirty-six years old. And you? How old are you?

TV Comedy. Part Two

GUIDE: I have very pleasant memories of this room.
CARMEN: Isn't it nice! But there are a lot of people here, aren't there?
GUIDE: Yes, too many.
JUAN: Yes, but this is your work, isn't it? You are a guide.
GUIDE: Sometimes.
CARMEN: But, aren't you a guide in the Alhambra?
GUIDE: Well, the Alhambra is my home as it were.
JUAN: What's the matter?
CARMEN: I don't know. I have something in my eyes.
JUAN: Would you like a handkerchief?
CARMEN: Thank you.
JUAN: (Is it better) now?
CARMEN: Yes, let's go.
GUIDE: This room is called the Room of the Kings because of the paintings on the ceiling.
CARMEN: Could you give me the book?
JUAN: What are you going to look at?
CARMEN: The photo of the king. They are identical.
JUAN: Not exactly identical. This man has a beard and the guide hasn't.
CARMEN: But look at the eyes. They are the same. How old is the king in the book?
JUAN: Thirty-five.
GUIDE: Let's go and visit another room.
CARMEN: How old are you?
GUIDE: Thirty-five. This is the room of the Two Sisters. It is Yasmina's favourite.
CARMEN: Yasmina? Your wife? Are you married?
GUIDE: Yes, I'm married.
CARMEN: That's it! [i.e. "Already it is!"] Look. Read this.
JUAN: "The King and Yasmina …"
CARMEN: You see? The king's wife is also called Yasmina, like the guide's (wife).
JUAN: Give me the book!
GUIDE: Sir! [i.e. "Teacher!"]
CARMEN: Juan! Juan!
JUAN: Where are you?
CARMEN: We are over here!
GUIDE: The stairs are over there.
CARMEN: What's the matter?
JUAN: Nothing.

GUÍA: Esos son los jardines del Generalife. Maravillosos, ¿verdad?
JUAN: Conoce usted muy bien este lugar...
CARMEN: ¿Dónde está?
JUAN: Aquí pasa algo raro.

SEÑOR: Perdone, ¿es usted el profesor Serrano?
JUAN: Sí, sí, soy yo, ¿y usted?
SEÑOR: Yo soy el guía.
CARMEN: ¿El guía?
SEÑOR: Sí, son las cuatro. Tenemos una cita a esta hora.

CARMEN: ¡Las cuatro!
JUAN: ¡Las cuatro!

PRESENTADOR: Adiós.

GUIDE: Those are the gardens of the Generalife. Marvellous, aren't they?
JUAN: You know this place very well ...
CARMEN: Where is he?
JUAN: Something strange is going on here.

MAN: Excuse me. Are you Mr Serrano, the teacher?
JUAN: Yes, yes. That's me. And you?
MAN: I am the guide.
CARMEN: The guide?
MAN: Yes. It's four o'clock. We have an appointment at this time.

CARMEN: Four o'clock!
JUAN: Four o'clock!

PRESENTER: Goodbye.

● **CAJÓN DE SASTRE**

① Notice the expression ¿me cobra?. This follows the pattern of the kind of requests which you have learned to express in this unit. It is used to call the attention of shop assistants, barmen, etc. when you want to pay.

② You have already learned two ways of inquiring as to someone's occupation: ¿qué es tu hermano? and ¿profesión?. Here is a third (more formal and less frequent) possibility for asking for the same information, combining the word profesión and the verb tener: ¿qué profesión tiene usted?

③ Remember that the Arabs lived in the Iberian Peninsula for several centuries (from the 8th century to the end of the 15th century). There are many important historic buildings and artistic treasures from this period, especially in the southern half of the country. One of the most representative is the Alhambra in Granada, which has been declared part of the world's heritage. You will see that most of the television unit takes place in this beautiful building.

④ The word entrada has two different meanings. One corresponds to 'entrance' or 'way in' in English (the opposite in this case being salida - 'exit' or 'way out'). The other meaning corresponds to English 'ticket' (cinema, theatre, places of entertainment in general).

12. Pero, ¿qué es usted?

● USTED YA PUEDE...

ask someone's occupation;	¿Qué es tu mamá?
and reply;	Empleada de banco.
express someone's occupation;	Soy periodista. Es profesora.
express possessions, properties and characteristics of people and things;	¿Tienes dinero? Tienen un barco. Tengo dos hijos. La casa no tiene ventanas.
ask someone to do something;	¿Abres la puerta? ¿Vienes conmigo?
ask someone's age;	¿Cuántos años tiene usted?
and reply;	Noventa.
indicate someone's age;	Tengo cuarenta y dos años.
ask someone's marital status and reply;	¿Está usted casada? No, estoy soltera.
express someone's marital status;	Estoy divorciado.
answer questions to fill in official forms (occupation, age, marital status).	¿Profesión? ¿Edad? ¿Estado civil?

In this unit you will learn how to ask whether shops and bars, etc. have what you want to buy. You will learn how to indicate where you live, what hotel you are staying at, and so on. You will also learn further expressions for interacting with other people.

I

Hay cerveza alemana.   We sell German beer. [i.e. "There is ..."]

This is how shops and bars, etc. indicate things they have for sale.

¿Tienen ensalada?   Do you have salad?

And this is how to ask for the same information.

rosa (f) = rose

hojas de reclamaciones (f. pl.) = complaints forms

paella (f) = paella

asado, -a = roast

1. Listen and put a cross against the following sentences as you hear them on the tape.

1. Hay cerveza alemana. ░
2. ¿Tienen ensalada? ░
3. ¿Tiene rosas rojas? ░

4. Hay hojas de reclamaciones. ░
5. Tenemos paella. ░
6. Hay pollos asados. ░

To ask whether a shop, bar, etc. sells what you want to buy, use hay, which you already know, followed by the name of the article in question:

¿Hay fresas?

You can also use tiene or tienen (from the verb tener), which, again, you already know:

¿Tienen camisas italianas?

Hay and tenemos (from the verb tener) are used in bars, shops, etc. to indicate articles they have for sale:

Hay queso de Burgos.

Hoy tenemos paella.

---

peine (m) = comb

bañador (m) = swimming costume

2. Imagine that you go into the shop on the camping site where you are spending your holidays in order to buy the articles on the list on the left. Ask whether they have those things.

EXAMPLES:

¿Tienen peines?   ¿Tienen colonia?
¿Hay peines?   ¿Hay colonia?

Pañuelos
Peine
Cepillos de dientes
Bañador
Jabón
Colonia
Helados
Camisa
Corbata

¿Tienen fres__as__?

Fresas = count noun - plural.

¿Tienen leche?

Leche = non-count noun - singular.

---

3. Imagine that you have a slight problem on your holiday and have to go to the chemist's. Ask whether they have something for:

la garganta, el estómago, las muelas, la cabeza, los ojos, los oídos.

EXAMPLE:

¿Tiene algo para la garganta?

THIS WILL HELP YOU: algo para... ➙ something for ...

garganta (f) = throat   **cabeza (f)** = head
estómago (m) = stomach   **ojo (m)** = eye
muela (f) = back tooth   **oído (m)** = ear

II **Vivo cerca de la estación.** I live near the station.

This is how to indicate the general area where you live.

Estoy en el Hotel Excelsior. I am (staying) at the Excelsior Hotel.

And this is how to indicate where you are staying temporarily.

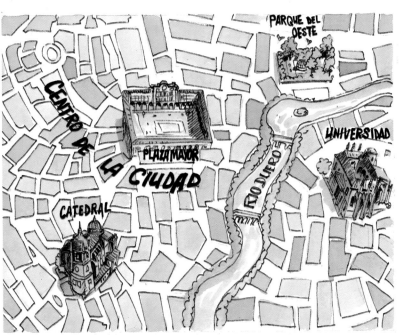

centro (m)	= centre
catedral (f)	= cathedral
universidad (f)	= university
río (m)	= river

cerca de	= near
lejos de	= a long way from
al lado de	= next to
enfrente de	= opposite
detrás de	= behind
delante de	= in front of

4. Listen and repeat when you hear the signal.

In Unit 2 you learned how to give your exact address, indicating la calle, el número, el piso and la puerta:

C/ Goya, 9, 4.° derecha.

But it is not always necessary to be so precise. You can also use expressions such as:

Vivo en el centro de la ciudad.

Ana vive cerca de la universidad.

5. Make sentences which express where the following people live. Use one element from each column below.

EXAMPLE: Ana vive cerca del río.

Ana	vivo	en	el centro.
Mis padres y yo	vives	cerca de	la catedral.
Tú	vive	lejos de	la universidad.
Antonio y María	vivimos	al lado de	el río.
Yo	vivís	delante de	el aeropuerto.
Vosotros	viven	enfrente de	la comisaría.
Mis abuelos		detrás de	la estación.
Mis amigos			una farmacia.
Enrique			la Plaza Mayor.

6. Ask one another where you live. You should reply by giving the approximate location.

EXAMPLE: —¿Dónde vives?

            —Detrás de la estación.

alojarse = to stay at (hotel, etc.)

To express where you are staying temporarily, use either alojarse (which is more formal) or estar:

            —¿Dónde se aloja usted?

            —En el hotel Escala, cerca de la universidad.

            —¿Dónde vives?

            —No soy de aquí. Estoy en un hotel. Al lado de la estación.

7. You will hear a conversation which has been adapted from the TV unit. Listen and try to follow without looking at the transcription.

8. Listen again to the conversation from the previous exercise. Write what is said in the spaces provided below. Stop the tape as often as you need.

AMPARO: —

JUAN: —

AMPARO: —

JUAN: —

AMPARO: —

JUAN: —

AMPARO: —

JUAN: —

9. Dramatise the dialogue from Exercise 7.

III | **EN EL RESTAURANTE** | AT A RESTAURANT

10. Read the text in the pictures below as you listen to the tape.

Well, then, I am going to have a salad for the first course; and for the second course, a steak.

This is how to order in a restaurant.

Private. Keep out.
I am sorry. I don't speak Spanish.
Do you speak German?

The bill, please.

This is how to ask someone to speak to you in another language.

This is how to ask for the bill in a restaurant.

Learn the following expressions.
To order in a restaurant, use de primero..., de segundo..., which may be preceded by voy a tomar:

> De primero, ensalada, y de segundo, ternera.

> Voy a tomar, de primero, ensalada, y de segundo, ternera.

Ask for drinks as follows: para beber...:

> Para beber, vino blanco. **To drink, (I'll have) white wine.**

To ask for the bill, say:

> La cuenta, por favor.

> ¿Me trae la cuenta, por favor?

cerdo (m) = pork
ternera (f) = beef
cordero (m) = lamb
filete (m) = steak
patatas fritas (f. pl.) = chips
tortilla (f) = omelette

entremeses (m. pl.) = hors d'oeuvres
postre (m) = dessert
frito, -a = fried
al horno = roast, baked
a la plancha = grilled

11. Look at the menu and place your order, using the expressions which you have learned here.

13. ¿Tiene algo para la garganta?

> If someone speaks to you in a language which you recognise but do not understand, say lo siento, no hablo… You can ask people to speak in another language by adding ¿habla usted…?:
>
> Lo siento, no hablo inglés, ¿habla usted español?

12. Dramatise the dialogue from Exercise 10.

> If you visit any Spanish-speaking country you will come across a wide variety of signs and public notices. Here are some which you will find useful:

1 = Private.
2 = Pull.
3 = Push.
4 = No smoking.
5 = Smoking not allowed.

6 = No dogs.
7 = Enter without knocking.
8 = Keep out.
9 = Please do not touch.

Y POR FIN…

You have now reached the end of the first stage of the Course. You have learned many different things in Spanish. Luis Cánovas will now help you to see how much you have achieved.

For example, you can now understand many things when people speak to you.

13. Listen to the tape and answer in Spanish.

1. What does Luis Cánovas give his friend?
2. Luis suggests they do something together. What?
3. Does his friend accept?
4. Does she like the present?

14. Read the sentences below. Then listen to the tape and indicate whether what you hear is true or false.

1. Luis Cánovas says hello at the beginning and then goodbye at the end.   T   F
2. There is a young couple to his left.   T   F
3. It is half-past two.   T   F
4. Luis Cánovas is going to have white wine.   T   F
5. He is going to have fruit for his dessert.   T   F
6. A young man and woman are talking in a very loud voice.   T   F
7. The restaurant is not very nice.   T   F
8. At one table there are three men.   T   F

You can also express many things in Spanish.

15. Use what you have learned in Spanish so far to express the following:

1. Introduce yourself.
2. It is morning. Greet someone.
3. Someone has given you a present. Thank him/her for it.
4. It is Friday evening. You say goodbye to a colleague at work. You will not see him/her again until Monday.
5. You enter a particular building because you want to see Mr. García. You ask a janitor if el señor García is available.
6. You are visiting a friend's house for the first time. You want to go to the toilet but you don't know where it is. Ask.

7. You and your husband/wife arrive at a hotel. Ask for a room.
8. You are in a cafeteria and want to have a coffee. Order one.
9. You have had a small party at home. When the party breaks up there is a jacket left lying on a chair. Ask who it belongs to.
10. You want to know if there is a king in Spain. Ask.
11. You are eating an ice-cream and a small boy is watching you enviously. Offer him un poco.
12. Tell your dog to come to you.
13. Someone says something to you but you do not understand. Ask them to repeat what they said.

14. You have finished your drink in a bar. You want to pay.
15. Ask for the bill in a restaurant.
16. You want to know the identity of el chico de la derecha. Ask someone standing next to you.
17. Now you want to know that person's nationality. Ask.

18. You have come out without a watch and want to know the time. Ask.

19. You go into a fruit shop and ask for un kilo de fresas.

20. You go into a clothes shop and ask for una camisa.

21. You see an object on the table in front of you but you don't know how to say it in Spanish. Ask what it is called.

22. You have just been introduced to someone. Ask him what his occupation is.

23. You now know the same person a little more. Ask his age.

24. You are having a meal at the home of some Spanish friends. You need the salt. Ask for it.

25. You enter a restaurant because you want to try paella. Ask if they have it.

You have also learned how to express many things in writing, as you will see in the following exercise.

EN UNA OFICINA   AT THE OFFICE

16. Listen and fill in the blanks in the following conversation:

LUIS CÁNOVAS: ¿ ▢▢▢▢ ▢▢▢▢ ?
SECRETARIA: ¡Pase! ¡Adelante! ¿ ▢▢▢ ▢▢▢ ▢▢▢ ?
LUIS CÁNOVAS: ▢▢▢ Luis Cánovas.
SECRETARIA: ¡Ah! ¿ ▢▢▢ ▢▢▢ D. Luis Cánovas? ▢▢▢ , por favor. Un momento, ¿ ▢▢▢ ▢▢▢ ? ¡Ah, sí, ▢▢▢ cajón! ▢▢▢ usted. ▢▢▢ , por favor.
LUIS CÁNOVAS: Mil, ▢▢▢ , tres mil, ▢▢ mil ▢▢▢ .
SECRETARIA: ¿De acuerdo?
LUIS CÁNOVAS: Sí, sí, ▢▢▢ . Perdón, ¿ ▢▢▢ ▢▢ Escudero?
SECRETARIA: ▢▢▢ . ▢▢▢ preguntar. Marta, ▢▢▢ Ana, ¿ ▢▢▢ ▢▢▢ ? ¿ ▢▢▢ verlo ahora el señor Cánovas? Gracias, Marta. ▢▢▢ y puede ▢▢▢ usted ahora. ▢▢▢ piso, ▢▢▢ puerta ▢▢▢ ▢▢▢ .
LUIS CÁNOVAS: ▢▢▢ gracias ▢▢▢ , señorita. ▢▢▢ .
SECRETARIA: Adiós. ▢▢▢ , ▢▢▢ piso, prime…
LUIS CÁNOVAS: Sí, sí. No ▢▢▢ . Muchas gracias. ▢▢▢ ▢▢▢ .

contar (v. i.) = to count
todo, -a = all
preguntar = to ask
recordar (v. i.) = to remember

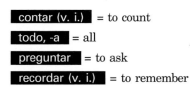

17. Dramatise the conversation from the previous exercise.

EN UN HOTEL   AT A HOTEL

18. Listen and fill in the blanks in the following conversation:

LUIS CÁNOVAS: Buenos días.

RECEPCIONISTA: Buenos días. ¿Qué ▒▒▒▒▒▒▒▒▒▒ ?

LUIS CÁNOVAS: Una ▒▒▒▒▒▒▒▒▒▒▒▒▒▒ .

RECEPCIONISTA: Un momento. ¿La quiere ▒▒▒▒▒▒▒▒▒▒▒ ?

LUIS CÁNOVAS: Sí, sí, claro, con baño.

RECEPCIONISTA: Muy bien. ▒▒▒▒▒▒▒ número 48. ¿▒▒▒▒▒▒▒ , por favor?

LUIS CÁNOVAS: Luis Cánovas.

RECEPCIONISTA: Cánovas...¿▒▒▒▒▒▒▒▒▒▒▒▒▒▒▒ , con "b" o con "v"?

LUIS CÁNOVAS: Con "v", con "v".

RECEPCIONISTA: ¿▒▒▒▒▒▒▒▒▒▒ su ▒▒▒▒▒▒▒▒▒▒ ?

LUIS CÁNOVAS: Un momento. ¿Dónde ▒▒▒▒▒▒ ?¡Ah, sí, está ▒▒▒▒▒ ! ▒▒▒▒▒ usted.

RECEPCIONISTA: Habitación 48.

LUIS CÁNOVAS: Sí, sí. Perdón, ¿▒▒▒▒▒▒▒▒▒ en la habitación?

RECEPCIONISTA: Sí, señor. ▒▒▒▒▒▒ las habitaciones ▒▒▒▒▒ teléfono y ▒▒▒▒▒ usted llamar directamente.

LUIS CÁNOVAS: Habitación 48, ¿verdad?

RECEPCIONISTA: Sí, ▒▒▒▒▒▒▒▒▒▒▒▒▒ . Señor, oiga, señor Cánovas.

LUIS CÁNOVAS: ¿Sí?

RECEPCIONISTA: ¿▒▒▒▒▒ suyas ▒▒▒▒ gafas?

LUIS CÁNOVAS: ¿▒▒▒▒▒ gafas?

RECEPCIONISTA: Éstas, ¿no ▒▒▒▒▒ ?

LUIS CÁNOVAS: No, no son ▒▒▒▒ .

RECEPCIONISTA: ¿De ▒▒▒▒▒▒▒ son?

LUIS CÁNOVAS: No sé. Mías no.

RECEPCIONISTA: Perdone. ▒▒▒▒▒▒▒ .

LUIS CÁNOVAS: No se ▒▒▒▒▒▒ . Hasta luego.

19. Dramatise the conversation from the previous exercise.

13. ¿Tiene algo para la garganta?

EN UNA REUNIÓN,
A LA MESA

HAVING A MEAL
WITH SOME FRIENDS

20. Listen and fill in the blanks in the following conversation:

LUIS CÁNOVAS: Oye, chico, ¿ _____ _____ la sal, por favor?

CHICO: Aquí no _____. Lo _____. Un momento. Oiga, señor, ¿me _____ usted la _____?

SEÑOR MAYOR: _____.

CHICO: _____ usted. _____ _____ la sal.

LUIS CÁNOVAS: Ah, muchas gracias. Perdona, _____ también un cuchillo.

CHICO: Por aquí no hay _____.

LUIS CÁNOVAS: Mira, _____, a la derecha _____ uno. Por favor, _____.

CHICO: Ese es _____ señor _____ _____ barba.

LUIS CÁNOVAS: ¿De _____ es?

CHICO: Del de la _____.

LUIS CÁNOVAS: ¡Ah! Vale, vale. Camarero, por favor, oiga ¿ _____ _____ un cuchillo? No tengo.

CAMARERO: ¡Huy! Perdone usted. Tome; su _____, señor.

LUIS CÁNOVAS: Muchas gracias.

CAMARERO: De nada.

CHICO: ¿ _____ está _____?

LUIS CÁNOVAS: Esto.

CHICO: Sí, claro. ¿Pero qué _____ _____?

LUIS CÁNOVAS: ¿ _____? Una ensalada tropical.

CHICO: ¿Y qué es una ensalada tropical?

LUIS CÁNOVAS: Esto. ¿ _____ un poco? Toma, _____.

CHICO: ¡Mm! ¿Puedo _____ _____ poco?

LUIS CÁNOVAS: Claro, claro. _____.

21. Dramatise the conversation from the previous exercise.

TRANSCRIPTION OF THE TV DIALOGUES
"¿TIENE ALGO PARA LA GARGANTA?"

Presentación. Primera parte

PRESENTADOR: Perdone.
CONDUCTOR: No hablo español… ¿Habla usted alemán?
PRESENTADOR: Lo siento, no hablo alemán.
CONDUCTOR: Ah… sí, gracias.
PRESENTADOR: Hola.
FLORISTA: Hola. ¿Qué desea?
PRESENTADOR: ¿Tiene rosas rojas?
FLORISTA: Sí. Mire.
PRESENTADOR: ¿Y margaritas? ¿Tiene margaritas? Ah, sí. Están allí. ¿Puede enviar un ramo a mi hotel? Margaritas y rosas.
FLORISTA: Sí, ¿dónde vive usted?
PRESENTADOR: En el Hotel Excelsior.
FLORISTA: Hotel…
PRESENTADOR: Sí, cerca de la Alhambra.

Telecomedia. Primera parte

AMPARO: ¡Hola, Pedro, amor mío! Perdón. Tú no eres Pedro.
JUAN: Pues no. Y lo siento.
AMPARO: Y yo también… Perdón. Me llamo Amparo.
JUAN: Encantado. Yo soy Juan.
AMPARO: No eres de Granada, ¿verdad?
JUAN: No, no.
AMPARO: ¿Pero vives aquí?
JUAN: No, vivo en Madrid. ¿Y tú, dónde vives?
AMPARO: Aquí, cerca de la estación. ¿Estás de vacaciones?
JUAN: No, estoy trabajando; pero… hoy voy a visitar la ciudad.
AMPARO: Hombre, pues yo también. Encantada.
JUAN: Adiós, encantado.
PEDRO: ¡Amparo!
AMPARO: ¡Pedro!
PEDRO: Toma.
AMPARO: Gracias.
CARMEN: ¿Quién es ésa?
JUAN: ¿Qué te pasa?
CARMEN: La garganta…
JUAN: ¿La garganta?
CARMEN: No voy a ir con vosotros.
JUAN: ¿Quéeeee? Oye, la visita es importante.
CARMEN: Ya, ya… Pero voy a ir a una farmacia. Necesito algo…
JUAN: ¿Te espero en el autobús?
CARMEN: No, no, no me esperes. Vete tú solo.
JUAN: ¿Yo solo? Hombre, no.
CARMEN: Pero yo no puedo hablar. Mira, yo voy a la farmacia.
JUAN: ¿Voy contigo?
CARMEN: No, hombre. Tú tranquilo.
JUAN: Bueno.
FARMACÉUTICO: Así que duerme usted mal, ¿no?
GUÍA: Cuatro días sin dormir. Cuatro.
FARMACÉUTICO: Bueno. Pues con esto va a dormir usted muy bien. Pero cuidado, tome una sola ¿eh? Una sola al día.
GUÍA: Gracias. ¿Cuánto es?
FARMACÉUTICO: Son quinientas diez pesetas.
CARMEN: ¿Tiene algo fuerte para la garganta?
FARMACÉUTICO: ¿Cómo?
CARMEN: Unas pastillas para la garganta.

Presentation. Part One

PRESENTER: Excuse me.
DRIVER: I don't speak Spanish. Do you speak German?
PRESENTER: I'm sorry. I don't speak German.
DRIVER: Ah, yes. Thank you.
PRESENTER: Hello.
FLORIST: Hello. Can I help you?
PRESENTER: Do you have any red roses?
FLORIST: Yes. Look.
PRESENTER: And daisies? Have you any daisies? Ah, yes. There they are. Could you send a bunch to my hotel? Daisies and roses.
FLORIST: Yes. Where do you live?
PRESENTER: In the Excelsior Hotel.
FLORIST: Hotel …
PRESENTER: Yes. Near the Alhambra.

TV Comedy. Part One

AMPARO: Hello, Pedro, my love! I'm sorry. You aren't Pedro.
JUAN: Well, no. And I'm sorry.
AMPARO: So am I. I'm sorry. My name is Amparo.
JUAN: How do you do. My name is Juan.
AMPARO: You aren't from Granada, are you?
JUAN: No; no.
AMPARO: But you live here?
JUAN: No. I live in Madrid. And you? Where do you live?
AMPARO: Here. Near the station. Are you on holiday?
JUAN: No, I'm working; but… today I'm going to visit the city.
AMPARO: "Hombre!" So am I. It's been a pleasure to meet you.
JUAN: Goodbye. It's been a pleasure.
PEDRO: Amparo!
AMPARO: Pedro!
PEDRO: Here.
AMPARO: Thank you.
CARMEN: Who is that?
JUAN: What's the matter?
CARMEN: My throat.
JUAN: Your throat?
CARMEN: I'm not going to go with you.
JUAN: Whaaat? The guided tour is important.
CARMEN: Yes, I know. But I'm going to go to a chemist's. I need something …
JUAN: Shall I wait for you on the coach?
CARMEN: No, no. Don't wait for me. You go alone.
JUAN: By myself? No!
CARMEN: But I can't speak. Look, I'm going to the chemist's.
JUAN: Shall I come [i.e. "go"] with you?
CARMEN: No! Don't worry.
JUAN: OK.
CHEMIST: So you are not getting any sleep, are you?
GUIDE: Four days without sleeping. Four.
CHEMIST: Well, you'll sleep very well with this. But be careful. Take only one, OK? Only one a day.
GUIDE: Thank you. How much is it?
CHEMIST: That's five hundred and ten pesetas.
CARMEN: Have you got something strong for my throat?
CHEMIST: Sorry?
CARMEN: Some tablets for my throat.

FARMACÉUTICO: Ah, ya. Espere un momento. Son trescientas veinte pesetas.

CARMEN: ¿Cuántas tomo?

FARMACÉUTICO: Dos cada dos horas.

CARMEN: Gracias.

AMPARO: Hola, Juan.

JUAN: Hola.

AMPARO: Vamos en el mismo autobús, ¡qué bien!

JUAN: Sí, estupendo.

GUÍA: ¡Hombre! ¡Vamos a viajar juntos! Sí, ya sé... la garganta. Vamos, tómese una pastilla y siéntese, por favor.

TURISTA 1: Lo siento, no hablo inglés. Lo siento, sólo hablo español. Ah, perdón. Es bonita Granada, ¿verdad? Muy bo-ni-ta Gra-na-da, ¿no?...

Presentación. Segunda parte

CAMARERO: Buenos días. ¿Qué desea?

PRESENTADOR: Voy a tomar de primero una ensalada.

CAMARERO: Muy bien. Hoy tenemos un pescado estupendo. ➡ ①

PRESENTADOR: Pues no sé... ¿Hay besugo?

CAMARERO: Sí, señor. Estupendo.

PRESENTADOR: Tienen besugo. Muy bien, de segundo besugo al horno.

CAMARERO: ¿Y de beber?

PRESENTADOR: ¿Tienen cerveza alemana?

CAMARERO: Sí, señor. Mire.

PRESENTADOR: Pues tráigame ahora una cerveza alemana, y para el besugo, vino blanco.

CAMARERO: Muy bien, señor.

PRESENTADOR: ¿Me trae la cuenta, por favor?

CAMARERO: ¿La cuenta? Enseguida, señor.

PRESENTADOR: Adiós, buenas tardes.

CAMARERO: Adiós, buenas tardes.

Telecomedia. Segunda parte

TURISTA: ¡Vamos! ¡Esas caras!

GUÍA: Señorita. Vamos a cenar. Es la hora. Señorita...

CARMEN: ¡Cumpleaños feliz!

GUÍA: Tranquila. ¿Le pasa algo? Enseguida llegamos al restaurante.

TURISTA 1: ¿Tienen cordero?

CAMARERO: Sí, muy bueno.

TURISTA 1: Pues yo voy a tomar de primero unos espárragos, y de segundo, cordero.

TURISTA 2: Yo voy a tomar unas ostras de primero y... ¿Hay besugo?

CAMARERO: Hoy tenemos un pescado estupendo.

TURISTA 2: Bueno. Y besugo de segundo.

TURISTA 3: Yo de primero quiero unos calamares y de segundo...

CAMARERO: Muy bien. ¿Qué desean ustedes?

TURISTA 3. ¿Tienen gambas fritas?

CAMARERO: No, hoy no tenemos.

GUÍA: ¿Tienen gazpacho?

CAMARERO: Sí, señor.

GUÍA: Pues yo, de primero gazpacho. ¿Y usted qué va a tomar?

CARMEN: Una cama, por favor.

CAMARERO: ¿Camarones? ¡Marchando!

GUÍA: Ésas no son sus pastillas; ésas son las mías. Las suyas son éstas. Lo siento mucho. No sé cómo... Lo siento, yo...

CHEMIST: Ah, yes. Just a moment. That's three hundred and twenty pesetas.

CARMEN: How many should I take?

CHEMIST: Two every two hours.

CARMEN: Thank you.

AMPARO: Hello, Juan.

JUAN: Hello.

AMPARO: We are going on the same coach. That's nice!

JUAN: Yes, very nice.

GUIDE: Well! We are going on the same trip. Yes, I know. Your throat. Come on. Take a tablet and have a seat, please.

TOURIST: I'm sorry. I don't speak English. I'm sorry; I only speak Spanish. Ah! Excuse me. Granada is beautiful, isn't it? Gra-na-da is ve-ry beau-ti-ful, isn't it?

Presentation. Part Two

WAITER: Good morning. What would you like?

PRESENTER: I'll have a salad for the first course.

WAITER: Very well. We have some lovely fish today. ➡ ①

PRESENTER: Well, I don't know. Do you have bream?

WAITER: Yes, sir. (It's) very good.

PRESENTER: They have bream. Very well, baked bream for the second course.

WAITER: And to drink?

PRESENTER: Do you have German beer?

WAITER: Yes, sir. Look.

PRESENTER: Well, bring me a German beer for now, and white wine with the bream.

WAITER: Very well, sir.

PRESENTER: Could you bring me the bill, please?

WAITER: The bill? Right away, sir.

PRESENTER: Goodbye. Good afternoon.

WAITER: Goodbye. Good afternoon.

TV Comedy. Part Two

TOURIST: Come on! Those faces!

GUIDE: Miss! We are going to have the evening meal. It's time. Miss! ...

CARMEN: Happy birthday to you!

GUIDE: Don't get upset. Is something wrong with you? We'll be in the restaurant right away.

1ST TOURIST: Do you have lamb?

WAITER: Yes. (It's) very good.

1ST TOURIST: Well, I'll have some asparagus for the first course, and some lamb for the second course.

2ND TOURIST: I'll have some oysters for the first course and ... Do you have bream?

WAITER: We have some very good fish today.

2ND TOURIST: OK. And bream for the second course.

3RD TOURIST: I'll have some squid for the first course and for the second course ...

WAITER: Very well. What are you going to have?

TOURIST: Do you have fried prawns?

WAITER: No, we don't have any today.

GUIDE: Do you have "gazpacho" [= cold soup]?

WAITER: Yes, sir.

GUIDE: Well, I'll have some "gazpacho" for the first course. And what are you going to have?

CARMEN: A bed, please.

WAITER: "Camarones?" [= kind of prawn] Right away!

GUIDE: Those aren't your tablets; those are mine. Yours are these. I'm very sorry. I don't know how ... I'm sorry. I ...

CARMEN: Voy a los servicios.
GUÍA: ¿Sola?
CARMEN: Claro. Sola.
GUÍA: Por favor, ¿me trae la cuenta? ➡ ②
CARMEN: ¡No puedo hablar! ¡No puedo hablar!
PRESENTADOR: Buenas noches. Buenas noches.

CARMEN: I'm going to the toilet.
GUIDE: Alone?
CARMEN: Alone, of course.
GUIDE: Could you bring me the bill, please? ➡ ②
CARMEN: I can't speak! I can't speak!
PRESENTER: Good night. Good night.

● CAJÓN DE SASTRE

① Pescado = fish (merluza = hake, besugo = bream, salmón = salmon, etc.) is an essential element in Spanish cooking, both at home and in restaurants. If you travel round Spain, try the many different varieties which you will find.

② The propina = tip is not obligatory in Spain but people frequently tip waiters, and so on, especially in restaurants. There are no hard and fast rules as to quantity or percentage. Nevertheless, if you are satisfied with the service, and so on, between 5 and 10 per cent of the total bill would be considered sufficient.

● USTED YA PUEDE...

ask whether shops and bars have what you want;	¿Tienen ensalada? ¿Hay paella?
and express the same information;	Tenemos cordero. Hay cerveza alemana.
express the approximate area in which you live;	Vivo cerca de la estación.
ask someone where he is staying temporarily;	¿Dónde se aloja usted? ¿Dónde estás?
and express the same information;	Estoy en un hotel.
order in a restaurant;	De primero... De segundo... De postre... Para beber...
ask for the bill in a restaurant;	La cuenta, por favor. ¿Me trae la cuenta, por favor?
ask someone to speak in another language;	Lo siento, no hablo inglés. ¿Habla usted español?
understand some signs and public notices.	Privado. Prohibido el paso. Perros no. etc.

GENDER

1. Common nouns in Spanish (i.e. those which are not proper nouns) must be either <u>masculine</u> or <u>feminine</u> in gender. For example, casa - house is feminine in gender and tren - train is masculine. In the vocabulary list for each unit and in the general vocabulary list at the back of the book you will find the following indications as to the gender of such nouns, (m) for <u>masculine</u> and (f) for <u>feminine</u>.

Masculine ending in:	Feminine ending in:
- O	- A
(nouns and adjectives)	
abogad<u>o</u> = lawyer perr<u>o</u> = dog alt<u>o</u> = tall	abogad<u>a</u> = (female) lawyer perr<u>a</u> = bitch alt<u>a</u> = tall
Consonant	- A
(adjectives of nationality and nouns)	
alemá<u>n</u> = German profeso<u>r</u> = teacher españo<u>l</u> = Spanish	aleman<u>a</u> = German profesor<u>a</u> = (female) teacher español<u>a</u> = Spanish

2. Most nouns referring to persons or animals, together with a large number of adjectives, have two forms: one for the feminine and one for the masculine.
It is important that you learn the basic patterns for the formation of the gender of these words in Spanish. They are as shown in the table on the left:

3. There are some nouns (among which are many indicating professions) together with some adjectives, which have only one form, valid for both the masculine and the feminine. These are indicated in the vocabulary list for each unit and in the general vocabulary list in the following way: (m. y f.).
In these cases the only formal indication of the gender of the noun or adjective is the agreement (or concord) which is seen in the form of other co-occuring words. For example:

<u>el</u> dentist<u>a</u> = the dentist   <u>la</u> dentist<u>a</u> = the (female) dentist
<u>el</u> médic<u>o</u> = the doctor   <u>la</u> médic<u>o</u> = the (female) doctor
<u>el</u> vestido azu<u>l</u> = the blue dress   <u>la</u> corbata azu<u>l</u> = the blue tie

4. You should remember that masculine plural forms may have two different meanings in Spanish, one referring to a set of exclusively masculine entities:

Tengo dos hij<u>os</u> y ninguna hija.   I have two sons and no daughter.
<u>Los</u> niñ<u>os</u> se llaman José y Pedro. The boys' names are José and Pedro.

and another inclusive meaning referring to a mixed set of both masculine entities and feminine entities:

Tiene cuatro hij<u>os</u>: dos niños y dos niñas.   He has four children: two boys and two girls.
<u>Los</u> niñ<u>os</u> se llaman María, Ana y José.   The children's names are María, Ana and José.

 GRAMMATICAL NUMBER IN NOUNS AND ADJECTIVES

Words whose singular form ends in:	form the plural by:
a vowel	adding -s
niñ<u>o</u> = boy cas<u>a</u> = house caf<u>é</u> = coffee pap<u>á</u> = daddy	niñ<u>os</u> = boys cas<u>as</u> = houses caf<u>és</u> = coffees pap<u>ás</u> = parents
a consonant	adding -es
alemá<u>n</u> = German españo<u>l</u> = Spanish ba<u>r</u> = bar ciuda<u>d</u> = city autobú<u>s</u> = bus	aleman<u>es</u> = German español<u>es</u> = Spanish bar<u>es</u> = bars ciudad<u>es</u> = cities autobus<u>es</u> = buses

1. Spanish words (nouns, adjectives, articles, possessives, demonstratives, etc.) vary in number i.e. they may occur in the singular (referring to a single entity) or in the plural (referring to more than one entity).

2. It is important that you learn the basic rules for the formation of the plural. These can be seen in the table on the left.

3. Remember that some words only occur in the plural. This is the case, for example, with gafas - glasses, entremeses - hors d'oeuvres, and so on. This is indicated in the vocabulary lists in each unit and in the general vocabulary list by means of (pl.).

❸ CONCORD

Those words which normally go together with a noun (adjectives, articles, possessives, demonstratives, etc.) must be used in the same gender as the noun i.e. they must agree with the noun. This is referred to as concord.

un chico italiano   una chica italiana
unos chicos italianos   unas chicas italianas

❹ ARTICLES

1. It is important that you learn the forms of the article in Spanish. These are as follows:

el   for the masculine singular: el niño = the boy
la   for the feminine singular: la niña = the girl
los for the masculine plural: los niños = the boys/the children
las for the feminine plural: las niñas = the girls

2. These words must agree with the words which they accompany, both with regard to gender (masculine or feminine) and with regard to number (singular or plural). You will have noticed this in the examples above.

3. Sometimes the noun may already have been mentioned and is omitted because it is taken as understood or is redundant. In such cases the articles will appear in the company of other classes of words, such as adjectives, possessives, and so on, or forming part of structures with de followed by a noun:

— ¿Qué camisa quieres?   — Which shirt do you want?
— La roja.   — The red one.

— Dame esas gafas, por favor.   — Give me those glasses, please.
— Éstas no son las tuyas; son   — These are not yours; they are
las mías.   mine.

— ¿Quién es Pedro?   — Which one is Peter?
— El chico de la derecha, el   — The boy on the right; the one with
de la camisa verde.   the green shirt.

4. Contracted forms: The masculine singular form of the article el is systematically fused with the prepositions a and de to form only one word, a + el becoming al and de + el becoming del:

Voy al cine.   I am going to the cinema.
Vienen del aeropuerto.   They are coming from the airport.

❺ DEMONSTRATIVES

1. Forms for the masculine and the feminine:

	singular			plural		
masculine	este	ese	aquel	estos	esos	aquellos
feminine	esta	esa	aquella	estas	esas	aquellas

2. Demonstratives must agree with the noun which they refer to, both in gender and in number:

este hotel   this hotel
esta calle   this street
estos hoteles   these hotels
estas calles   these streets

3. The forms are the same whether followed by a noun or not (though in the latter case the written form appears with an accent):

ese hotel   that hotel
Ése es mi hotel. That is my hotel.

—¿Qué camisa quieres?   — What shirt do you want?
—Ésa.   — That one.

4. Forms for the neuter:

esto	eso	aquello

These words are equivalent to <u>esta</u>, <u>esa</u> or <u>aquella</u> <u>cosa</u> respectively, and are used to refer to something when we do not know what it is, we cannot remember its name, or we do not wish to mention its name:

¿Qué es eso?	What is that?
¿Cómo se llama aquello?	What is that called?
Esto es una cámara de vídeo.	This is a video camera.

5. Spanish divides space into three separate planes: este, ese, aquel.

- este: the area which is relatively close to the speaker:
  Estas gafas no son mías.   These glasses are not mine.
- aquel: the area which is relatively distant from both the speaker and the hearer:
  Aquél es mi coche.   That (one) is my car.
- ese: an intermediate area or, alternatively, that area which is relatively close to the hearer:
  Esos zapatos son bonitos.   Those shoes are nice.

⑥ POSSESSIVES

1. The forms of possessives are determined by the following factors:

1.a. Who the possessor is (<u>yo</u> - I, <u>tú</u> - you, <u>él</u> - he, <u>nosotros</u> - we, etc.)
1.b. Whether the noun which expresses the thing possessed is masculine or feminine in gender, and also whether it is in the singular or in the plural with regard to number.
1.c. Whether it appears before the noun it refers to or not.

This gives rise to a complex variety of different forms. Do not worry if it takes you some time to fully familiarise yourself with them.

2. Forms:

Before the noun
(Example: mi hijo - my son)

Person of the possessor		with a singular noun		with a plural noun	
		masc.	fem.	masc.	fem.
yo	I	mi	mi	mis	mis
tú	you	tu	tu	tus	tus
él	he				
ella	she	su	su	sus	sus
usted	you				
nosotros-as	we	nuestro	nuestra	nuestros	nuestras
vosotros-as	you	vuestro	vuestra	vuestros	vuestras
ellos	they				
ellas	they	su	su	sus	sus
ustedes	you				

After the noun or when the noun is absent because it is taken as understood.
(Examples: Esa botella es <u>mía</u>.   That bottle is mine.
Ahí hay dos relojes;   There are two watches
dame el <u>mío</u>.   there; give me mine.)

Person of the possessor		with a singular noun		with a plural noun	
		masc.	fem.	masc.	fem.
yo	I	mío	mía	míos	mías
tú	you	tuyo	tuya	tuyos	tuyas
él	he				
ella	she	suyo	suya	suyos	suyas
usted	you				
nosotros-as	we	nuestro	nuestra	nuestros	nuestras
vosotros-as	you	vuestro	vuestra	vuestros	vuestras
ellos	they				
ellas	they	suyo	suya	suyos	suyas
ustedes	you				

3. Observations:

3.a. Examples of variation in form due to the fact that the possessive does not appear in front of a noun or the noun is taken as understood:

<u>Mi</u> café es éste; ése no es <u>mío</u>. My coffee is this one; that one is not mine.

—Hay un papel en <u>tu</u> coche.   — There is a piece of paper on your car.
—Y en el <u>tuyo</u> también.   — And on yours too.

Note that the change in form which we are discussing here does not affect <u>nuestro</u> and <u>vuestro</u>:

<u>Nuestra</u> cámara es ésta; ésa   Our camera is this one; that one is not
no es <u>nuestra</u>.   ours.

3.b. Examples of variation in form due to the gender and number of the thing possessed:

<u>Su</u> documentación y <u>sus</u> billetes, señor,	Your papers and your tickets, sir.
—El reloj es <u>suyo</u>, pero las gafas no.	—The watch is his, but the glasses are not.
—¡Ah!, ¿no son <u>suyas</u>?	— Oh! Aren't they his?

Variation in number (i.e. whether singular or plural) affects all forms, but variation in gender is not reflected in <u>mi, tu, su</u>. In no case is the form of possessives affected by the gender of the possessor:

<u>Su</u> documentación y <u>sus</u> billetes, señora.	Your papers and your tickets, madam.

3.c. Examples of variation in form brought about by the grammatical person of the possessor:

Toma <u>tu</u> bolígrafo y dame el <u>mío</u>.	Take your ballpoint and give me mine.
Ellos van a ir en <u>su</u> coche y nosotros en el <u>nuestro</u>.	They are going to go in their car and we (are going) in ours.
Usted en <u>su</u> habitación y vosotros en la <u>vuestra</u>.	You in your room and you in yours.

As you will have noticed, the forms for <u>él, ella, usted</u> coincide with those used for <u>ellos, ellas, ustedes.</u>

7   INDEFINITE EXPRESSIONS

Here are some frequent words which indicate indeterminate quantity :

1. Un, una	un cuchillo	a knife
	una cuchara	a spoon
Unos, unas	unos paquetes	some parcels
	unas cervezas	some beers

There is an obvious relationship between "<u>el</u> bar" and "<u>un</u> bar", for which reason un and una are also called indefinite articles. The forms of the plural are slightly different in nature and are more restricted in use. For the moment, use them only when instructed to do so.
If there is no noun accompanying un, this word adopts the form uno:

¿Tienes hijos?	Do you have any children?
Sí, tengo uno.	Yes, I have one.
¿Qué bolígrafo quieres?	What ballpoint do you want?
Uno rojo.	A red one.

2.Algún, alguna	algún bar	a/some bar
	alguna ciudad	a/some city
Algunos, algunas	algunos amigos	some friends
	algunas monedas	some coins
Algo (= alguna cosa)	Dame algo.	Give me something.
Alguien (only for people)	Hay alguien.	There is someone.

The corresponding negative forms are as follows:
Algún ➡ ningún, ninguna (**there is no plural**):

	ningún cuchillo	no knife
	ninguna cuchara	no spoon
Algo ➡ nada:	—¿Qué hay ahí?	— What is there there?
	— Nada.	— Nothing.
Alguien ➡ nadie:	—¿Quién hay ahí?.	— Who is there there?
	— Nadie	— No one.

Note how these negative forms combine with no:

<u>No</u> hay <u>ningún</u> cuchillo.	There is no knife.
<u>No</u> hay <u>nada</u>.	There is nothing.
<u>No</u> hay <u>nadie</u>.	There is nobody.

If there is no noun accompanying <u>algún</u> and <u>ningún</u>, these words adopt the forms alguno and ninguno **respectively**:

Necesito un taller. ¿Hay alguno por aquí?	I need a garage. Is there one near here?
— ¿Cuántos plátanos hay?	— How many bananas are there?
— Ninguno.	— None.

3. Poco	poco café	little coffee
Poca	poca leche	little milk
Pocos	pocos libros	few books
Pocas	pocas cervezas	few beers
Poco	come poco. (with a verb)	Eat little.
	poco grande (with an adjective)	not very big [i.e. "little big"]
	poco bien (with an adverb)	not very well [i.e. "little well"]
Un poco	un poco de leche	a little milk
	un poco grande	a little big
	descansa un poco.	Rest a little.

4. Mucho	mucho café	a lot of coffee
Mucha	mucha leche	a lot of milk
Muchos	muchos libros	a lot of books
Muchas	muchas cervezas	a lot of beers
Mucho	come mucho. (with a verb)	Eat a lot.
Muy	muy grande (with an adjective)	very big
	muy cerca (with an adverb)	very near

5. Todo	todo el libro	all the book
Toda	toda la leche	all the milk
Todos	todos los chicos	all the boys
Todas	todas las calles	all the streets
Todo (= todas las cosas)	dame todo.	Give me everything.

Note that the article appears with the forms of <u>todo</u> when there is an accompanying noun.

 NUMBERS

1	uno, -a	11	once	21	veintiuno, -a
2	dos	12	doce	22	veintidós
3	tres	13	trece	23	veintitrés
4	cuatro	14	catorce	24	veinticuatro
5	cinco	15	quince	25	veinticinco
6	seis	16	dieciséis	26	veintiséis
7	siete	17	diecisiete	27	veintisiete
8	ocho	18	dieciocho	28	veintiocho
9	nueve	19	diecinueve	29	veintinueve
10	diez	20	veinte	30	treinta

31	treinta y uno, -a	500	quinientos
40	cuarenta	600	seiscientos
50	cincuenta	700	setecientos
60	sesenta	800	ochocientos
70	setenta	900	novecientos
80	ochenta	1.000	mil
90	noventa	2.000	dos mil
100	cien	3,000	tres mil
101	ciento uno, -a	1.000.000	un millón
200	doscientos, -as	2.000.000	dos millones
300	trescientos		
400	cuatrocientos		etc.

Observations:

a) Note that all numbers which end in <u>uno</u> vary according to gender, and the same is also true of hundreds:

veintiuna pesetas	- veintiún bolígrafos
doscientas treinta pesetas	- doscientos bolígrafos

b) Note the difference between <u>veintiuno</u>, on the one hand, and <u>treinta y uno, cuarenta y uno,</u> etc., on the other. The word <u>y</u> is always obligatory when tens are combined with units:

    58 = cincuenta y ocho
    479 = cuatrocientos setenta y nueve
    1.683 = mil seiscientos ochenta y tres

However, the word <u>y</u> cannot appear in other cases:

    101 = ciento uno
    470 = cuatrocientos setenta
    2.008 = dos mil ocho

c) Before a noun, <u>uno</u> becomes <u>un</u>:

    veintiún libros

d) Note that where English uses a comma to separate thousands from hundreds (viz. 2,000; 30,000) Spanish uses a full-stop (viz. 2.000; 30.000).

El Rincón de la Gramática

9 **ORDINAL NUMBERS**

primero (1.º), primera (1ª)	sexto (6.º), sexta (6.ª)
segundo (2.º), segunda (2.ª)	séptimo (7.º), séptima (7.ª)
tercero (3.º), tercera (3.ª)	octavo (8.º), octava (8.ª)
cuarto (4.º), cuarta (4.ª)	noveno (9.º), novena (9.ª)
quinto (5.º), quinta (5.ª)	décimo (10.), décima (10.ª)

Before a noun primero and tercero become primer, tercer:

primer piso	first floor
piso primero	first floor
primero	first

10 **PERSONAL PRONOUNS**

A	B	C	D	E
yo	me	me	me	yo
tú	te	te	te	tú
usted	lo, la	le	se	usted
él, ella	lo,la	le	se	él, ella
nosotros, -as	nos	nos	nos	nosotros, -as
vosotros, -as	os	os	os	vosotros, -as
ustedes	los,las	les	se	ustedes
ellos, -as	los,las	les	se	ellos, -as

1. You should learn the pronouns in the table on the left.

2. The pronouns in column A are used when these words are the subject of the verb:

Yo soy de Barcelona, ¿y tú? I am from Barcelona. And you?

Note that these subject pronouns do not normally appear with the verb because the forms of the verb are sufficient to indicate the subject by themselves:

tengo ➡ yo I have

Tengo dos hijos - I have two children, Estoy comiendo - I am eating, etc, are therefore more frequent than Yo tengo dos hijos or Yo estoy comiendo. Sometimes, however, it is necessary for these subject pronouns to appear, but do not worry about this point for the moment.

3. The pronouns in column B are direct object pronouns:

Necesito un libro. I need a book.
Lo necesito. I need it.

Bear in mind that direct object pronouns have different forms for the masculine and the feminine of the third person:

Necesito este libro. ➡ Lo necesito.	I need this book.	I need it.
Necesito la camisa. ➡ La necesito.	I need the shirt.	I need it.
Necesito los billetes. ➡ Los necesito.	I need the tickets.	I need them.
Necesito las gafas. ➡ Las necesito.	I need the glasses.	I need them.

4. The pronouns in column C are indirect object pronouns:

Dale ese libro. Give him that book.
¿Nos cobra esto? Would you charge us for this?

The indirect object is normally the receiver or the person who benefits or suffers from the action which is expressed by the verb.

5. The pronouns in column D are used in reflexive sentences (Juan se está duchando - Juan is having a shower [i.e. "is showering himself"]), and for this reason they are referred to as reflexive pronouns. They are also used with those verbs which are conjugated with a pronoun (i.e. those which end in -se - see the vocabulary lists): Me siento aquí - I sit here; Se llama Juan - He is called Juan [i.e. "He calls himself Juan"], etc.

6. The pronouns in column E appear after the following prepositions: para, con, en, etc.; para mí, cerca de ti, en él, con nosotros, etc. Note that in the case of con there are special forms for the first and second persons singular:

Vengan conmigo. Come with me.
Están hablando contigo. They are talking to you.

7. Direct object pronouns, indirect object pronouns, and reflexive pronouns (columns B, C, and D) normally appear before the verb: <u>La</u> encontramos - We find it; <u>Me</u> dan -Tthey give me; <u>Se</u> llama - He is called. However, they should be placed after the forms of the imperative: Dé<u>me</u> un kilo de fresas - Give me a kilo of strawberries; Lláme<u>nos</u> mañana - Call us tomorrow, etc.

In structures with <u>estar + -ndo</u> and <u>ir a + -r</u> these pronouns may be placed either before the first verb:

<u>Me</u> están llamando por teléfono.	They are phoning me.
<u>Lo</u> voy a leer.	I am going to read it.

or after the second verb:

Están llamándo<u>me</u> por teléfono.	They are phoning me.
Voy a leer<u>lo</u>.	I am going to read it.

Note that the pronoun which appears after the verb is combined with the verb to form one word only.

⑪ THE FORM SE

The word <u>se</u> is a marker of the so-called impersonal construction; that is to say, it is used on those occasions on which, for some reason, one does not want to or cannot say who is the exact person or the persons who are carrying out the action of the verb, or when this action is attributed to people in general. Note the difference between:

Felipe habla español.	Felipe speaks Spanish.

where the particular, specific person who carries out the action of speaking - hablar is <u>Felipe</u>, and:

En Argentina <u>se</u> habla español.	Spanish is spoken in Argentina.

where the sentence says that in a general indeterminate way Argentina is a country in which Spanish is spoken. The same difference can be seen between the following:

No puedo aparcar aquí.	I cannot park here. (because it is not allowed)

referring to <u>yo</u> - I, a particular, specific person, and

No <u>se</u> puede aparcar aquí.	Parking is not allowed here.

in which the sentence expresses a prohibition which applies to everyone in general.

2. The verb is normally used in the third person singular (the form which corresponds to the pronouns él, ella). You can see this in the examples above. Nevertheless, if the verb is followed by a noun in the plural, you should use the third person plural form (i.e. that which corresponds to the pronouns <u>ellos</u> and <u>ellas</u>). You can see this in the following examples:

<u>Se</u> necesita<u>n</u> secretaria<u>s</u>.	Secretaries (are) needed.
¿<u>Se</u> puede<u>n</u> hacer foto<u>s</u> aquí?	Is it possible to take photos here?
En España <u>se</u> lee<u>n</u> mucho<u>s</u> libro<u>s</u>.	Many books are read in Spain.

⑫ INTERROGATIVES

1. Forms:

quién, quiénes
cuál, cuáles
qué
cuánto
cuánto, cuánta, cuántos, cuántas
dónde
cómo

2. Uses:

2.a. Quién (masculine and feminine singular) and quiénes (plural) are used to ask who someone is:

— Quién es esa chica?	— Who is that girl?
— Carmen.	— Carmen.
— ¿Quiénes son esos señores?	— Who are those people?
— Mis padres.	— My parents.

2.b. Cuál (masculine and feminine singular) and cuáles (plural) also vary according to number, but not gender. They are used to indicate or identify one thing among two or more things of the same class which are present together:

— ¿Cuál es tu vestido?	— Which one is your dress?
— El de la derecha.	— The one on the right.
— ¿Cuáles son tus zapatos?	— Which ones are your shoes?
— Los negros.	— The black ones.

This form may be used in place of quién/quiénes to indicate one or more persons among a group of several people:

¿Cuáles son tus padres?   Which ones are your parents?

2.c. Qué is an invariable form followed by a noun:

¿Qué vestido?	What dress?
¿Qué camisa?	What shirt?
¿Qué zapatos?	What shoes?
¿Qué gafas?	What glasses?

It expresses the same meaning as cuál/cuáles:

¿Qué vestido es el tuyo?
¿Cuál es tu vestido?   ⎤⊢ Which dress is yours?

¿Qué zapatos son los tuyos?
¿Cuáles son tus zapatos? ⎤⊢ Which shoes are yours?

Qué is also used when there is no accompanying noun. When this form refers to people it is used to inquire about someone's occupation or profession. Note the difference between:

	Qué es tu padre?	What is your father?
and:	Quién es tu padre?	Who is your father?

When referring to things this form is used to ask what something is. Alernatively, it has the neutral value of ¿qué cosa?, in sentences such as:

¿Qué desea?	What would you like?
¿Qué van a tomar?	What are you going to have?
¿Qué hay en la maleta?	What is there in the suitcase?
¿Qué estás haciendo?	What are you doing?
¿Qué es eso?	What is that?
¿Qué es un transistor?	What is a transistor?
¿Qué pasa?	What is the matter?

2d. Cuánto is the interrogative form which inquires about quantity. It may have an invariable neuter use (=how much) when occurring without an accompanying noun in sentences like the following:

¿Cuánto es?	How much is it?
¿Cuánto es todo?	How much is everything?
¿A cuánto están las naranjas?	How much are the oranges?
¿Cuánto cuesta?	How much does it cost?

Alternatively, it may occur with an accompanying noun and suffer changes of form like an adjective: cuánto, -a, -os, -as (= how much, how many):

¿Cuánto dinero tienes?	How much money do you have?
¿Cuánta agua hay?	How much water is there?
¿Cuántos años tienes?	How old are you? [i.e. "How many years do you have?"]
¿Cuántas hermanas tienes?	How many sisters do you have?

2.e. Cómo - how is the interrogative of manner in Spanish. This form is used to ask how something is or how something is done. It is invariable in form:

¿Cómo se escribe tu nombre? — How do you spell [i.e. "write"] your name?

Cómo and qué are used in order to ask someone to repeat what they have said.

2.f. Dónde - where is the interrogative which is used to ask where something is or where something takes place. This form is invariable:

¿Dónde está el baño? — Where is the bathroom/toilet?
¿Dónde vives? — Where do you live?

It may be preceded by a preposition:

— ¿A dónde vas? — Where are you going to?
— A casa. — Home.
— ¿De dónde vienes? — Where have you been? [i.e. "Where are you coming from?"]
— De la oficina. — In the office. [i.e. "From the office."]

⑬ CONJUGATION OF VERBS

The infinitive of verbs in Spanish may end in -AR (as in necesitar), in -ER (as in comer) or in -IR (as in vivir). In other words, verbs may belong to the 'first' conjugation (ending in -AR), to the 'second' conjugation (ending in -ER) or to the 'third' conjugation (ending in -IR).

This information is important because the forms of a verb vary according to the conjugation to which it belongs. The variations in form of 'regular' verbs always follow the same pattern (see the relevant section in this appendix). If the verb is 'irregular', it differs in some respects from the regular pattern. This is indicated in the vocabulary lists by (v.i.). The differences can be seen in the relevant section of this appendix.

⑭ VARIATIONS IN VERB FORMS

Spanish verbs have a complex variety of forms. You will gradually become acquainted with these throughout this Course. Variations in verb forms are governed by the following factors:

1. The existence of three conjugations, i.e. of three different patterns of inflection depending on whether the infinitive ends in -ar, in -er or in -ir.

2. The existence of different tenses (present, past, etc.) and moods (indicative v. subjunctive). In this first coursebook you will learn present indicative forms and imperative forms. You will also learn some uses of the gerund (comprando, comiendo, viviendo) and of the infinitive.

3. Variations in person and number due to their concord with the subject, i.e. whether the subject is yo, tú, él, nosotros, etc.
These factors give rise to a great variety of forms. You should not worry if you take some time to become fully familiar with them.

⑮ VERBAL CONCORD

One of the variations in form of verbs in Spanish is due to concord; the verb must be in that form which corresponds to the person and number of the subject.

The exact form here depends on the conjugation to which the verb belongs (infinitive ending in -ar, -er or -ir). As an example, consider the present indicative of the verb vivir, which is shown in the table on the left.

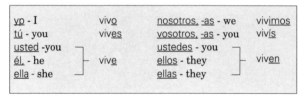

yo - I	vivo	nosotros, -as - we	vivimos
tú - you	vives	vosotros, -as - you	vivís
usted -you		ustedes - you	
él. - he	vive	ellos - they	viven
ella - she		ellas - they	

THE PRESENT INDICATIVE

1. When a verb is 'regular' it forms the present indicative in the same way as one of the three verbs which are given in the following table:

	comprar	comer	vivir
(yo)	compro	como	vivo
(tú)	compras	comes	vives
(él ella usted)	compra	come	vive
nosotros, -as)	compramos	comemos	vivimos
vosotros, -as)	compráis	coméis	vivís
(ellos ellas ustedes)	compran	comen	viven

2. Some verbs (so-called pronominal or reflexive verbs) are conjugated in the same way, but add a pronoun. See the following example:

LLAMARSE

me	llamo	nos	llamamos
te	llamas	os	llamáis
se	llama	se	llaman

You can easily recognise these verbs because the infinitive has -se added on to the end: llamarse, sentarse, alojarse.

3. The present indicative of irregular verbs:

The verbs abrir - to open, escribir - to write and leer - to read are irregular in some respects, but they form the present indicative in exactly the same way as regular verbs.

	yo	tú	él,ella usted	nosotros, -as	vosotros, -as	ellos,ellas ustedes
abrir: The present is formed according to the pattern of regular verbs in -ir.						
cerrar:	cierro	cierras	cierra	cerramos	cerráis	cierran
contar:	cuento	cuentas	cuenta	contamos	contáis	cuentan
dar:	doy	das	da	damos	dais	dan
encender:	enciendo	enciendes	enciende	encendemos	encendéis	encienden
encontrar:	encuentro	encuentras	encuentra	encontramos	encontráis	encuentran
escribir: The present is formed according to the pattern of regular verbs in -ir.						
estar:	estoy	estás	está	estamos	estáis	están
hacer:	hago	haces	hace	hacemos	hacéis	hacen
ir:	voy	vas	va	vamos	vais	van
irse: The same as ir, but placing me, te, se, nos, os, se before.						
jugar:	juego	juegas	juega	jugamos	jugáis	juegan
leer: The present is formed according to the pattern of regular verbs in -er.						
poder:	puedo	puedes	puede	podemos	podéis	pueden
poner:	pongo	pones	pone	ponemos	ponéis	ponen
probar:	pruebo	pruebas	prueba	probamos	probáis	prueban
probarse: The same as probar, but placing me, te, se, nos, os, se before.						
querer:	quiero	quieres	quiere	queremos	queréis	quieren
recordar:	recuerdo	recuerdas	recuerda	recordamos	recordáis	recuerdan
saber:	sé	sabes	sabe	sabemos	sabéis	saben
salir:	salgo	sales	sale	salimos	salís	salen
sentarse:	me siento	te sientas	se sienta	nos sentamos	os sentáis	se sientan
ser:	soy	eres	es	somos	sois	son
tener:	tengo	tienes	tiene	tenemos	tenéis	tienen
traer:	traigo	traes	trae	traemos	traéis	traen
venir:	vengo	vienes	viene	venimos	venís	vienen
ver:	veo	ves	ve	vemos	veis	ven
volver:	vuelvo	vuelves	vuelve	volvemos	volvéis	vuelven

IMPERATIVE FORMS

1. The following are the imperative forms for regular verbs. The underlined endings apply respectively to all regular verbs ending in -ar, -er and -ir:

tú	➡	habla	bebe	sube
usted	➡	hable	beba	suba
vosotros -as	➡	hablad	bebed	subid
ustedes	➡	hablen	beban	suban

2. Negative forms (i.e. those preceded by no) are the same as the affirmative forms for usted and ustedes, but this is not so for tú and vosotros, -as:

tú	➡	no hables	no bebas	no subas
usted	➡	no hable	no beba	no suba
vosotros, -as	➡	no habléis	no bebáis	no subáis
ustedes	➡	no hablen	no beban	no suban

3. Imperative forms for irregular verbs:
The table below gives the imperative forms for those irregular verbs which appear in this first coursebook.
The order in which they appear is as follows: affirmative forms for tú, usted, vosotros, -as and ustedes, and negative forms for tú and vosotros, -as.
The verbs abrir - to open, escribir - to write and leer - to read are irregular in some respects, but they form the imperative in exactly the same way as regular verbs.

	tú	usted	vosotros, -as	ustedes	(no) tú	(no) vosotros, -as
abrir: This follows the pattern of regular verbs in -ir.						
cerrar:	cierra	cierre	cerrad	cierren	no cierres	no cerréis
contar:	cuenta	cuente	contad	cuenten	no cuentes	no contéis
dar:	da	dé	dad	den	no des	no déis
encender:	enciende	encienda	encended	enciendan	no enciendas	no encendáis
escribir: This follows the pattern of regular verbs in -ir.						
hacer:	haz	haga	haced	hagan	no hagas	no hagáis
ir:	ve	vaya	id	vayan	no vayas	no vayáis
irse:	vete	váyase	(idos)	váyanse	no te vayas	no os vayáis
jugar:	juega	juegue	jugad	jueguen	no juegues	no juguéis
leer: This follows the pattern of regular verbs in -er.						
poner:	pon	ponga	poned	pongan	no pongas	no pongáis
probar:	prueba	pruebe	probad	prueben	no pruebes	no probéis
probarse:	pruébate	pruébese	probaos	pruébense	no te pruebes	no os probéis
recordar:	recuerda	recuerde	recordad	recuerden	no recuerdes	no recordéis
salir:	sal	salga	salid	salgan	no salgas	no salgáis
sentarse:	siéntate	siéntese	sentaos	siéntense	no te sientes	no os sentéis
ser:	sé	sea	sed	sean	no seas	no seáis
tener:	ten	tenga	tened	tengan	no tengas	no tengáis
traer:	trae	traiga	traed	traigan	no traigan	no traigáis
venir:	ven	venga	venid	vengan	no vengas	no vengáis
ver:	(ve)	vea	ved	vean	no veas	no veáis
volver:	vuelve	vuelva	volved	vuelvan	no vuelvas	no volváis

4. Remember that unstressed pronouns are placed after affirmative imperative forms of the verb: ¡Tráelo! - Bring it; ¡Dadme! - Give me; ¡Escríbenos! - Write to us. With negative forms, pronouns are placed as normal, i.e. before the verb: ¡No lo traigas! - Don't bring it; ¡No me deis! - Don't give me; ¡No nos escribas! Don't write to us.

5. The following patterns of the pronominal verbs sentarse and probarse show how pronouns combine with imperative forms:

	siéntate		pruébate
	siéntese		pruébese
sentad + os ➡	sentaos	probad + os ➡	probaos
	siéntense		pruébense

THE GERUND

Regular verbs form the gerund as follows:

comprar	➡	comprando
comer	➡	comiendo
vivir	➡	viviendo

2. Of the verbs which appear in this book, the following have an irregular gerund:

ir	➡	yendo
irse	➡	yéndose
leer	➡	leyendo
poder	➡	pudiendo
traer	➡	trayendo
venir	➡	viniendo

For the moment, however, you are likely to need only the gerund for the verb leer.

 FORMS OF ADDRESS: TÚ - USTED

1. There are two forms of address for speaking to other people in Spanish. If there are differences between the speakers with regard to socioeconomic status and especially age, it is likely that the form usted will be used (or the plural ustedes). On the other hand, when such differences do not exist or are ignored (for example, in speaking to members of the family, friends, colleagues), the form used will normally be tú or the plural forms vosotros and vosotras. The use of tú or tuteo is gaining ground in Spain; nevertheless, you should be careful in using this form. If in doubt, use usted or ustedes.

This norm refers to that variety of Spanish which has been adopted as the model in this Course. However, there are other varieties in Spain and in Latin America in which the forms vosotros or vosotras are not used. In these varieties ustedes is the only form of address used in the plural.

2. Note that these forms of address affect the form of other words: verbs, possessives, and unstressed pronouns which are added on to the end of the verb. The details here are as follows:

2.a. The forms of verbs, possessives and unstressed pronouns which correspond to usted are the same as those which correspond to él (or ella), and those of ustedes are the same as those which correspond to ellos (or ellas):

usted vive	———————	ustedes viven	
él vive	———————	ellos viven	
su billete	———————		
el billete es suyo	———————	de él, de ella, de usted	

él	➡	se llama
usted	➡	se llama

2.b. There are also differences between the forms of the imperative which are used with tú and vosotros, -as, on the one hand, and those which are used with usted and ustedes, on the other hand:

tú	➡	habla	vosotros	➡	hablad
usted	➡	hable	ustedes	➡	hablen

3. Personal subject pronouns (yo, tú, etc.) are normally avoided. Nevertheless, usted and ustedes appear more frequently than other pronouns: ¿Cómo te llamas? - What is your name? as against ¿Cómo se llama usted? - What is your name?

⑳   SER AND ESTAR

1. Spanish differentiates between two verbs, ser and estar, where English uses only one verb, 'to be'. In this first coursebook you have seen the following uses of these verbs:

2. Ser is used:

2.a. to identify and to introduce people; i.e. this use is related to the question ¿quién? - Who?

— ¿Quién <u>eres</u>?	— Who are you?
— <u>Soy</u> Andrés.	— I'm Andrés.
<u>Es</u> mi hermana.	She is my sister.
Éste <u>es</u> mi jefe.	This is my boss.
<u>Es</u> el niño moreno.	He is the dark-haired boy.

2.b. to identify things, or to say what they are called; i.e. this use is related to the questions ¿qué? - What? or ¿cuál? - Which one?

— ¿Qué <u>es</u> eso?	— What is that?
— Ésta <u>es</u> la catedral.	— That is the cathedral.
— Eso <u>es</u> un kiwi.	— That is a kiwi.
— ¿Cuál <u>es</u> tu libro?	— Which is your book?
— <u>Es</u> el verde.	— It is the green one.
— <u>Es</u> el de la derecha.	— It is the one on the right.

2.c. to express possession; i.e. this use is related to the question ¿de quién? - Whose?

— De quién <u>es</u> esta maleta?	— Whose is this suitcase?
— <u>Es</u> mía.	— It's mine.
Este libro <u>es</u> de Luis.	This book is Luis's. [i.e. "is of Luis"]

2.d. to express someone's occupation or profession:

— ¿Qué <u>es</u> usted?	— What are you?
— <u>Soy</u> profesor.	— I am a teacher.

2.e. to express where people and things are from; i.e. this use is related to the question ¿de dónde? - Where from?

— ¿De dónde <u>es</u>?	— Where is he from?
— <u>Es</u> de Barcelona.	— He is from Barcelona.
<u>Soy</u> italiano.	I am Italian.

2.f. to express both what day it is and what time it is:

¿Qué <u>es</u> hoy?	What is today?
Mañana <u>es</u> jueves.	Tomorrow is Thursday.
— ¿Qué hora <u>es</u>?	— What time is it?
— <u>Son</u> las dos y media.	— It is half-past two.

2.g. to ask how much something is and to express the price of something:

— ¿Cuánto <u>es</u> ?	— How much is it?
— <u>Son</u> cuatrocientas pesetas.	— It is four hundred pesetas.

3. Estar is used:

3.a. to express where people and things are; i.e. this use is related to the question ¿dónde? - Where?

¿Dónde <u>está</u>?	Where is it?
El jefe <u>está</u> en el bar.	The boss is in the bar.
La cocina <u>está</u> allí.	The kitchen is there.

3.b. to ask if the person we are looking for is available and to supply the same information:

— ¿<u>Está</u> tu padre?	— Is your father in?
— No, no <u>está</u>.	— No, he's not.

3.c. in constructions with the gerund (estar + -ndo):

— ¿Qué <u>estás</u> haciendo?	— What are you doing?
— <u>Estoy</u> comiendo.	— I'm eating.

3d. to express the date:

— ¿A qué <u>estamos</u>?	—What date is it?
— <u>Estamos</u> a quince.	— It is the fifteenth.

3.e. to inquire about and to express the price of articles which are variable in price:

¿A cuánto <u>están</u> las fresas?	How much are the strawberries?
Las naranjas <u>están</u> a doscientas el kilo.	The oranges are two hundred a kilo.

3.f. to express marital status:

— ¿<u>Está</u> usted casado?	— Are you married?
— <u>Estamos</u> solteros.	— We are single.

Vocabulary

The number which appears in brackets after each word refers to the unit in which that word appears for the first time.

abajo (9) = below
abogado, -a (12) = lawyer
abrigo (m) (4) = overcoat
abrir (v. i.) (6) = to open
abuelo, -a (9) = grandfather, -mother
aceite (m) (5) = oil
adelante (3) = After you
adiós (1) = Goodbye
aeropuerto (m) (2) = airport
agua (f) (4) = water
ahí (3) = there
ahora (10) = now
a la plancha (13) = grilled
alemán, -a (9) = German
al horno (13) = roast, baked
al lado de (13) = next to
allí (3) = over there
alojarse (13) = to stay (hotel, etc.)
alto, -a (9) = tall
amarillo, -a (9) = yellow
amigo, -a (1) = friend
año (m) (12) = year
apagar (12) = to switch off
aparcamiento (m) (5) = car park
aparcar (6) = to park
apellido (m) (2) = surname
aquí (3) = here
arriba (9) = above
asado, -a (13) = roast
así (4) = like this, this way
atún (m) (11) = tuna fish
autobús (m) (5) = bus
avería (f) (7) = breakdown
azúcar (m) (6) = sugar
azul (m. y f.) (9) = blue
bailar (10) = to dance
bajar (5) = to go/come down
bajo, -a (9) = short
banco (m) (5) = bank
bañador (m) (13) = swimming costume
baño (m) (3) = toilet
bar (m) (4) = bar
barato, -a (11) = cheap
barba (f) (9) = beard
barco (m) (7) = ship, boat
beber (7) = to drink
Berlín (3) = Berlin
billete (m) (3) = ticket

billete (m) (4) = bank note
blanco, -a (9) = white
bocadillo (m) (11) = roll
boda (f) (9) = wedding
bolígrafo (m) (3) = ballpoint pen
bolso (m) (11) = handbag
bonito, -a (9) = pretty, nice
botella (f) (4) = bottle
Bruselas (3) = Brussels
buenas noches (1) = good night
buenas tardes (1) = good afternoon / good evening
buenos días (1) = good morning
cabeza (f) (13) = head
café (m) (4) = coffee
café con leche (4) = white coffee
café solo (4) = black coffee
cajón (m) (3) = drawer
calcetín (m) (11) = sock
calle (f) (2) = street
cámara de vídeo (f) (6) = video camera
camarero, -a (12) = waiter, waitress
camisa (f) (9) = shirt
camping (m) (5) = camping site
carne (f) (11) = meat
carné (m) (4) = identity card
caro, -a (11) = expensive
cartero (m) (9) = postman
casa (f) (6) = house, home
casado, -a (12) = married
casete (m) (12) = cassette recorder
catedral (f) (13) = cathedral
centro (m) (13) = centre
cepillo de dientes (m) (11) = toothbrush
cerca (5) = nearby
cerca de (13) = near
cerdo (m) (13) = pork
cerrar (v. i.) (12) = to close
cerveza (f) (4) = beer
champú (m) (11) = shampoo
chaqueta (f) (4) = jacket, coat
chico, -a (5) = boy, young man; girl, young woman
chocolate (m) (5) = chocolate
cigarro (m) (8) = cigarette
cine (m) (5) = cinema
ciudad (f) (7) = city
coche (m) (4) = car

cocina (f) (7) = kitchen
coger (5) = to take, to pick up
colonia (f) (11) = eau de cologne
comer (5) = to eat
comisaría (f) (4) = police station
comprar (6) = to buy
contar (v. i.) (13) = to count
corbata (f) (9) = tie
cordero (m) (13) = lamb
correr (6) = to run
cosa (f) (6) = thing
costar (v. i.) (11) = to cost
cuarto de baño (m) (7) = bathroom
cuarto de estar (m) (7) = sitting / living room
cuarto de hora (m) (10) = quarter of an hour
cuchara (f) (6) = spoon
cuchillo (m) (6) = knife
cuidado (2) = Be careful
cumpleaños (m) (10) = birthday
cura (m) (9) = priest
dar (v. i.) (4) = to give
delante de (13) = in front of
delgado, -a (9) = thin, slim
de nada (2) = Don't mention it
dentífrico (m) (11) = toothpaste
dentista (m. y f.) (7) = dentist
dentro (9) = inside
deporte (m) (5) = sport
derecha (f) (2) = right-hand side
descansar (10) = to rest
despacio (5) = slowly
detrás de (13) = behind
día (m) (2) = day
dinero (m) (7) = money
dirección (f) (2) = address
director, -a (3) = manager
divorciado, -a (12) = divorced
docena (f) (11) = dozen
doctor, -a (3) = doctor
documentación (f) (4) = identification papers
domingo (m) (2) = Sunday
don, doña (3) = Polite forms of address used to superiors. These forms always appear together with the

forename.

ducha (f) (4) = shower
edad (f) (12) = age
empleado, -a (12) = employee
encantado, -a (1) = How do you do
encender (v. i.) (12) = to switch on
encontrar (v. i.) (7) = to find
enfermero, -a (12) = nurse
enfrente de (13) = opposite
ensalada (f) (6) = salad
entrada (f) (12) = entrance, way in
entrar (5) = to go/come in
entremeses (m. pl.) (13) = hors d'oeuvres
escribir (v. i.) (4) = to write
escuchar (6) = to listen
España (3) = Spain
español, -a (9) = Spanish
esperar (6) = to wait
estación (f) (2) = station
estado civil (m) (12) = marital status
estar (v. i.) (3) = to be (in a certain place)
estómago (m) (13) = stomach
Europa (3) = Europe
falda (f) (9) = skirt
farmacia (f) (5) = chemist's
feo, -a (9) = ugly
filete (m) (13) = steak
flor (f) (10) = flower
folleto (m) (7) = brochure
foto (f) (3) = photograph
francés, -a (9) = French
fresa (f) (11) = strawberry
frigorífico (m) (5) = fridge
frito, -a (13) = fried
fruta (f) (5) = fruit
fuego (m) (8) = a light (for cigarette)
fuera (9) = outside
fumar (5) = to smoke
gafas (f. pl.) (3) = glasses
garaje (m) (12) = garage
garganta (f) (13) = throat
gasolina (f) (7) = petrol
gasolinera (f) (5) = filling station
gordo, -a (9) = fat
gracias (2) = Thank you
gramo (m): g. (11) = gram
grande (m. y f.) (9) = big
gris (m. y f.) (9) = grey
guapo, -a (9) = good-looking, pretty
habitación (f) (4) = room

habitación con baño (4) = room with a bathroom
habitación con ducha (4) = room with a shower
habitación doble (4) = double room
habitación individual (4) = single room
hablar (6) = to speak
hablar alto (8) = to speak in a loud voice
hablar bajo (8) = to speak quietly
hablar despacio (8) = to speak slowly
hablar rápido (8) = to speak quickly
hacer (v. i.) (6) = to do
hacer (v. i.) deporte (5) = to practise sport
hasta luego (1) = See you later
hasta mañana (2) = See you tomorrow
helado (m) (10) = ice-cream
hermano, -a (1) = brother/sister
hijo, -a (1) = son/daughter
hojas de reclamaciones (f. pl.) (13) = complaints forms
hola (1) = Hello
hombre (m) (5) = man
hora (f) (10) = hour
hospital (m) (2) = hospital
hotel (m) (2) = hotel
hoy (10) = today
huevo (m) (5) = egg
iglesia (f) (5) = church
inglés, -a (9) = English
invitar (10) = to invite, to treat
ir (v. i.) (5) = to go
irse (v. i.) (10) = to go, to leave
italiano, -a (9) = Italian
izquierda (f) (2) = left-hand side
jabón (m) (11) = soap
jamón (m) (11) = ham
japonés, -a (9) = Japanese
jardín (m) (12) = garden
jefe (m. y f.) (3) = boss
jersey (m) (11) = jersey
jueves (m) (2) = Thursday
jugar (v. i.) (6) = to play
kilo (m): Kg. (11) = kilo
lata (f) (5) = tin
leche (f) (4) = milk
leer (v. i.) (6) = to read
lejos de (13) = a long way from
libro (m) (4) = book
limón (m) (11) = lemon
litro (m): l. (11) = litre

llamar (8) = to call
llamarse (2) = to be called
llave (f) (8) = key
llegar (8) = to arrive
llegar pronto (10) = to arrive early
llegar tarde (10) = to arrive late
llevar (10) = to take
Londres (3) = London
lunes (m) (2) = Monday
luz (f) (12) = light
madre (f) (1) = mother
Madrid (3) = Madrid
maleta (f) (4) = suitcase
mamá (f) (9) = Mummy
manzana (f) (11) = apple
mañana (2) = tomorrow
mañana (f) (10) = morning
máquina de fotos (f) (6) = camera
marido (m) (1) = husband
marrón (m. y f.) (9) = brown
martes (m) (2) = Tuesday
más. (10) = more
mecánico (m) (9) = mechanic
media hora (f) (10) = half an hour
médico (m. y f.) (7) = doctor
medio, -a (11) = half
merluza (f) (11) = hake
mes (m) (12) = month
mesa (f) (3) = table
meter (5) = to put in
miércoles (m) (2) = Wednesday
minuto (m) (10) = minute
mirar (5) = to look
momento (m) (10) = moment
moneda (f) (3) = coin
moreno, -a (9) = dark-haired
moto (f) (3) = motorbike
muela (f) (13) = back tooth
mujer (f) (1) = wife
mujer (f) (5) = woman
naranja (f) (4) = orange
necesitar (8) = to need
negro, -a (9) = black
nieto, -a (9) = grandson/-daughter
niño, -a (2) = boy/girl
no (2) = no
noche (f) (10) = night
nombre (m) (2) = name
novio, -a (1) = boyfriend, girlfriend
nuevo, -a (8) = new
número (m) (2) = number
oficina (f) (3) = office

oído (m) (13) = ear
ojo (m) (13) = eye
otro, -a (10) = another
padre (m) (1) = father
padres (m. pl.) (1) = parents
paella (f) (13) = paella
pan (m) (5) = bread
pantalones (m. pl.) (9) = trousers
pañuelo (m) (8) = handkerchief
papá (m) (9) = Daddy
papel (m) (8) = paper
paquete (m) (6) = parcel, packet
parar (6) = to stop
París (3) = Paris
parque (m) (5) = park
pasaporte (m) (4) = passport
pasar (5) = to pass
pastel (m) (11) = small cake
patata (f) (11) = potato
patatas fritas (f. pl.) (13) = chips
peine (m) (13) = comb
película (f) (10) = film
pelo (m) (9) = hair
pelota (f) (12) = ball
pequeño, -a (9) = small
perdón (1) = Excuse me / I'm sorry
periódico (m) (6) = newspaper
periodista (m. y f.) (12) = journalist
perro, -a (2) = dog; bitch
pescado (m) (11) = fish
peseta (f) (3) = peseta
pila (f) (12) = battery
piso (m) (2) = floor
plátano (m) (5) = banana
playa (f) (5) = beach
plaza (f) (2) = square
poder (v. i.) (3) = to have permission to
policía (f) (7) = police
policía (m. y f.) (12) = policeman / -woman
pollo (m) (6) = chicken
poner (v. i.) (5) = to put
por aquí (5) = around here
por favor (1) = please
postal (f) (11) = postcard
postre (m) (13) = dessert

precio (m) (11) = price
preguntar (13) = to ask
primo, -a (9) = cousin
probar (v. i.) (5) = to try
probarse (v. i.) (11) = to try on
profesión (f) (12) = profession
profesor, -a (3) = teacher
pronto (10) = early, soon
propina (f) (13) = tip
pueblo (m) (5) = village
puerta (f) (12) = door
¿qué tal? (1) = How are you?
querer (v. i.) (5) = to want
queso (m) (11) = cheese
radio (f) (6) = radio
rápido, -a (8) = quickly
rato (m) (10) = short while
recepcionista (m. y f.) (12) = receptionist
recordar (v. i.) (13) = to remember
regalo (m) (10) = present
reloj (m) (6) = watch, clock
rey, reina (7) = king; queen
río (m) (13) = river
rojo, -a (9) = red
Roma (3) = Rome
rosa (f) (13) = rose
rubio, -a (9) = fair-haired, blond
sábado (m) (2) = Saturday
saber (v. i.) (11) = to know
sal (f) (6) = salt
salida (f) (12) = exit, way out
salir (v. i.) (8) = to go/come out
secretario, -a (3) = secretary
sello (m) (11) = stamp
semana (f) (2) = week
sentarse (v. i.) (5) = to sit down
señor, -a (3) = man, sir, Mr.
señorita (f) (3) = young woman, Miss
ser (v. i.) (1) = to be
sí (2) = yes
sobre (m) (3) = envelope
sobrino, -a (9) = nephew; niece
¡socorro! (8) = Help!
soltero, -a (12) = single
subir (5) = to go/come up

taller (m) (5) = garage
también (5) = too, also
tarde (10) = late
tarde (f) (10) = afternoon, evening
tarta (f) (11) = cake, gateau
taxi (m) (2) = taxi
té (m) (4) = tea
teléfono (m) (4) = telephone
televisión (f) (3) = television
tenedor (m) (6) = fork
tener (v. i.) (4) = to have
ternera (f) (13) = beef
tienda (f) (11) = shop
tío, -a (9) = uncle; aunt
todavía (7) = still
todo (11) = everything
todo, -a (13) = all
tomar (4) = to take, to have (= eat, drink)
tomar una copa (10) = to have a drink
tomate (m) (5) = tomato
tortilla (f) (13) = omelette
traer (v. i.) (12) = to bring
tren (m) (5) = train
trozo (m) (11) = piece
último, -a (9) = last
universidad (f) (13) = university
vaso (m) (4) = glass
vendedor, -a (12) = vendor
venir (v. i.) (5) = to come
ventana (f) (12) = window
ver (v. i.) (6) = to see
verde (m. y f.) (9) = green
vestido (m) (9) = dress
viejo, -a (9) = old
viernes (m) (2) = Friday
vino (m) (4) = wine
vino blanco (m) (11) = white wine
vino tinto (m) (11) = red wine
visitar (7) = to visit
viudo, -a (12) = widower; widow
vivir (2) = to live
volver (v. i.) (6) = to go/come back
zapato (m) (8) = shoe
zumo (m) (4) = (fruit) juice
zumo de naranja (4) = orange juice

Key to the Exercises

● UNIT 1

1 Luis Cánovas — Soy Luis Cánovas — Juan Serrano — Soy Juan Serrano — Carmen Alonso — Soy Carmen Alonso — Carmen y Juan — Somos Carmen y Juan.

3 Andrés Cueto — Rafael — Carlos Pérez López — María.

4 1. Soy   2. Somos   3. Soy   4. Somos   5. Soy.

5 Use the form soy when giving your own name, and the form somos when giving your own name and someone else's name at the same time.

6 Hola — ¿qué tal? — adiós — hasta luego.

7 Buenos días — buenas tardes — buenas noches — hola — ¿qué tal? — hola, ¿qué tal? — hola, buenos días — hola, buenas tardes — hola, buenas noches.

8 1. Hola.   2. WOMAN — Adiós/Hasta luego. MAN —Adiós.   3. días.   5. MAN — tardes. WOMAN — buenas tardes.   6. MAN — noches. WOMAN — Buenas noches/Hola/¿Qué tal?

9 The order in which you hear them is as follows: ¿Qué tal? — hasta luego — buenas noches — adiós — hola — buenos días — buenas tardes.

10 1. Buenas tardes; Buenas tardes.   2. Adiós.   3. **You can use any expression for greeting someone or for saying goodbye.**

11 Perdón — por favor — oiga — ¿sí? — dígame.

13 Ésta es mi hermana — Luis Cánovas — encantada — ¿qué tal?

15 1. —Oiga, por favor. —Sí, dígame.   2. —Éste es mi hermano… Elena López. Encantado. Encantada.   3. —Manolo… María… —Encantada. —¿Qué tal?   4. —Buenos días. Soy Luis Cánovas. —Buenos días; dígame.   5. —Hola, buenas tardes. —¿Qué tal? **You should therefore have put a cross against 2 and 3.**

16 **There are many possible combinations. The following are a few examples:** Mi hija / Ésta es mi hermana / Mis padres / Estos son mis padres / Elena / Soy José Pérez, **etc. Replies should be with** encantado, -a or ¿qué tal?.

● UNIT 2

1 Me llamo Luis Cánovas - ¿cómo se llama usted? - Mercedes Sánchez - ¿y usted? - ¿cómo se llama usted? - Andrés Martín.

2 Cómo - llamo - se - llama.

3 1. MAN.— ¿Cómo se llama usted?   2. MAN.— Me llamo   3. WOMAN.— Mi hijo se

5 Carmen Alonso Casaseca - Juan Serrano Ribera - Óscar Muñoz López - Marta Pérez Martín.

6 ¿Dónde vive? - en Madrid - vivo en Madrid - en la calle de Alcalá - en el número 8 - en la calle de Alcalá, 8.

7 Uno - dos - tres - cuatro - cinco - seis - siete - ocho - nueve - diez - primero - segundo - tercero - cuarto - quinto - sexto - séptimo - octavo - noveno - décimo.

8 Elena, calle de Málaga, número 8 - Emilio Prieto, Plaza Mayor, 5, primero - Alfonso Muñoz, calle Goya, 9, cuarto piso, derecha - Marta Pérez López, plaza de América, 7, séptimo izquierda.

9 1. vive - En - calle   2. en - número   3. vive - la   4. en - En - calle - izquierda.

10 ¿Dónde viven ustedes? - ¿Nosotros? Vivimos en Sevilla -¿Y usted? - Yo vivo en Madrid.

13 and **14** **The voice on the tape says:** ¿Apellidos? - ¿nombre? - ¿dirección?.

16 ¿Está libre? - Sí - ¿A dónde vamos? - A la calle de Alcalá, 8.

17 ¡Cuidado! - ¡Cuidado con el niño!

18 Perdón - lo siento - Nada, nada - no se preocupe.

19 Gracias - muchas gracias - De nada.

20 Hasta mañana - Adiós - hasta mañana - adiós, hasta mañana.

21 Viernes, uno - sábado, dos - domingo, tres- lunes, cuatro - martes, cinco - miércoles, seis - jueves, siete - viernes, ocho - sábado, nueve - domingo, diez.

22 **The following dates:** 5 - 9 - 8 - 4.

23 Número 1 , hospital - número 2, Hotel Imperial - número 3, estación - número 4, aeropuerto.

24 | ¿A dónde vamos? - (al Hotel Imperial) - ¿A dónde vamos? - (a la estación) - ¿A dónde vamos? - (al aeropuerto).

25 | 1. Perdón / perdone / lo siento   2. ¡Cuidado! / ¡Cuidado con el perro!   3. Gracias / Muchas gracias   4. ¿Está libre?   5. Sí / No.

26 | Muchas gracias - (de nada) - hasta mañana - (adiós/hasta mañana) - lo siento - (nada, nada/no se preocupe) - ¿cómo se llama usted? - (Say your forename or your **forename** and surname) - ¿a dónde vamos? - (Use the **word** a followed by an address or the name of a place) - ¿dónde vive usted? - (Use the word en followed by your **address** or the name of the place where you live).

● UNIT 3

1 | ¿Dónde están mis gafas? - Ahí, en la mesa - El bolígrafo está en el cajón - Las fotos están en el sobre - ¿Dónde está Luis? -En la oficina - En el baño - ¿Dónde **está** Madrid? - Está en España - ¿Dónde están Londres y Bruselas? - Roma y Berlín están en Europa -¿Dónde están París y Madrid?

2 | 1. T   2. T   3. T   4. T   5. F   6. T

3 | 1. Dónde - en   2. Dónde - En   3. en   4. está - **Está**   5. están   6. están - **Están.**

4 | aquí - el sobre está aquí - ahí - el sobre está ahí - allí - **el** sobre está allí - aquí - el hotel está aquí - ahí - el hotel **está** ahí - allí - el hotel está allí.

6 | 1. Somos. Estamos   2. Soy. Estoy   3. Es. **Está   4.** Son. Están.

7 | ¿Está el señor Escudero? - No, no está - Y la **señorita**

Barrio, ¿está? - Sí. Un momento, por favor.

8 | director - directora - secretario - jefe - señor - señorita.

9 | ¿Está el señor Ibarra? - ¿Está la señorita García?, etc.

10 | **For** señor Ibarra, señorita García, señora Alonso and don **Roberto Mauri the answer is:** Sí, sí está. For don Julio **Nieto** and doña María Prado: the answer is: No, no está.

16 | 1. YOUNG WOMAN: Está JANITOR: está   2. YOUNG WOMAN: Es MAN: soy - está   3. YOUNG WOMAN: es SR. PRADO: soy   4. YOUNG WOMAN: Está SR. PRADO: está - Está   5. SR. PRADO: Cómo.

19 | **The numbers and the order in which they appear are as follows:** veinte - once - dieciocho - quince - dieciséis - doce - diecisiete - trece - cinco - diecinueve - siete - diez - catorce.

● UNIT 4

1 | ¿De quién es esta maleta? - es del señor Cánovas - **esa** maleta es mía.

2 | 1. T   2. F   3. T   4. F

3 | La chaqueta es de Julio - El coche es **de Marta -** Las maletas son de Rafael - Los bolígrafos **son de** Elena.

4 | nuestras casas - sus coches - sus gafas - su **bolígrafo - su** chaqueta - sus maletas - mis billetes - su libro.

5 | Las gafas son suyas - La casa es suya - Los **libros son** suyos - La chaqueta es suya - El coche es mío - **El bolígra-** fo es suyo - Los billetes son nuestros - El **abrigo es mío.**

6 | 1. BELLBOY: suyas - WOMAN: son   2. POLICEMAN: **suyo** - MAN: es mío.

7 | Este bolígrafo - esta chaqueta - esas maletas - aquellos coches - aquella casa.

8 | 1. Mr. López is at the very back of the picture.   2. The customer wants the glasses he has in his hand.

12 | Con uve - con jota - con hache - con uve - con ce - con jota - con ce.

14 | 1. Una habitación individual.   2. Una habitación doble. 3. Dos habitaciones dobles / una habitación doble y dos habitaciones individuales.

15 | Picture 1 (¿Me da su pasaporte?) - Picture 2 (Una habitación individual con baño) - Picture 3 (documentación, por favor).

16 | 1. En un bar   2. En una comisaría   3. En un bar   4. En

un bar   5. En un hotel   6. En un bar   7. En una comisaría   8. En un bar.

17 CUSTOMER 1: Un vaso de leche - CUSTOMER 2: Un zumo de naranja.

19 Ochenta y nueve (89) - veintidós (22) - cincuenta y seis (56) - setenta y tres (73) - cien (100).

21 1. El treinta - diez - veintiuno   2. El treinta - cero siete - treinta y ocho   3. El treinta - cero seis - sesenta y siete.

● UNIT 5

1 ¿A dónde va usted - ¿a dónde va? - a Salamanca - voy a Salamanca.

2 1. T   2. F   3. F   4. F   5. T   6. F   7. T

3 1. va; a; gracias; nada   2. vamos; voy   3. al   4. favor va. ¿Qué hay? - ¿qué hay en el frigorífico? - una botella de leche - hay leche - hay una botella de leche - tres naranjas - aquí hay tres naranjas.

6 Un plátano - tomates - chocolate - fruta - aceite - huevos - pan - una lata.

7 The following numbers should have been ticked: 1, 3, 4, 6, 7, 8.

8 1. Una farmacia   2. Una iglesia   3. Un banco   4. Un hospital.

9 1. hay una farmacia   2. hay…iglesia   3. hay…banco… un hospital   4. hay…gasolinera.

10 A: por…algún   B: hay…en   A: hay   B: ninguno.

12 ¿Un café? - ¿quiere usted un café? - sí, gracias - ¿quieren ustedes un café? - ¿quieren un café? - no, gracias.

14 ¿Puedo? - ¿puedo sentarme ¿puedo sentarme aquí? - sí - sí, claro.

15 1. ¿Puedo…?   2. ¿Puedo…?   3. A.—¿Puedo…? B.—claro.   4. A.—¿Podemos…? B.—Bueno.   5. ¿Puedo…?

17 Coma - coma una naranja - no fume - bueno.

18 The following pictures should have been indicated, in the order given here: 6, 1, 3, 2, 4, 5.

19 Accept by saying "bueno, muy bien, de acuerdo" or "vale".

20 Haga deporte - vaya despacio - mire - no fume - pruebe este café - tenga cuidado.

21 1. ¿A dónde va ese tren?   2. Voy a Madrid.   3. ¿Qué hay aquí?   4. ¿Dónde hay una farmacia?   5. ¿Hay algún banco por aquí / cerca?   6. ¿Un café? or ¿quiere usted un café?   7. ¿Puedo entrar? or ¿se puede?   8. Pruebe estas / esas naranjas.   9. No fumes.

● UNIT 6

1 ¿Quieres agua? - Y tú ¿dónde vives? - ¿Es tuyo? - ¿Me da su pasaporte? - ¿Cómo se llama usted?

4 Sentence 1 Picture 3 - Sentence 2 Picture 1 - Sentence 3 Picture 2 - Sentence 4 Picture 4 - Sentence 5 Picture 5 - Sentence 6 Picture 2.

5 To CARLITOS: 1. ¿Cómo te llamas? - ¿Tienes teléfono? - ¿Dónde vives? To D. ANTONIO AND Dª ANA: ¿Cómo se llaman? - ¿Tienen teléfono? - ¿Dónde viven? (The word ustedes **is frequently placed immediately after the verb:** ¿Cómo se llaman ustedes? etc.) To FELIPE AND MERCEDES: ¿Cómo os llamáis? - ¿Tenéis teléfono? - ¿Dónde vivís?

7 ¿Qué están haciendo? - Están jugando - Está comiendo - Están corriendo - Está escribiendo.

8 jugar - leer - escuchar - hablar - radio - periódico.

9 Complete sentences are as follows: 1: Estoy comprando el periódico.   2: ¿Qué está haciendo María? - Está hablando por teléfono.   3: ¿Qué están haciendo los niños? ¿Están viendo la televisión? - No, están leyendo.   4: Estamos esperando el autobús.   5: Estoy abriendo este paquete.

10 El hermano de Felipe está hablando con una mujer - Mis padres están escuchando la radio - Luis está comiendo - El señor Fernández está aparcando el coche - Aquel chico está fumando.

12 To D. CARLOS AND D. RAFAEL: Pasen. To YOUR CHILDREN: Escuchad. To ANTONIO: Para. To THE TOURISTS: Miren. To DAVID: Espera.

13 para - pare - come - comed - escriba - escribid - siéntate - venga - vuelve.

14 To DON FELIPE: Siéntese. To MANUEL: ¡Corre!. To LUIS: Ven. To ISABEL AND DIEGO: Coged.

15 1: No fumes. 2: No habléis. 3: No cojas ese bolígrafo.

16 **Examples with** tú: fuma; no fumes - baja; no bajes - escribe; no escribas - juega; no juegues - habla; no hables - come; no comas - mira; no mires - lee; no leas - sube; no subas - entra; no entres - escucha; no escuches - ven; no vengas.

18 The underlined words are the odd ones out:
Group 1: vino - cerveza - <u>pollo</u>
Group 2: <u>pan</u> - cuchara - tenedor
Group 3: sal - <u>cuchillo</u> - azúcar
Group 4: ensalada - tomates - <u>café</u>

20 conmigo - venid - corráis - Miren - haciendo - Estoy - Qué - Toma - Me pasa - Tome - Qué es - esto es.

● UNIT 7

1 ¿De dónde? - ¿de dónde viene ese barco? - de Valencia - viene de Valencia.

2 1. vienes - del - vengo - de   2. venís - vengo - taller - del.

3 1. F   2. F   3. F   4. F   5. T   6. T   7. T

4 del - vengo del.

6 ¿Se puede fumar aquí? - no se puede - no se puede fumar - todavía no se puede fumar.

7 1. No se puede fumar   2. No se puede pasar   3. No se puede beber   4. No se puede hablar   5. No se puede aparcar   6. Se puede aparcar.

8 1. ¿Se puede coger un folleto?   2. ¿Se puede comer en el cine?   3. ¿Se puede meter la maleta aquí?   4. ¿Se puede aparcar en esta calle?   5. ¿Se puede visitar la catedral?

10 1. MAN: ¿Qué pasa? WOMAN: Que - gasolina   2. WOMAN: que - aparcando.   3. YOUNG MAN: ¡Mi dinero! 4. WOMAN: avería.

11 1. la.   2. es - el.   3. el - es - la - la.   4. el.   5. la - es - el.
6. es.   7. es - la.   8. es - la.   9. son.   10. son - los.

12 1. Éste es el cuarto de estar.   2. Ésta es la cocina.
3. Éste es el cuarto de baño.   4. Ésta es mi habitación.
5. Ésta es la habitación de la niña.

14

100x	222	301	500x	601	775x
121x	243x	350x	555	625x	803x
169	300	499x	600	765	901x

16 1. TOTAL BEFORE TAX: novecientas cinco pesetas. TOTAL AFTER TAX: novecientas noventa y seis pesetas.   2. TOTAL BEFORE TAX: ochocientas diez pesetas; TOTAL AFTER TAX: ochocientas noventa y una pesetas.   3. TOTAL BEFORE TAX: ochocientas cincuenta pesetas; TOTAL AFTER TAX: novecientas veintiséis pesetas.

17 1. ¿De donde viene ese autobús?.   2. ¿A dónde va ese autobús?   3. ¿Se puede entrar? or ¿Se puede pasar?.   4. ¿Qué pasa?   5. ¿Cómo? or ¿cómo dice? or, possibly, ¿qué?   6. Que Pepe Gómez está aquí or Que Pepe Gómez está en la ciudad   7. Use ése and its various forms with the name of the thing you indicate.

● UNIT 8

1 Voy a leer el periódico - ¿vas a hacer una foto? - va a comer - vamos a ir al hotel - ¿vais a entrar? - van a venir mañana

2 1., 2. and 3. va a.

3 1. van a hacer deporte   2. va a entrar   3. va a sentarse
4. va a llegar.

4 El lunes va a ir al banco - el martes va a comprar fruta, café y cervezas - el miércoles va a ir al dentista y va a llamar por teléfono a María - el jueves va a comer con Andrés y sus amigos - el viernes va a escribir a Felipe - el sábado va a esperar a sus padres en la estación de autobuses - el domingo va a hacer deporte y va a visitar a su hermano.

6 unos zapatos nuevos - libros nuevos - papel - un coche -

las llaves - un cigarro - un pañuelo.

7 1. Necesita un abrigo   2. necesita agua   3. necesitan unos zapatos   4. necesita un bolígrafo   5. necesita un pañuelo.

8 1. Necesito un cuchillo   2. necesito una cámara de vídeo   3. necesito un / mi pasaporte   4. necesito un periódico   5. necesito una habitación doble.

9 ¿me das el periódico? - dame el periódico - ¿me das tu pasaporte, por favor? - ¿nos da dos cafés con leche? - dénos dos cervezas, por favor - dame un cigarro.

10 ¿Me das una cebolla? - ¿Me das el limón? - ¿Me da una revista? - ¿Me das un pañuelo? - Necesito un martillo -Necesitamos un fontanero - Dame la llave inglesa - ¿Necesitas el destornillador?

11 1. Déme un abrigo / ¿Me da un abrigo?   2. Déme (un poco de / un vaso de / una botella de) agua / ¿Me da (...) agua   3. Dénos unos zapatos / ¿Nos da unos zapatos? 4. Déme un bolígrafo / ¿Me da un bolígrafo?   5. Déme un pañuelo / ¿Me da un pañuelo?

12 **There are two possibilities for sentences here: Dame... or ¿Me da...? . After that you should add the name of the thing you ask for.**   1. Dame el periódico / ¿Me das el periódico?   2. un cigarro   3. fuego   4. las llaves del coche.

15 1. Pasa, pasa / Tú primero   2. **and** 3. Pase, pase / Usted primero.

17 1. ¿Puede hablar más alto? / Más alto, por favor. 2. ¿Puede hablar más bajo? / Más bajo, por favor. 3. ¿Puede hablar más despacio? / Más despacio, por favor.

18 ¿Cuánto es? - ¿cuánto es todo? - ¿cuánto es esto?

19 1. ¿Cuánto es? - **the box of handkerchiefs** - ¿cuánto es? - **the bottle of milk** - ¿cuánto es? - **the ball**.

21 1. ¿Cómo se llama usted?   2. ¿Es suyo este coche? 3. ¿Dónde están los cigarros?   4. ¿Cómo se escribe su apellido?   5. ¿De quién son estas gafas?   6. ¿A dónde va este tren?   7. ¿Quiere usted una cerveza?   8. ¿Hay alguna farmacia por aquí?   9. ¿Qué es eso?   10. ¿Me pasas el tenedor, por favor?   11. ¿Qué pasa?   12. ¿De dónde viene David?   13. ¿Cuánto es todo?   14. ¿Se puede fumar aquí?

22 a) 8 - b) 1 - c) 14 - d) 5 - e) 2 - f) 9 - g) 10 - h) 4 - i) 11 - j) 13 - k) 3 - l) 6 - m) 7 - n) 12.

23 Felipe García Sánchez - No, no es mío - En el cajón de la mesa-Con ce-Son suyas-A Barcelona-Sí, gracias-No, no hay ninguna-Esto es un zumo de naranja - Toma - Que no se puede fumar aquí - De la calle - 1.450 pesetas - No, no se puede.

● **UNIT 9**

1 ¿Quién es aquel señor? - El padre de la novia - ¿Quiénes son éstos? - Son Carmen y Juan.

2 Carlos es sobrino de Juan y de María: **T** - Los tíos de Carlos son Juan y María: **T** - Carlos es primo de Carmen y de Julián: **F** - Carlos es primo de Ana: **T** - Los abuelos de Carlos se llaman Carmen y Julián: **T** - Carlos es nieto de Ana: **F**.

3 You: ¿Quién es? - Tape: El cartero - You: ¿Quién es? - Tape: El profesor de su hijo - You: ¿Quién es? - Tape: El mecánico - You: ¿Quién es? - Tape: la policía.

4 ¿Cuál es su vestido? - ése - ¿cuál es la madre del novio? - la señora de la izquierda; la del vestido azul.

5 1. ¿Cuál es el bolígrafo de Juan?   2. ¿Cuáles son mis gafas? or ¿Cuáles son las mías?   3. ¿Quién (or cuál) es Pepe?   4. ¿Quién (or cuál) es María?

6 Tape: Dame el bolígrafo. - You: ¿Qué bolígrafo? - Tape: Dame las gafas. - You: ¿Qué gafas? - Tape: Dame el dinero. - You: ¿Qué dinero? - Tape: Dame el periódico.

You: ¿Qué periódico? - Tape: Dame la cuchara. You: ¿Qué cuchara?

7 **On the tape:**   1. ¿Cuál es la chica? - La de la derecha. 2. ¿Cuál es el coche de Juan? - El último.   3. ¿Cuál es el bolígrafo de Ana? - El segundo por la derecha. 4. ¿Quién es el chico? - El de la izquierda.   5. ¿Cuáles son tus gafas? - Las de arriba.
Solutions: 1: **Number 2 in Picture 1**   2: **Number 4 in Picture 4**   3: **Number 4 in Picture 2**   4: **Number 1 in Picture 1**   5: **Number 1 in Picture 3.**

8 1. La de la derecha   2. El último   3. El segundo por la derecha   4. El de la izquierda   5. Las de arriba.

9 Voice 1: ¿Quién es Juan Serrano? Voice 2: No es el moreno - No es la rubia - No es la de la corbata marrón - No es el de la barba - No es la de los zapatos negros - No es el de la camisa blanca - No es el de los pantalones verdes - Juan Serrano es el de la falda amarilla.
Solution: 1 - 3 - 4 - 2 - 6 - 5 - 7 - 8.

10 Juan es el de la camisa blanca - Luis Cánovas es el de la corbata azul - El novio de Carmen es el de los zapatos negros - David es el de los pantalones rojos.

11 1. El de la camisa blanca   2. El de la corbata azul   3. El de los zapatos negros   4. El de los pantalones rojos.

12 1. ¿Cuál es el coche de Juan? - el pequeño; ¿Cuál es el coche de Carmen? - el grande   2. ¿Quién (or cuál) es Diego? - el gordo; ¿Quién (or cuál) es José? - el delgado   3. ¿Quién (or cuál) es la hija - la alta; ¿quién (or cuál) es la madre? - la baja   4. ¿Cuáles son los zapatos de David? - los viejos; ¿Cuáles son los zapatos de Oscar? - los nuevos   5. ¿Quién (or cuál) es Julio? - el guapo; ¿Quién (or cuál) es Víctor? - el feo   6. ¿Cuál es la corbata de Emilio? - la bonita; ¿Cuál es la corbata de Pepe? - la fea.

13 1. es el   2. es la   3. son los.

14 2. Diego es el gordo y José es el delgado   3. La hija es

la alta y la madre es la baja   4. Los zapatos de David son los viejos y los de Oscar son los nuevos   5. Julio es el guapo y Víctor es el feo   6. La corbata de Emilio es la bonita y la de Pepe es la fea. **In all cases the second occurrence of** ser **could be omitted.** Diego es el gordo y José, el delgado.

15 1. son   2. eres   3. sois   4. es.

16 2. Son de Francia. Son franceses   3. Son de Inglaterra. Son inglesas   4. Son de Italia. Son italianos   5. Es de Alemania. Es alemán   6. Es de Japón. Es japonesa 7. Son de Brasil. Son brasileños   8. Es de Marruecos. Es marroquí.

18 LUIS: quién. FOTOGRAFO: padre - la - de - la - mujer. LUIS: la - del - azul. FOTOGRAFO: madre. LUIS: dónde. JOVEN: vestido. LUIS: Cuál. JOVEN: novia. LUIS: bonito - quién - es. JOVEN: Quién. LUIS: el - de.

● UNIT 10

1 ¿Qué día es hoy? - jueves - ¿qué día es hoy? - veintiocho - hoy es lunes - hoy es veinticinco - hoy es sábado - hoy es treinta.

2 To THE GIRL: Hoy es martes or hoy es cuatro. To THE BOY: Hoy es sábado or hoy es quince. To THE OLD WOMAN: Hoy es lunes or hoy es diecisiete. To THE MAN: Hoy es viernes or hoy es veintiuno. **In all the answers you can omit** hoy es.

4 1. Sí   2. Sí   3. No   4. Veintitrés.

5 ¿Qué hora es? - son las cinco - son las cinco menos veinte - son las doce.

6 1. Reloj número 5   2. Reloj número 2   3. Reloj número 4   4. Reloj número 1   5. Reloj número 3.

7 Reloj número 1: son las nueve y cuarto. Número 2: son las nueve y veinticinco. Número 3: son las diez menos cinco. Número 4: es la una y media. Número 5: son las dos menos diez. **In all the answers you can omit the verb.**

8 **The tape says the following:** En Madrid son las dos de la tarde - en Las Palmas es la una de la tarde - en Moscú son las cuatro de la tarde - en Tokio son las diez de la noche - en Pekin son las nueve de la noche - en Nueva York son las ocho de la mañana en Buenos

Aires son las diez de la mañana. **The times should therefore be distributed in the following way:** Madrid: 14.00. Las Palmas: 13.00. Moscú: 16.00. Tokio: 22.00. Pekín: 21:00. Nueva York: 8:00. Buenos Aires: 10:00.

9 1: las doce y veinticinco.   2. La una menos veinte. 3. La una.   4. Las dos y media.   5. Las siete menos veinte.   6. Las siete menos cuarto.

10 1-2: un cuarto de hora.   3-4: hora y media.   5-6: cinco minutos.

11 1. T.   2. F: she is there five minutes.   3. T.   4. F: Rosi does not arrive.

14 1C - 2F or B - 3E - 4B - 5D - 6A.

16 The tape says: 1. ¿Vemos esa película?   2. Te invito a un helado.   3. ¿Bailamos? 4. ¿Quiere usted un café? So, situation 1 is the result of sentence 3, situation 2 is the result of sentence 4, situation 3 is the result of sentence 1, and situation 4 is the result of sentence 2.

17 1. Por el regalo.   2. Bailar or ¿Bailamos?   3. Sí.

18 1. Jueves.   2. Doce.   3. A un café.   4. Las seis menos veinte.

19 es - jefe - las cinco - Diego - bailan - llega or entra.

● UNIT 11

1 ¿Qué precio tiene el jersey? 2. ¿Qué precio tiene el bolso? 3. ¿Qué precio tienen las postales? 4. ¿Qué precio tiene la merluza?

2 Ocho mil seiscientas - Siete mil quinientas cincuenta - Veinticinco - Tres mil cien.

4 The price you give will obviously be modified by inflation, etc. However, the following answers would be possible here: Son muy caras - es barato or es muy barato - es muy barata - es muy cara - son baratos or son muy baratos.

5 ¡Qué caras! - ¡qué barato! - ¡qué barata! - ¡qué cara! - ¡qué baratos!

6 You can say the name of the article after replying to the greeting. For example: Buenos días. Una docena de huevos. You can also place déme in front of the things you ask for. For example: Buenos días. Déme una docena de huevos. Or you can use a a question. For example: Buenos días. ¿Me da una docena de huevos?

7 You can greet the shopkeeper and then say póngame followed by the name of the article you ask for. For example: Buenos días. Póngame un bocadillo de queso. You can also use a question: Buenos días. ¿Me pone un bocadillo de queso?

8 You should have put a cross against all articles except the following: un kilo de pescado, un bocadillo de jamón, una docena de huevos, un trozo de tarta and una botella de agua.

11 ¿Cuántas? - ¿cuántos? - ¿cuánto? - ¿cuánta? - ¿cuántos? - ¿cuántos? - ¿cuánta? - ¿cuánta? - ¿cuánto? - ¿cuántos?

17 Me - ¿Cuántas? - están - caras - Que - medio - kilo - y - llama - Cuánto.

18 1. Fresas - manzanas. 2. Kilo y medio. 3. 175 - 110 - 130 - 160.

● UNIT 12

1 ¿Qué es tu padre? - ¿qué es su novia? - ¿qué es usted? - soy profesor - Elena es médico - son mecánicos - somos policías.

2 Profesora - cartero - enfermero - vendedora - periodista - empleado de banco - camarera.

3 Antonio es médico - Pepe es mecánico - Lucía es abogada - Rosi es policía - Víctor es dentista - Paquita es camarera - Ricardo es cura.

5 Tiene dos coches - tengo dos coches - ¿tienes dinero? - tenemos una máquina de fotos - no tienen televisión - ¿tenéis radio? - no tengo reloj.

6 Andrés no tiene camisa - Carlos tiene camisa - Pepe tiene zapatos - María no tiene zapatos - Cristina tiene reloj - Miguel no tiene reloj - Antonio tiene una pelota or Antonio tiene pelota - Eduardo no tiene pelota.

7 These are the questions you hear: ¿Tiene usted coche? - ¿Tiene usted casa? - ¿Tiene usted cámara de vídeo? - ¿Tiene usted televisión? - ¿Tiene usted casete? - ¿Tiene usted dinero? - ¿Tiene usted un bolígrafo? - ¿Tiene usted teléfono? In all cases you can answer either: Sí tengo or no tengo.

9 1. F 2. T 3. F 4. F 5. F

10 Un año tiene cincuenta y dos semanas - un año tiene doce meses - un año tiene trescientos sesenta y cinco días - un mes tiene treinta or treinta y un días - una semana tiene siete días - un día tiene veinticuatro horas.

11 These are the questions you hear: ¿Tiene usted hijos? - ¿Tiene usted jefe? - ¿Tiene usted sobrinos? - ¿Tiene usted amigos? - ¿Tiene usted amigas? You can answer either: No, no tengo or sí tengo or sí, tengo dos / muchos / cuatro…

12 Vengan conmigo - ¿vienen conmigo? - compra el periódico - ¿compras el periódico? - trae unas cervezas - ¿traes unas cervezas?

13 1. ¿Llevas los niños a casa? 2. ¿Me traen or me trae usted la maleta? 3. ¿Apagáis la radio? 4. ¿Coges el paquete? 5. ¿Enciendes la luz? 6. ¿Abre usted or abres la ventana? 7. ¿Cierra usted la puerta? In all cases you may add por favor at the end of the request.

16 ¿Cuántos años tienes? - tengo treinta y siete años - Julia tiene doce años.

17 and **18** In your answer you should use the following: the name of the person in question + tiene + the corresponding number + años.

20   1. Elena está viuda.   2. Lali y Pepe están casados.
3. Alfonso está divorciado.   4. Luisa está soltera.
5. Ana y Andrés están casados.

23   **You hear the following questions:**   ¿Nombre? - ¿apellidos? - ¿dirección? - ¿teléfono? - ¿profesión? - ¿edad? - ¿estado civil?

24   1. Luis Cánovas no tiene hijos.   2. La mamá de los niños es enfermera.   3. Están comprando un libro.
4. El libro tiene fotos.   5. El libro cuesta mil seiscientas pesetas.   6. En el bolso, Carmen tiene una máquina de fotos.   7. Sí. Luis Cànovas está soltero.   8. Luis Cánovas tiene treinta y seis años.

● UNIT 13

1   **You hear:** ¿Tiene rosas rojas? - Hay cerveza alemana - Tenemos paella - Hay hojas de reclamaciones - ¿Tienen ensalada? -Hay pollos asados.
Solutions: 3 - 1 - 5 - 4 - 2 - 6

2   ¿Tienen? **or** ¿Hay? pañuelos - peines - cepillos de dientes - bañadores - jabón - colonia - helados - camisas - corbatas.

4   Vivo cerca de la estación - Luis Cánovas está en un hotel - ¿Dónde vive usted? - En el centro de la ciudad - ¿Dónde estás? - En un hotel, al lado de la universidad.

5   Ana vive… - Mis padres y yo vivimos… - Tú vives… - Antonio y María viven… - Yo vivo… -Vosotros vivís… Mis abuelos viven… - Mis amigos viven… - Enrique vive…
For the remaining part of the sentences you can combine any word from column 3 with any word from column 4.

7   Mujer: Hola. Me llamo Amparo. Hombre: Encantado. Yo soy Juan. Mujer: No eres de Granada, ¿verdad? Hombre: No, no. Mujer: Pero vives aquí. Hombre: No; soy de Madrid y vivo en Madrid. ¿Y tú, dónde vives? Mujer: Aquí, en Granada. Cerca de la estación. ¿Y tú, dónde te alojas, dónde estás? Hombre:También cerca de la estación, en el hotel Imperial.

13   1. Un regalo   2. ¿Bailamos?   3. Sí.   4. Sí.

14   1. T   2. F   3. F   4. T   5. T   6. F
7. F   8. T

15   1. Soy…   2. Buenos días   3. Gracias **or** Gracias por el regalo   4. Hasta el lunes   5. ¿Está el señor García?
6. ¿Dónde está el baño   7. Una habitación doble, por favor   8. Un café, por favor **or** ¿Me pone un café? **or** Póngame un café   9. ¿De quién es esta chaqueta?
10. ¿Hay rey en España? 11. ¿Quieres un poco? 12. Ven
13. ¿Cómo? **or** ¿Cómo dice? **or** ¿Perdón? **or** ¿Qué?
14. ¿Cuánto es?   15. La cuenta, por favor **or** ¿Me trae la cuenta, por favor?   16. ¿Quién es el chico de la derecha? 17. ¿De dónde es? 18. ¿Qué hora es? 19. Un kilo de fresas **or** ¿Me pone un kilo de fresas? **or** Póngame un kilo de fresas   20. Quería una camisa   21. ¿Cómo se llama esto?   22. ¿Qué es usted? **or** ¿Qué eres?
23. ¿Cuántos años tienes? **or** ¿Cuántos años tiene?
24. ¿Me pasas la sal, por favor? **or** Pásame la sal, por favor   25. ¿Tienen paella? **or** ¿Hay paella?

16   Luis Cánovas: ¿Se puede? Secretaria: ¿Qué desea usted? Luis Cánovas: Soy Secretaria: ¿Es usted - Siéntese - ¿dónde está su sobre? - está en el - Tome - Cuente el dinero Luis Cánovas: dos mil - cuatro - y cinco mil. Luis Cánovas: gracias. - ¿está el señor Secretaria: Un momento. Voy a - soy - ¿está tu jefe? ¿Puede - Sí está - verlo - Segundo - primera - a la derecha. Luis Cánovas: muchas - por todo - Adiós. Secretaria: Recuerde, segundo Luis Cánovas.- se preocupe - Hasta luego.

18   Recepcionista: desea Luis Cánovas: habitación individual Recepcionista: con baño - Habitación - Su nombre - Cómo se escribe - Me da - pasaporte Luis Cánovas: está - aquí Tome Luis Cánovas: hay teléfono Recepcionista: Todas - tienen - puede Recepcionista: la cuarenta y ocho Recepcionista: Son -estas Luis Cánovas: Qué Recepcionista: son suyas Luis Cánovas: mías Recepcionista: quién - Lo siento Luis Cánovas: preocupe.

20   Luis Cánovas: me pasas Chico: hay - siento - pasa - sal Señor mayor: Toma Chico: Tome - Aquí está Luis Cánovas: necesito Chico: ninguno Luis Cánovas: ahí - hay - dámelo Chico.- del - de la Luis Cánovas: quién Chico: barba Luis Cánovas: puede traerme Camarero: cuchillo Chico: Qué - comiendo - es eso Luis Cánovas: Esto - Quieres - prueba. Chico: coger otro Luis Cánovas: Toma.